STATE

of the

NATION

STATE

of the

NATION

BY JOHN DOS PASSOS

ILLUSTRATED BY F. STROBEL

GREENWOOD PRESS, PUBLISHERS
WESTPORT, CONNECTICUT

The Library of Congress has catalogued this publication as follows:

Library of Congress Cataloging in Publication Data

Dos Passos, John, 1896-1970.
   State of the nation.

   1. United States--Description and travel--1940-1960.
2. United States--Social conditions--1933-1945.
I. Title.
E169.D68   917.3   73-718
ISBN 0-8371-6782-5

Copyright 1943 and 1944 by John Dos Passos

Originally published in 1944
by Houghton Mifflin Company, Boston

Reprinted with the permission
of Elizabeth H. Dos Passos

First Greenwood Reprinting 1973

Library of Congress Catalogue Card Number 73-718

ISBN 0-8371-6782-5

Printed in the United States of America

ACKNOWLEDGMENT

Grateful acknowledgment is made to HARPER'S MAGAZINE, to FORTUNE, and to LIBERTY MAGAZINE for permission to reprint some of the material included in this book.

CONTENTS

CHAPTER I

A Letter to a Friend in the Theatres

Y OUR LETTER gave me an idea of what you men in uniform are thinking about this country. It made me feel the widening of the rift between the man in the service and the civilian. So much of the youth and energy of the country has been committed to these wars that what kind of citizens you people become as you grow up in warfare is going to determine in a very large measure what kind of a country we shall have when the wars are over. I've lived through enough years of shift and change by now to know that it is not the professed aims people are striving to achieve that set the pattern of the future but the habits of behavior they take on in the process. It will be the methods we use in industry and in the services to cope with the things that are happening to us now that will determine the shape of our society in the years to come. Whether this nation is going to continue to develop as a selfgoverning community ruled by laws that depend on the people's consent or whether it is going to be sucked back under that rule by the club of a boss and his gang which has been the commonest scheme of government since mankind began, depends on the behavior of every American citizen alive today.

We must not forget that the survival and growth through the centuries of the English system of equality for individual men before the law, and its development on this continent into our peculiarly American institutions has been a sort of a miracle. It represents the longest stretch in history during which any large group of the population has lived under political liberty. Miracles only happen when enough people want them to happen. When we cease to want liberty hard enough to be willing to work for it this miracle of freedom and equality before the law will fade away and despotism will again become the universal pattern of human society.

I know that our system has never been perfect and that all sorts of injustices have flourished under it, but I don't think you'll deny that during the hundred and sixtyeight years of the existence of the United States the ordinary run of men here have had a better chance to develop and to live their lives as they wanted to than during any other period we know about anywhere else in the world.

During that time our liberties have weathered storms. We are now in the midst of the greatest of them. It is we Americans now alive who are going to determine out of our strength and our weakness, out of our good sense and our folly, what the whole future course of the United States is going to be.

The test finds us far from ready to meet it. We haven't the leadership, the education, the theoretical background or the political formula we need. Still, in defiance of historical logic, I believe we are going to meet it.

One reason is that we have to meet it. The people of this country have a common language and have developed a common aptitude for the use of machinery, but we have none of the ingrained cohesive habit and tradition of the old ethnic groups. What holds us together as a nation is our system of liberties. These liberties have continually to be adapted as changing methods of industrial production and changing relationships with the other peoples of the world change the shape of our society. To survive in the coming world at all we shall have to learn how to continue to be a nation of free men.

For us to win this war that underlies the military wars we have got to be clear in our minds about what each individual man can

do to make selfgovernment work.   Americans, in spite of conflicts of interest, racial, economic and regional, have got to retain
enough basic common aims and beliefs to hold them together.
We have got to develop as clear notions about the shape of our
country and what we want it to become as the eighteenth century lawyers and country squires who laid the foundations for
us had of their America.   We've got to determine clearly what
proportion of a man's time should be devoted to the duties of citizenship and what proportion to his own affairs.   To accomplish
that we have all got to rub a lot of smeary political phrases off the
slate and you people in uniform have got to remember that in
spite of the Articles of War you are still citizens.

There are many things going on at home you might complain
of very justly, but in your letter I think you are complaining
about the wrong ones.   You say that workers in industry are
making too much money, that the concerted effort of working
people to get a larger share of the profits of industry is treason in
wartime, that the farmers are thinking of nothing but their own
pocketbooks, and that, as you are being regimented within an
inch of your life, you don't see why civilians shouldn't be regimented too.   And you end up with a list of people you want shot
without trial.

Leaving out the shooting without trial, which was the first
thing free institutions were set up to prevent, can't you see that
the functioning of a selfgoverning republic depends upon the dignity and independence of the great mass of its citizens?   Ever
since our cities began to fill up with factory workers and office
workers it has been obvious that the first requirement for a return to decency in government was an improvement in the social
status of the average worker for wages.   The quickest way a man
can raise himself in his own eyes and in the eyes of his neighbors,
according to our national standards, is by earning more money.
If the men and women who work for wages in industry are to
hold their end up as citizens against the increasing concentration
of the power of wealth in a few hands they've got to have an increasing share of the profits of industry.   In using what means

he has to better himself how is a working man striking for higher
wages any more a traitor than a manufacturer holding out until
he gets a favorable contract with the government for his product?
It's only by their insistence on higher prices for their crops that
the farmers have been able for the first time in many years to bail
themselves out and to get our rural economy back onto a sound
financial basis. So long as we live in a money system you
shouldn't blame the people left at home for continuing to play
the game according to the rules. You do have a right, at a time
when your independence, and that of all the young men in the
country, has been taken away from you, to blame us for not
striking a proper balance between the part of our lives we give to
public service and the part we keep for our own profit. If you
had had the chance that I've had during the last year to travel
around among the various types of people in this country, I think
you would agree with me that it is neither the farmers nor the
factory workers who have been the worst offenders in putting
their own interests before those of the country as a whole.

You mustn't forget either that the day you get your discharge
you will start to profit personally from any gains in higher wages
and better working conditions those union leaders you say such
hard things of have managed to obtain for wageworkers, or that
even in uniform your standard of life is higher than that of the
troops of our allies because of the standard that has been set in
industry by the demands and the general cussedness of generations of American working men. If we let into civilian life too
much of the regimentation that is generally admitted to be necessary in the army we will be destroying at home the very liberties
you are defending against foreign enemies.

Regimentation means regimenters. Our entire American system of government is based upon the conviction that no man is
good enough to be trusted with more than very limited power over
his fellow men. It was the aim of the framers of our constitution
to balance power against power. Even the lobbying and the tugs
of war in Washington between various group interests that you
complain of as being so shocking in a time of national peril are

part of the system that has grown up out of the constitution. Though we certainly can't claim any kind of perfection for it the one thing we can say about our system as a whole is that it is getting results. Our outstanding victory so far has been the immensity of production on the farm and in the factory and the fact that it has been attained with such an amazingly small dislocation of our normal habits of life. Any military victories we win abroad will be based upon this initial victory at home.

People will tell you that individual liberty as our fathers and grandfathers knew it was only possible in a country of constantly expanding frontiers. They'll wag their heads and tell you that now that the Pacific coast is settled the great days are over. It is just not true. With each new advance in technology the possibilities of our lives expand at a terrifying rate. The most casual trip through any six of the fortyeight states will show you that the country has been barely settled yet. Our people are still frontiersmen. Compared to the encrusted centers of habit and ritual and tradition that are being blasted into heaps in the wars across the seas even our oldest cities are the provisional bivouacs of a raw and fluid civilization that has not yet stiffened into a frame. The people of this country can still change their occupations, their way of living, their settlements as easily as they can eat their breakfasts. We are still jacks of all trades, eager to learn new skills and to adapt ourselves to new social arrangements. In this national fluidity lie possibilities for good and for evil. Now that plentiful production of food and of goods is just about a solved problem, the chances for the survival of the miracle of a republic of free men should be much better now than they were when the country started in the age of handicrafts and scarcity. The question isn't whether we have the opportunity to continue building on the foundations the men of the thirteen colonies laid for us. The question is whether we have the will and the brains to use the opportunities which the new skills and the new knowledge and the new frontiers are opening up to perfect and develop the institutions of selfgovernment ...

Provincetown, Massachusetts, April, 1944

WHEN I PUSHED MY WAY in through the swinging green curtains of the Pullman washroom, two men were sitting on the broad leather seat across the end. One of them had a splotchy concave spudlike face under skimpy sandy hair and smoked a cigarette with much nervous flicking of the ash into the bright spittoon at his feet. The other, a small broadshouldered man with a grizzly closecropped head and a grizzly closecropped mustache, wore a blue flannel shirt and smoked a corncob pipe. They sat jiggling and lurching as the train jounced over the uneven roadbed. Their eyes were fixed on the white metal washbasins in front of them. The man with the cigarette was talking, but the man with the corncob pipe didn't look like a man who was listening. When I started to move jerkily in their direction, they made room for me between them on the bench without looking up.

'Thanks,' I said.

'Well,' intoned the man with the cigarette, as if summing up for my benefit what he'd been saying before, 'I been on the road six weeks and it's too long. . . . With my car I could have finished up in four and given everybody better service all around. . . . What did you say your line was?'

I backed up against the wall to let the question go past me to the grizzly man with the corncob pipe. He took his pipe out of his mouth and looked at it fixedly for a moment before answering in a rather mournful musical tone, 'Presses. We install presses.'

'They tell me pressers and cleaners are having a hard time with priorities . . .'

Laughter began to bubble up deep inside the man who was smoking the corncob pipe. Not a muscle of his face moved, but he began to shake all over. He drew on his pipe and let the smoke out through his nose with an air of great satisfaction. 'Not pants presses . . . Our presses tailor sheet metal, armorplate, that sort of thing.'

'Oh,' said the man in the corner, profoundly impressed.

It took him some time to think up another question. 'How do you find people?' Without waiting for an answer he answered it himself: 'I find 'em crabby. Our customers are all retailers. 1 have to go around and explain to 'em why we can't fill their orders or can only supply half or a third of what they need and I'm expected to make 'em like it. Salesmanship in reverse. I find people crabby. So you don't find 'em crabby?'

The grizzly man's pipe crackled. He looked pleased, but he didn't answer. The man in the corner lit another cigarette and addressed himself to me.

'You travellin'?'

'In a way.'

'What line?'

I felt my face getting red.

'For a magazine,' I stammered.

'Sellin' books?'

'No, I'm writing articles just at present. I'm trying to do some articles about what it's like in this country in wartime.'

'So you're the guy who knows all the answers,' growled the grizzly man through his pipestem.

'No, I ask other people. They tell me the answers.'

'Maybe you got some dope.' The man in the corner flicked at his cigarette so hard with a thin yellowed finger he flicked the whole end off. 'Maybe you've got a hunch about when this goddam war's going to end.'

'All I know is what I read in the papers, as they say in Washington.'

The grizzly man was shaken with silent laughter again.

'So you are one of these guys that goes around and asks questions? Tell me one thing,' he asked, in a confiding tone of voice. 'Did you ever learn anything from anybody by asking questions?'

'I'm not so much on asking questions . . . Sometimes you can just sit around listening to what people have to say of their own accord.'

'But how are you going to get the answers you need without asking about the things you want to know about?'

'That's the question.'

That shut us all up. We sat there silent in a row looking at the polished washbasins until the porter came to tell us our berths were made up.

CHAPTER 2

Yankee Mechanics

T HE WHISTLE BLOWS. At the wide sliding doors of the long building shaped like a shoebox with oblong windows stained dark-blue figures appear. One man runs out, then two, then three, cantering across the broad stretch of cinders in the windy winter sunlight. More follow until hurrying lines are converging on the low shed where they punch their timecards. The morning shift is off. A black dense crowd now is pushing slowly out through the gates. Their faces are gray and yellowish under the dirt of eight hours' work. They wear visored caps pulled down over their foreheads, heavy gloves well grimed, thick clothes bunched at the waist under coveralls, or woollen trousers tucked into arctics. There are a few redchecked breeches or green and red plaid shirts, and occasional red deerhunters' caps that have a look of the north woods. They wear their pictures on oval identification badges pinned to their caps or to the breasts of their shirts. They are in a hurry. It's cold. Their bodies, baggy with sweaters and heavy woollen pants, move sluggishly. As they flow in a packed mass out the gate and across the railroad track, you begin to make out the difference in faces. The clothes, the boots, the caps, the gloves are more or less interchangeable. But the faces are sharp or blunt, ruddy or pale, old or young. They all have a fixed intent look. Some of them are women. It's surprising how many women. Middleaged women. Young girls. They wear the same clothes, their faces are bleared under the same grime; it's hard to tell them from the men and boys.

Home After Work

As the crowd reaches the sidewalk, it dissolves suddenly into brisk individuals hurrying in different directions, threes and fours chatting as they walk or groups stamping their feet waiting along the counter of the hotdog stand or filtering into the shabby lunch-room across the street. They line up for busses. They scatter among the parked cars that are ranked in all the open lots and line all the streets as far as you can see. The streets that were empty a few minutes before are jammed now with slowmoving strings of cars. A procession of cars two abreast fills the right lane of the tall soaring girderwork bridge that crosses a great tidal river swirling brown and silvery past purple rocks rimmed with ice to the high opposite bank tufted with bright white birches and green firs.

The cars are packed tight with bodies in bulky clothes. As the cars cross the bridge, every face turns to look downstream at the long buildings and the iron spiderwebs of the ways and at the destroyers lying alongside the wharf, spare gray pointed hulls still streaked and checkered with yellow underpaint, narrow decks encumbered with temporary housing where the shipfitters are at work. The boat that shows a string of red white yellow blue bunting fluttering in the sharp wind was launched yesterday. That's the end product of their work.

They are in a hurry to get home. More than half of them still live out from town, in big white oldtime farmhouses linked by a kitchenwing and a woodshed to their great barns, standing back from the road maybe at the top of a rolling grasslot, with the woods behind them; or in rough board shacks with belching stove-pipes in clearings in the woods; or in the small gray gabled houses grouped sedately round the seaweedy rocks of the old fishing-coves where dories and powerboats are anchored off wormeaten wharves. Some of them live in gingerbread bungalows with scalloped composition roofing beside fillingstations along highways, or in halfslums of gawky long unpainted red and yellow fourfamily houses that radiate from shoefactories and old textile mills in the patchwork industrial towns at the falls of the rivers. Some of them have moved in near their work and are camping in tourist cabins and in rows of silvery trailers nailed down to the ground with tarpaper to keep the drafts out from under; or in the rooming and boardinghouses of the shipyard town itself; or in the moderately comfortable dwellings left over from the last war; or in the carefully designed colonies of wellequipped brick houses that were laid out a couple of years ago in the last flicker of social ardor of New Deal housing, or in the rows of prefabricated barracks on stilts that are now being slapped together with little regard for the climate or the standard of living. A few hopelessly incurable individualists live in shacks they tacked together themselves out of old packingcases and odd boards and sheetiron and cardboard from the town dump. Their shacks huddle in a welter of frozen mud and stripped trucks and brokendown jalopies and piledup tincans and blowing papers out on a promontory crowned with tall hemlocks which overlooks the river and the bridge and the shipyards and the town strung along the ridges behind with its wellspaced white gables and its white lanterns and cupolas standing up against the blue among the bare twigs of the elms, and its sharp white spires.

How Do They Spend Their Money?

This town, with its handsome upper street of old houses set behind elms in broad lawns and gardens flanked by barns and carriagehouses and vinecovered summerhouses, testifying to the lumbering woodworking shipbuilding prosperity of a hundred years or more ago, and its brick business streets dating from the beginning of iron shipbuilding after the Civil War, seems somewhat aghast at the new wave of life that's welled up around it. The upper street is about the same, perhaps a little better kept up than ten years ago; but the business section, which used to maintain a certain grim decorum, looks as if a tornado had struck it. Everywhere litter and trash, small gimcrack stores, unswept lunchrooms with jukeboxes, decrepit sodafountains have taken the place of the establishments of the solid merchants. Cigarette ads and crudely lettered signs reading, 'Beer to Take Out,' are in the shopwindows instead of stocks of goods.

If you go into a store to inquire about the beer, the bleakfaced gray man with redrimmed eyelids behind the counter can't wait to tell you that you can't drink it on the premises. 'There'll be nothin' of this sort after the first of the year,' he adds, with every air of grim satisfaction, 'and the hotels will damn well have to close their cocktail lounges ... The state liquor store'll be the only place they can git it.'

'Then they aren't blowing much of their money in?'

'Don't see how they could be ... Movie theatres' doin' some business. Only one of 'em's any good.'

'How about bowling alleys and poolrooms?'

'Well, there's only one bowlin' alley now. Other one had ter close because they couldn't git any pinboys. Most likely this 'un'll have ter close down soon.'

'At least there must be a nice little housing boom.'

He puckered his mouth up as if he'd gotten a sudden sour taste in it. The pucker spread across every feature of his face. He stared at me without speaking for some time with a look of stony antagonism in his eyes. Then he started to talk, biting off his words and spitting them out:

'There's some federal housin' if that's what you want to call it. They sure put up a fight against it. You see people here don't think this is goin' to last. They were stung last time. In the last war they built two hundred extry houses and when peace come there warn't nobody to live in 'em. Been six or seven hundred houses empty for the last fifteen years.'

'But why don't the merchants carry any stock of goods?'

'What's the use? they say. People buy whatever they've got anyway. They can't get their orders filled. Most likely some of

'em feel they've made as much profit as they kin with the new
taxes, so why should they make the effort?'

'If they aren't blowing it in, how are the shipyard workers
spending their money?' I asked a solid citizen in the vestibule
of the town hall, a redfaced man in a new light gray tweed suit
that matched silvery hair slicked back on his head. He stood with
his legs apart and his tan bluchers firmly planted on the board
floor, and wagged his head judiciously as he thought up his
answer.

'They eat up a lot of it,' he said. 'Food's high . . . Only the
other day my wife was at the meatmarket worryin' how she could
afford a roast of beef, and a feller we know, shipyard worker, come
in and bought a twelvepound roast right out from under her nose
. . . last one they had in the store . . . Didn't even ask the price
. . . Just said wrap it up and pulled out a roll of bills and paid
for it. My, she was mad.'

'I suppose they drink more than they did.'

'Those that drink drink more and better liquor, I guess . . .
Some of these fishermen are awful heavy drinkers . . . But to tell
the truth none of 'em blow much of it in . . . If you're workin'
eight hours seven days a week — and that's what you have to do;
it's the overtime piles up the money — and it takes you an hour
each way to get to work, you don't have much time for raisin'
hell. The people around this section have just been holdin' on by
their eyelashes since the last war prosperity. Now they're bailin'
themselves out, payin' off old storebills, and back taxes, cuttin'
down the mortgage on the old home. Some of 'em are buyin' homes
and furniture. The dentists are doing a raging business. There've
been more new false teeth put in in the last year than in the last
ten . . . I guess you can class that under capital gains.' He gave
a creaky laugh. 'They're buyin' what they can, paintin' up and
patchin' up, but most of the money's goin' for dead horses.'

'Oh yes, I'm losing mortgages all the time,' said a banker in a
small town nearby in answer to the same question. 'I guess the
first thing people are doing is getting themselves out of debt.'

The Women Come Out

Inside the shipyard there is much more enthusiasm. Newly hired women and boys bustle about their work with a brighteyed look as if they found it novel and enlivening. Out of tens of thousands employed, only a couple of thousand ever worked in a shipyard before. Many of them never worked in industry at all. They have the satisfaction of seeing a destroyer which is the end product of their work slide into the brown river every twentyone days.

'It's really exciting,' the large-eyed lady in a frilly blouse who is personnel director for women said to me. 'I've only been here three months. I came in to take a welding course and now ...' she paused with a little toss of her head. From where we sat at her desk we could see through the open office door the raw girls waiting in line at the application desk in the hall. 'They all feel the same way,' she said. 'Way back in women suffrage days the girls were all agitated about equal work for equal wages. Well, they've got it now and nobody's had a parade or anything.'

'You seem to be a case of upgrading yourself ... I was just going to ask you about upgrading.'

She laughed happily. She was obviously a woman of some education and business experience. No, she said she had never done anything of this kind before. She had done professional and secretarial work. 'And a great deal of housework raising children ... that's good training for anything,' she said. 'It's quite a revolution, isn't it?' she went on. 'It's all on account of welding — women never could have done riveting — welding and stream-lined assembly methods ...' She went on to talk about how well the women were doing their work. 'These Maine women have so much stuff,' she kept saying. It was expected that they would be useful as messengers and for winding asbestos covering on steam pipes and for cleaning up and painting and similar light work, but it was a surprise to everybody that they should turn out to be firstrate welders, that there would be three women dressing tools in the blacksmith shop, or that they would be running lathes and

drillpresses, or doing complicated layout work and operating a
platerolling machine. 'In this yard women work in every department, from the toolroom to shipfitting on board the launched
hulls.'

'Where do they come from?'

Well, about a third of them were young wives of men in the
service who had to support themselves and wanted to make their
work count . . . A great many of them were hardworking farmers'
wives, a lot were millhands from textile and shoe factories. Some
of them were tough little numbers from juke joints and dancehalls.
Of course the management was very much afraid of allure . . .
afraid that sex would raise its grisly head . . . but actually some
of the best welders were from among these tough little girls. On
the whole, women with some sort of artistic or craftworking skill
and jazzy babies made the best welders. The little girls were
particularly useful for getting into tight corners in shipfitting. In
fact, in some yards it was said they were trying to get midgets.
The stout old biddies were harder to train and usually ended cleaning up or painting. 'And let me tell you that it takes stuff to
handle a welding arc all day long . . . stuff and skill . . . They are
most of them scared to death of it at first on account of the roar
and splutter and the fumes, but after three or four days they get
used to it and will weld two steel plates together as coolly as
they'd sew a hem on a dress.

'And don't think there have been any concessions made to the
weaker sex . . The only concession has been to put in new wash-
rooms and toilets in charge of a matron . . . The matron is in-
dispensable . . . We couldn't get any plumbing fixtures, so we
gave them the orchidcolored fittings the firm had on hand for a
yacht they were building . . . for that man . . . you must know his
name . . . that man who had so many wives. The girls are mad
about them.'

The Farmer Is a Mechanic

The new men naturally have been quicker to break in, as they
were most of them what the manager called Yankee mechanics to

begin with: parttime farmers and fishermen who were accustomed to tinkering with their own cars and farming machinery and marine engines. Others were garage men and fillingstation attendants. Some came from the building trades and from textile mills. There is a sprinkling of schoolteachers, clerks from stores and officeworkers. All of them, almost without exception, came from inside the state, and the great majority from within a radius of thirty miles around the shipyard. It's surprising how many of the old men have come out. Many of them had been foremen or skilled operators in shipyards during the last war. It's the old men who contribute the traditional knowhow and form the backbone of the training system that is turning shoeclerks, fillingstation attendants, and farmhands into efficient operators of machine tools, so fast that even under the constant crippling loss of trained men to the draft, with the coupling of new methods with old skills the efficiency of the yard has been increased month by month.

The Old Men Leave Their Rockingchairs

Though the old men had played a part in the building of steel ships, it's in the small yards that have sprung up in every tidal inlet, to build wooden barges and tugs and minesweepers, that they have really come into their own. Outside of a few yachts and fishingboats there had been no wooden ships built along the New England coast since the oversize schooners built during the last war. At the yard I visited they told me that when the promoters of it, who operated a small marine railway, came back from Washington with the money to build some wooden ships, they couldn't find a man who knew how to handle an adze.

Only gradually, out of lobstermen's shacks and fishing coves and farmhouses the old shipcarpenters began to show their grizzled and mustached faces. They knew how to shape oak timbers. From the laying of the first keel they made building the ship a trainingschool for the medley of lumbermen, granite workers, housecarpenters, farmers, and fishermen. As they worked, the science of building wooden hulls had to be invented all over again.

The management had the government orders and the financial setup and the great oaks ready marked to be cut in the forested river valleys, but they couldn't go ahead until they got the know-how out of the heads of the old men. They never managed to get together more than a hundred real shipcarpenters. The young-sters of them were in their sixties. The oldest in the yard I visited was eightyfour.

It was a magnificent day; a slaty sky full of cotton clouds and a bright sunlight that shimmered on the bluesteel bay so full of is-lands densely set with dark fir and silvery balsam. A sharp wind ruffled the scalloped waves to indigo with speeding catspaws. The air smelt of cold seawater and rankly of freshsawed green oak and steamed planking. From the sawmill up the hill there came the muffled whir of buzzsaws, above every other sound rose the clear ringing crack of the adze on sound timber. The ribs of the row of big coalbarges stood up along the edge of the water a glistening cold yellow from out of crisscrossed scaffolding and runways. The bustle of men in lumbermen's clothes about the oaken skeletons of the ships, and the old red brick of the buildings across the narrow shining tongue of the harbor and the white gables and the churchspires of the old downeast town climbing up a spur of a big wooded hill gave you the feeling of being in a steel engraving of a hundred years ago.

They were getting ready to launch a minesweeper. The pen-nants, run up in a string fore and aft from the spar above the pilothouse, were fluttering briskly over the tubby vessel that glistened with new gray paint. Two men in a sharppointed little ochrecolored dory that danced prettily on the small sparkling waves were hammering at the forward part of the cradle. Then they drew away with a couple of strokes of the oars and the gray boat started to slide gently forward. The bow bit into the water as she gathered speed, rose a little, and the boat, gliding free of the tangled timbers of the cradle, went skimming smoothly as a duck out into the bay.

Work meanwhile continued on the other hulls. Except for

a small group from the office, a yachtsman, a shipchandler, an
architectural draftsman all turned boatbuilders for the war, who
stood stamping their feet from the cold on the dock round the tiny
bashrul figure of the little girl who had broken the bottle on the
boat's prow, no one had even looked around. The bundledup
figures of men and women perched on the scaffolding about the
huge oaken skeletons of the barges kept hammering and sawing.
Girls in baggy pants and sweaters ran to and fro with pots of
paint or rolls of asbestos covering for the steampipes. In the new
ways where a keel had just been laid down an old man, with a
hooked nose sticking out blue into the wind between the visor of
his black serge cap and the muffler that was wound across his
white whiskers, was slowly and carefully with curved back whit-
tling at a great oak timber between his feet with a curved adze
that flashed bright every time he lifted it in the cold sunlight of
the winter noon.

Labor and Management

In a yard outside of one of the small east coast cities where they
were building freighters we were sitting at a desk in a glassedin
office, looking out at the great blurred shapes of the hulls on the
ways and the row of busy tall cranes that kept swinging pieces of
ship in front of our eyes as we talked and at the gray sky and
the stretch of harbor water beyond.

I was asking an executive of the company whether in his
opinion management and labor were working together for war
production as well as they might. They had a long ways to go he
said. On instructions from Washington they had set up a labor-
management committee. He couldn't see that it had done much
yet. The first problem they'd tried to tackle was unnecessary absences from work. They had a long ways to go on that. This
was an independent crowd. It was hard keeping a man from
taking a couple of days off to paint his house, or a woman from
staying out till she got her dishes washed and her laundry done.
The hunting season was the worst. It was mighty hard to keep

a downeaster from goin' duckin' when he'd a mind to or goin' up
into the woods to shoot him some deermeat for the winter.

This was a union yard and you had to be careful not to let the
union run away with it. That was the trouble with these committees from management's point of view.

'What about this triangular duel between the company and the
two big labor organizations?'

'Of course that's in the other yard,' he answered sharply.
'Never been any trouble here.'

The executive was a sharpfaced young man with a keen lawyer's manner. He got up and lit a cigarette and took a couple of
paces back and forth across the room. 'Now get this straight, the
company hasn't anything to do with it,' he said emphatically. 'Is
it our fault if we have two yards and if the A.F. of L. has gotten
into one and the C.I.O. into the other? We are willing to do business with one union or both if they'd just make up their minds to
agree.'

'How do the men here feel about it?'

'Now you don't need to believe what I say, but the average man
working here feels just the way the management does . . . a plague
on both your houses. They feel — at least they tell me they feel —
that the whole thing's a put-up job of the Administration. This is
an A.F. of L. town from way back, but the Administration wants
the C.I.O. in here for political reasons. Now I'm not saying that.
Don't get me wrong . . . It's the men I've talked to on the job
who are saying that. Most of the men working in these yards
aren't any different from you and me, a great many of them are
farmers and small businessmen . . . But if I should go out and
tell them what they'll tell you, "To hell with this row between the
unions and let's get to work," I'd be interfering with the Wagner
Act and like as not end up in jail.'

I got up to go. While I had been sitting there a brandnew
deckhouse had been dropped onto the hull of the nearest Liberty
ship. The man I'd been talking to saw me looking out. His face
broadened into a smile. 'That's the fun of shipbuilding,' he said.
'You can see them grow. It's a very simple proposition really . . .

People love to work in a shipyard . . . That's one reason I don't
like this union business . . . For God's sake, don't quote me . . .
I know it has to be . . . Having to think of the management as the
enemy all the time kind of takes the pleasure in his work away
from a man.'

Back in town at the office of one of the union locals the secretary
leaned back in his chair and said: 'We're getting along fine considering that this used to be one of the most antiunion sections
of the country. Businessmen used to blow right up in your face
if you mentioned the word union. And the workingman wasn't
sold on the idea either. They are not yet, you heard that guy. . . ?'

He was referring to a ruddy sharpfeatured middleaged man
who had been arguing with him when I came into the office. He
was a shipyard worker. He was arguing about whether he should
ask for a raise directly or whether he should do it through the
shopsteward. He'd been working four months at one job and he
felt it was time for him to get a raise and said his idea was to go
up to the foreman and ask him for it. No, the secretary had kept
insisting, he ought to ask for it through the shopsteward who
represented the union.

'But I work with this foreman every day. He's a touchy kind
of feller. I wouldn't want him to think I'd gone over his head.'

'But that's what you pay the dues for, to have the union take
up grievances for you.'

'But askin' for a raise isn't a grievance . . . Now if I asked for
a raise an' didn't git it, I might have a grievance.'

'Then what's the use of having the union?'

The man had finally gone away saying reluctantly he guessed
he'd try the shopsteward. You could see that it gave him real
pain to feel he couldn't go up to his foreman, man to man, and ask
him for a raise if he wanted one.

'Now what can you do with a man like that?' the secretary
asked me with a wry unsmiling shake of his head after the man
had gone. 'But on the whole,' he added, rolling his eyes up, 'it's
all harmonious . . . considering that the idea of paying high wages,
even if it's Uncle Sam's money, keeps the management awake

nights. The one thing we tell 'em the guys really believe is that management is soaking away the dough. We don't let 'em forget there's a war on either.'

Old-Time Concern

In a famous old shipyard in Massachusetts where they still had what amounted to a company union the secretary of the labor-management committee gave me, as he talked about his work, management's picture in that part of the world of harmony with labor. He was evidently an old shipbuilder himself. He was a ruddyfaced grayhaired man with a clear skin younger than his years and clear gray eyes that looked straight at you. What he enjoyed most in life you could see was getting ships built. He talked with pleasure of the great expansion of the yard in the last ten years since naval building had started up again. That had meant a labor force doubling and tripling and expanding almost indefinitely. In spite of that, the oldtimers still dominated the yard. It pleased him that so many of the men who had worked in the yard during the expansion of the last war had come back, and that their sons were coming to work, and that, now that girls and women were being employed, most of them were the wives and daughters of old employees who'd been drafted. Of course some troublemakers and union-minded mavericks had come in, among so many you had to have some bad eggs, but on the whole they'd been able to keep it in the family.

In fact the majority of their workmen still lived within trolley distance. Several thousand families had moved into the adjoining towns, to be sure, but surprisingly few of them came from outside of the state or even from very far. This was a densely populated area of sprawling towns that were all each other's suburbs, fairly well linked up by trains, busses, and streetcars. Streets and streets of big glum houses left over from the realestate booms oi the past. Along the beaches and rocky necks of the shore there were thousands of vacant seaside cottages. They were planning to fill them up with shipyard workers. Everybody was very proud that this region contained such a wealth of housing as well as of skilled labor. If outsiders only kept their noses out, they could handle their war problems very nicely by themselves.

We got back to the subject of cooperation between management and labor. They were proud of their record in this yard, no labor trouble in twentytwo years. Yes, they had a union, an independent union — sure, it was independent; the office was across the street off company property — which had won two elections from the C.I.O. Half the production committee, as they called the labor-management committee here, was appointed by the union from its membership and half represented management. To tell the truth it wasn't so very different from the old employee representation plan. All these committees had been set in motion at the suggestion of Donald Nelson's W.P.B. Sure, it was worth the time spent at the weekly meetings, some very useful suggestions had been made by individual workers, and it certainly tended to keep up morale. Yes, he thought it was there to stay. Of course, in some places union organizers had made trouble in the production committees, but here, where it was all in the family, the system worked.

When I asked him whether what they read in the papers or heard over the radio had any effect on the men's efficiency and enthusiasm, he said the question was a poser. He guessed not many of 'em took much stock in the newspapers. No, he never heard much talk about the news. Of course Pearl Harbor had given us all a shock; we knew we were in for it then; we knew the war had to be won, in fact we couldn't imagine not winning it. No, not even the North African landings had caused much of a ripple. 'But I'll tell you what does, when one of the ships we built ourselves is sunk, that has an effect . . . That aircraft carrier, now, the men sure felt her loss. There are men here in the yard who knew every bolt and rivet on that ship. They knew the crews too. Skeleton crews are attached to the ships as soon as they are started. Losing that carrier really brought the thing home. There wasn't a man here who wasn't crazy to get to work on a new one. They circulated a petition and sent it to the Navy

Department asking to have the new one called the Pearl Harbor.'

This was a man who had spent his life in shipbuilding. The last thing I asked him was how the workmen they had now compared with those who had come into the yards during the last war. He said flatly there had been an improvement. Of the young men who came as apprentices and beginners, more had had at least a year of highschool; they learned quicker, dressed better, were generally better behaved, a higher type of man than the bunch of raw laborers who couldn't speak English who had flocked there to work twentyfive years ago.

'So our educational system has done a job?'

'Yes, sir, a great job.'

Modern production methods made more demands on skill and less on strength, he said. In the old days the worker had the knowhow in his arms, now he has to learn it in his head.

'But there's less skill required, isn't that so?'

'Yes,' he said, after a moment's thought. 'The real truth is that the knowhow is in the machine.'

'Won't that mean that in the long run the workingman will have less to sell to management than he did before and that management will be able to drive a harder bargain?'

He wouldn't pick the notion up. 'We got to win the war before we start to worry about things like that,' he said, smiling amiably.

Small Business in New England

'But what's the matter with small business?' you ask the white-haired man with haggard brow and yellow teeth and a nervous twitching manner who sits in tweeds behind a cluttered desk in a highceilinged office in the handsome Ionic building of the Chamber of Commerce.

'Nothing the matter with it. It's just dead,' he shouts back hoarsely from across piles of yellowed folders and withering pamphlets out of other days.

'But where's the money going? It's pouring into town every payday.'

'If you ask me I think they are putting it in their socks . . . They aren't spending much, honestly they're not. They buy furs and jewelry. Cheap novelty goods sell out. Clothing stores do well . . . But on the whole small business has lost its roots. There's no sap in it . . . Gosh, I oughtn't to be talking like this.'

'Could it be that New England businessmen hate the Administration so much they wouldn't be prosperous if they could, wouldn't give the government the satisfaction?'

'Cutting off their nose to spite their face, eh? I don't think so . . . The small businessman just can't cope with all these regulations. He can't do the paperwork required. He can't get the office staff. He's just shutting up shop and going into war work. That's what Washington intended . . . If you ask me, Washington does not intend to let the small businessman ever show his face again.'

'But there must be ways of finding something to sell. People have got all the money in the world to buy it.'

The secretary of the Chamber of Commerce shakes his head: 'Black market stuff. The decent New England merchant just won't stoop that low. The foreignborn go in for that sort of thing. They are reaping a harvest.'

'Is it as bad as that?'

'People like us have taken a licking,' he says. 'It'll be years before we know how bad a licking we've taken.'

After I had left him I stood under the columned porch of the building looking out at the noontime traffic under the bare elms along the street of old brick houses. The setting, in spite of the streetcars and the busses and the automobiles, was still Federalist New England. Opposite, a greenishgray church steeple rose up into the murky early winter sunlight. A smell of burning leaves came from the common down the block. In the wooden pediment over my head starlings in a row were carrying on their arrogant chatter, squawking and fluttering and pouting their glossy breasts into the sunlight. High above the city gulls were circling. The sparrows in the bushes looked cosy and plump. Only the people scurrying along the street looked drab and gray and driven. They were warmly dressed, they looked wellfed, but still as they passed by they looked helpless and fragile and faceless as dry leaves blown along the gutter by a gust of wind.

It's tough on people to live in a time of too many changes, I was thinking. But then I remembered the man I had met in a small inland town in Maine who was driving a taxi. As he drove us around, he told us how he happened to be there driving that taxi. He spoke without bitterness or regret, telling the story as if it were about somebody else. At home, in another downeast town that had no war industries to keep it alive, he'd run a hardware store for many years and before that had edited the newspaper. Recently his store hadn't done so well, couldn't get anything to sell. He was a dignified portly man with steelgray hair, the very type of smalltown Rotarian. He spoke cheerfully of his adventures as if they were just what a successful businessman had to expect. When he'd found he couldn't make both ends meet at home (he had two boys in the army and their leaving had made things kind of empty), he'd driven his car up here and licensed it as a taxi. Yes, he rather enjoyed the change. He'd been making quite a lot of money transporting warworkers and servicemen. Now the trouble was that after the first of January he understood taxis were only to be allowed three gallons of gas a day. He wouldn't be able to make a living at that and would have to find some other job.

The prospect didn't seem to worry him. A reporter for the local newspaper was in the cab. As we were getting out, the driver turned to him and said, 'Say, how about getting me a job on your paper?' 'Could be,' said the reporter. 'Better come in and talk to the boss.' I left them with their heads together at the door of the newspaper office.

The Old Seaport Blooms

Finding I had a couple of hours to spare, I began to walk around the town. In the rosy haze off the bay the quiet streets of stately mansarded houses that led toward the wharves and the bare elms and the old brick warehouses began to take on that look of being

in a weathered steel engraving. On one broad empty street I came
upon an oldtime barber college. Gone were the strapping lady
barbers and the blearyeyed youths who in the old days would
have been standing in a row rasping the fur off the chins of hungry
bindlestiffs or drunken lumberjacks who'd blown in their pay, o'
cutting hair and putting ears and noses in jeopardy with click-
clacking scissors. Nobody was lolling in the chairs waiting for a
fifteen cent shave. The soap had dried in the mugs, the mirrors
were streaked brown and murky with grime. Only in the darkest
corner an elderly man in his shirtsleeves was laboriously scraping
the upturned cheek of another tattered relic of the Hoovervilles of
the past. I guess there was nobody else in town broke enough to
be there. Another small business casualty.

Up on the hill the shopping streets were full of midday bustle.
Women with bundles were coming in and out of shops. People
were holding small children up to the showwindow of a depart-
mentstore to see a big dummy Santa Claus continually shaking
with mechanical laughter. Candy stores, restaurants, and sodafountains were full of sailors from the nearby naval base. As I
still had an hour before traintime, I set out to find a cocktail
lounge to settle down to read the paper in. Cocktail lounges there
were, but so lugubriously untenanted I decided to go somewhere
else. Sauntering farther along the main street, I came to a vaude-
ville theatre that advertised 'Songs from the Gay Nineties.'
People were filing past the ticket office. The stout young woman
in a fur neckpiece and a shovelshaped black hat who was in line
ahead of me cried out in surprise when she reached the window.
'You? . . . Why, goodness, how long have you been working
here?'

'Three days,' the blackeyed girl inside said rather proudly.

'Why on earth don't you go to the shipyard? Lil's there and
everybody.'

The girl, who evidently thought better than that of herself,
flashed her eyes as she rattled the changemaking machine and
said peevishly, 'To hell with the shipyard.'

'I bet you are not making your carfare.'

The girl behind the ticket window didn't answer. She dropped her eyes to her tickets.

The stout young woman tossed her shovelshaped hat and chanted as she flounced off into the theatre, 'In the shipyard you'd be doing better for yourself, dearie.'

Portland, Maine, December, 1942

IT WAS in one of those jerrybuilt Washington hotels that have been plastered with decoration out of some bargaincounter of eroded ornament so sleazy that you feel depravity seeping out of the stippled walls as if some of the turpitude that afflicted the builders, from the banker who did the financing and the architect who fudged the blueprints right through to the man who ran the cement mixer, had actually gotten into the tile and mortar and stucco. Walking along the corridor on the ninth floor, past the two colored maids with their rolling basket of soiled towels, differences in the earlymorning staleness of the steamheated air began to be noticeable as you passed the various rooms. From one door came a whiff of breakfast coffee, from another the smell of a freshlit cigar, or shaving soap, or toilet water, or a suspicion of rye, ever so slight indications that the lives writhing feebly in the sameness behind the identical doors had some individuality.

This morning it's a man in an official position who has written a book about democracy I'm looking for as I count my way down the numbers to his door. The door is ajar. I knock. 'Come in,' calls a voice from the bathroom.

The room is like all the other rooms. There is the same scattering of toilet articles on the bureau, the briefcase on the desk, the soft brown leather bag open on the baggage rack. On the rumpled bedspread there's a red and blue airline envelope with a sheaf of pale green tickets spilling out of it. On a chair with a raincoat thrown over the back of it a portable tyewriter stands open in its case. There's a race of men who spend their lives between their hotel rooms and their offices in the national capital and conferences in more hotel rooms and planeflights and sleepingcar nights sandwiched between speeches at meetings and conferences in hotel rooms and conversations in other offices and other hotel rooms from one end of the country to the other. Their emblem is the briefcase and the envelope full of airline tickets.

After a moment the man who had written a book about democracy came out of the bathroom to greet me, bringing with him an aroma of shaving soap. He was a tall kangarooshaped man in white shirtsleeves with a high receding forehead and a massive nose over a small chin.

'Excuse me,' he said effusively apologetic. 'You must excuse me ... I didn't get in till late last night ... A higher priority grounded me in Indianapolis. I had to come on by train ... so now I've got to telescope my day. If you don't mind we'll talk as I pack. I have to deliver an address tomorrow in Buffalo ... Today I'll have to cut all my appointments short ... You wanted to ask about something?'

'I wanted to ask how labor-management committees were working out.'

'Of course you know that this has been a matter very dear to my heart ... the Board has issued a directive ...'

The telephone rang. While he was talking I worked a small cigar out of its cellophane and lit it. From the telephone he walked with a determined stride back into the bathroom. When he reappeared he had his coat and vest on.

'... a directive,' he went on as if there had been no interruption, 'which has been backed up by circulars and mimeographed matter giving directions as to the functioning and formation of such labor-management committees. The results of the directive have not been quite what we had hoped, but they have been better than some of our members expected who didn't have any confidence in anything of this kind at all ...'

The telephone rang again. On the way over to answer it, he dropped a pair of folded pyjamas into his suitcase. When he'd finished the call, he hurried back into the bathroom and went on talking from there: 'Now for many years there has been a feeling in the progressive wing of the labor movement that, if we are to reverse the trend which many authorities deem to exist in this country against democratic selfgovernment, industry is the place to start. Though of course I wouldn't like to be quoted as saying this publicly because the industry members of the Board are extremely touchy about it. The way they put it is that it's just helping labor to get a foot in the stirrup ...'

The telephone rang again. He emerged from the bathroom with his shaving case packed and a bathrobe over his arm. Halfway through his telephone conversation he looked up at me and whispered plaintively, 'You don't see a pair of slippers anywhere, do you?' While he went on talking, I groped under the bed and found the slippers. I waved them in his direction and set them on his bathrobe on the foot of the bed. He smiled and tried to make his eyebrows say thank you while his mouth went on talking into the telephone. When he hung up he went on, 'And of course between you and me that's just what they don't want. We had to go clear to the White House to get the original directive through at all.' As he talked, he was stuffing his bathrobe and his slippers into his suitcase. He started pressing down the top of the suitcase. 'In my opinion the mere fact that the labor-management committees do exist even if in some cases only on paper constitutes one of the most impressive victories that have been gained on the liberal front.' As he came to a period, he strode up to me with his hand outstretched. 'Well, this has been delightful. You must excuse me ... If there's any further information, documentation, literature, or anything of that sort you must be sure and let me know.' Shaking his hand I was backing out the door. My cigar was out. I hadn't had time to relight it.

CHAPTER 3

The Men Who Make the Motors

U NDER THE WHITE SKY of winter on the level lands that stretch northward from the Mississippi and Ohio to the shore of the Great Lakes the snow dissolves horizons, planes out unevenness, obliterates ponds and rivers, blurs the outlines of gullies, fences, farm buildings, smudges the tracery of wooded tracts with a swirl of whiteness. Across the smooth plains, behind locomotives that jet cottony blobs of steam, move long trains capped with level streaks of snow of varicolored boxcars, tankcars, gondolas carrying shapes of machines hooded under tarpaulins, and always the caboose with its little stovepipe merrily jouncing along at the end. Between yellowish piles of snow thrown up by the snowplows, trucks stumble in long queues through the highways among the beetlelike shapes of passenger cars and the lowhung streamlined busses. Roads and railroad tracks crisscross and converge under the straight parallel scratches of telegraph and telephone wires and hightension lines looped from steel stanchion to steel stanchion. The tracks come together into freight yards beside oblong masses of industrial buildings levelled down by the snowy horizontals of their roofs until they seem part of the plain. The roads dive under concrete bridges; open out into broad main stems of towns between gridirons of streets of small frame houses; pass garish blocks of storefronts noisy with lettering, and open lots

ranked with thirdhand jalopies sealed under their white icing, and
the fanciful suburban architecture of servicestations, realestate
offices, garages, hamburger stands, roadside restaurants and fruit-
markets now boarded up and forgotten; to emerge again onto
snowy plains where great manufacturing plants jut up among
their parkinglots like mesas in the desert; to swerve round steelmills that smear the sky with brown smoke out of tall cylindrical
chimneys in fours and sixes; and to lose themselves in murky
canyons between warehouses, grain elevators, apartments, office
buildings leaking light from a thousand windows, hotels with
flashing signs, in the packed perpendicular mass of the mountain-
ous cities.

Production Man

We are driving out through the murk of a winter afternoon up a
deepcut snowy valley full of railroad tracks where the steel mills
glow like oldfashioned wood stoves beside rows of black cylindrical
stacks. From smaller chimneys jet little blobs of pink and sul-
phuryellow steam that hang under the pall of brown smoke from
the tall stacks.

'So you want to see production one hundred percent efficient,
eh?' asks the man who's driving me. 'Well, we think the feller
who runs our plant has got that problem licked. Absenteeism,
well, for him it just ain't. Labor turnover? You wait till you see
him. You'll probably be trying to get a job with him yourself.
That's what happened to me first time I saw him.'

This man, he goes on to explain, eats, drinks, breathes, and
sleeps production. Went to work in a machine shop when he was
fourteen years old. Knew the labor side of the fence because he'd
been a union organizer himself. Before he went into manufacturing he organized a local of the machinists' union. Was a labor
man for years; still reprints in the company's house organ editorials he wrote in the labor press; says he won't take back a word he
said then. He's made everything from automatic razors to diesel
engines. Now it is airplane starters and automatic pilots. He

started this concern with an old wreck of a factory building and a
hundred men. Now he has several thousand men spread out over
five plants. And with a third less plant than the famous old concern that produces the same automatic pilot he is turning out
three times as many units, so perfect that the armed services have
stopped inspecting them. 'Look' — the voice of the man who is
driving me grows warm with pride and affection — 'That's one of
our plants.' We are passing a new redbrick and glasstile building
set in snowy acres of parked cars. 'We put that one up in fortyseven days.'

At the main plant a few miles farther out he parks his car and
ushers me past the guard at the door and up a narrow stairway.
From the shops beyond the partition comes a whir of machines
and the brisk tune of '*This is the army, Mister Jones*' coming over
the public address system. 'But where are the offices?' I'm asking.
My guide laughs. 'All inside his head ... Here we are.'

We have crossed a narrow corridor and already I am being
introduced to his private secretary. She is a stout youngish
woman with a pretty skin and frizzy dark hair and a cosy manner.
She tells me cordially that I'm expected. 'He's out in the shop,
he's always out in the shop, but he'll be right back.' Then she
makes me a present of a souvenir pencil made of red white and
blue plastic with the name of the company on it, and adds confidentially, 'I know you'll think he's wonderful too ... Everybody does. You know he's always here. The rest of us work only
twelve hours, but he's here all the time. It's just wonderful to
work here. He's so wonderful to everybody.'

She ushers me into an office that opens right off the vestibule.
There are no doors. The place is airy and well lighted with a
comfortable up-to-date look. In the middle facing the entrance
stands a small desk with a microphone beside it. 'He can talk
to all the plants with that. He talks directly to every man at his
bench ... or right here. Nobody ever waits. Anybody can
walk right in.' She points to a glass cabinet with machine parts
laid out along the shelves. 'He calls these his toys.' She points to
a stuffed sailfish on the wall above. 'He caught that himself.

On a blue cloth on a table the other side of the room is a bisected airplane starter, its bright metal parts shining in the glow from the fluorescent light in the ceiling. 'That's it, that's what we make,' she says in a reverential tone. She settles you comfortably in a leather chair with a glazed paper booklet to read.

After a while the man himself walks in slowly from the plant. He's a stocky man in his fifties with graying blond hair. He wears a light easyfitting suit and a soft brown shirt open at the neck. He has a machinist's face and large opaque porcelain blue eyes. His hands are broad and stubby. He has a slightly abstracted look and the slow movements of a person who is accustomed to getting very little sleep and to resting as he goes. He shakes hands with the distantly intimate fatherly manner of someone who is accustomed to dealing with a great many different sorts of men in a day.

Somewhat conscious that this is a man who lives in a different world from mine. I start to explain to him what kind of articles I am trying to write. 'I see,' he says, without irony, 'you are merely writing generalities.'

Then he goes on, in the tone of one who has explained all this before and is a little weary of explaining it, but is still anxious to make himself plain, telling in a slow careful voice how he does it: 'The first thing to do is to eliminate fear in the shop. I worked in shops myself so I know how I used to feel, how I'd feel today. We eliminate all the little things that cause irritation without any reason.' He drew one leg out from under his desk and pointed out his shoe. 'The first thing I do when a new man comes in here is buy him a nice comfortable pair of shoes like these I wear. Men ruin their feet standing up all day in cheap old shoes and sneakers. It makes them uncomfortable. They get tired easy. We work in two shifts, twelve hours each, seven days a week. We haven't a time clock in the place. Every man who comes to work here promises to produce as much as he can, that's all.'

'How long have you been on these hours?'

'Ever since we started. We have a hundred percent union shop. of course, it's eight hours with overtime.'

'How about absenteeism?' I asked and stumbled over the word. 'A tenth of one percent. Some days we don't have any. The associates won't stand for it. If you go out early or come in late, they give you the wolf call. Nobody wants to get that twice.'

'Don't the men want to take a day off now and then?'

He looked up gravely. Evidently the shop was his life. He couldn't imagine being happy anywhere else even for a day. 'They don't seem to. If a man gets to feeling fagged, he can take a turkish bath and get a rubdown. We have expert masseurs. You'll see the baths later. If a man who's had no absences seems to be running down, I'll send him and his wife to Florida for a couple of weeks, or in summer to a camp on Georgian Bay. After loafing and fishing for a while, he'll come back fit as a fiddle ... That sort of thing does me good, so I know it must do them good. Everybody gets a nice hot lunch and there are coffee urns all around the plant ... A man can get him a cup of coffee and a doughnut or hot bouillon whenever he wants it. There's always somebody around for him to tell his troubles to. I've had three cups of bouillon with different men this afternoon.'

'Even so I should think a twelvehour day week after week would wear them out.'

His face set hard. His big opaque eyes looked straight ahead of him. 'It don't wear me out ... You ought to see the boys bowling nights, or playing baseball in summer ... We have a kind of clubhouse over here — everybody chips in for the upkeep. Getting tired's all in the conditions under which a man works. If you can make him comfortable and happy, he don't get so tired ... let him have a smoke if he wants it ... give him plenty of light and room ... Fear and obscurity make for fatigue and sloppy work.'

'You mean most men like to work.'

He smiled. 'I do myself. Don't you? ... The trouble with so many of these big plants is the management gets all balled up with social life, getting the better of somebody else ... all sorts of things that have nothing to do with production ... they used to call it keeping up with the Joneses. That don't worry us here.

Everybody who works here is an associate. We call you by your first name from the day you start in . . . This is what we make.'

He picked up a beautifully finished piece of metal and balanced it in his hand. His stubby fingers held it delicately. The film had gone off his eyes. He was enjoying himself. He made me lift it. 'See how light it is. My partner designs these things. He's a genius.' He made me balance it in one hand. Then he turned to the starter against the wall with the expression of a painter pulling the cover off a painting on his easel. 'That's the finished product,' he said, leaning back in his chair and letting his eyes run lovingly over every polished curve. 'Now I'll find somebody to show you around.'

'First . . . excuse me.' He pressed a button on his desk. The mike of the public address system hummed. 'Attention, Associates . . . Anybody who wants help in making out his income tax report should find Joe Jones. He's got all the dope . . . He'll be around the shop all afternoon . . . Don't nobody forget now that we are going to the Golden Gloves tonight. Everybody turn out . . .' He cut the thing off. He turned to me cosily smiling: 'They like to know I'm close by.'

'Say, Tom,' he called to the man who had brought me out.

'What is it, Bill?' the man answered from outside in the hall.

'Take this gentleman around the shop . . . Let him talk to anybody he wants to talk to.'

'Sure I will, Bill.'

The Upper Brackets

Your feet numb from wading through the deep slush of the downtown streets, your ears gnawed by the lashing sleety wind, you dive through the revolving doors into the warm lobby of the big hotel. Bellhops and doormen, freshfaced farmboys stuffed into silly pale blue uniforms out of superannuated musical comedies stand against the wall. Welldressed women hurry across the deep carpets under the eyes of frogfaced men with cigars in the corners of their mouths bogged into the soft upholstery of easy chairs

From the cocktail room comes a clinking of ice and a smell of zest of lemon and martinis and rye whiskey. From the restaurant comes a mellow smell of food. There are streaks of rich cigarsmoke in the air.

The lobby is crowded. Men and women are waiting around in twos and threes. People are pouring up the redcarpeted stairway that leads to the grand ballroom. There's a look of silk and real wool about their clothes, their shoes are solid and wellshined. they wear expensive neckties. It's a crowd out of the upper brackets: executives, topflight production engineers, personnel managers, public relations men, owners. They stand straight and walk confidently, with fat wallets on their hips. Their bodies are wellbuilt, wellexercised, they take good care of themselves. These are men who've reached the top, who have married monied and attractive wives, who are accustomed to giving orders, who expect subordinates to do what they say. They'll tell you that they have come up the hard way; they expect to stay up. Their hands are accustomed to the electric feel of the levers of power. This is their country. Tonight they are on a mission of patriotism. They are waiting to get a glimpse of the hero, the great flyer who has come back from the dead.

Soon the voice of the lean tense man home from out of several kinds of hell on earth starts to shrill out of every radio. He stands between the magnates of motorproduction as he talks. His voice is sobbing with earnestness. It was such a little time ago he was with the men dodging shellfragments in sweaty foxholes. He has seen them blinded and smashed to pieces. He has seen how they die. He has seen a young fellow die by inches beside him. He has himself been saved by a hundred-to-one chance. He can't understand how during this total war any part of the nation can still be doing the same things, thinking the same thoughts, nagging at the same wrangles as in times of peace:

'If you could understand,' he cries out, 'what our boys are doing in these hellholes throughout the Pacific and in the burning sands of Africa that your way of life may be preserved, you wouldn't worry about eight hours a day, overtime or double time for Sundays . .' Applause thunders out, clattering in the loud-speakers. 'Good boy . . . that's straight from the shoulder. Labor can't duck that one,' you can hear the salaried men and executives say one to another.

'If necessary to make us appreciate our duties, bring back the troops, place them in the factories, take the warworkers and place them in the foxholes with the filth and the Japanese, and I guarantee to you that production will be increased and much of it doubled within thirty days . . ' This is strong stuff. The listeners breathe deep . . . 'This is a life-and-death struggle for the welfare of our nation, none of us is doing so much that he can't do more . . .' Men and women are listening with wet eyes, people sitting round their radios swallow hard. What he says is true. Many a man promises himself he will do better. And as for those blankety blanks in the shops . . .

Afterwards the hotel lobby is more crowded than ever. There's a feeling of exultation about the people coming down the stairs out of the grand ballroom. They have been rubbing elbows with power. They have been hobnobbing with events. As men hurry past you hear fragments of talk. 'These damned unions' . . . 'Put labor in its place' . . . 'Slap every mother's son of them in the army an' make 'em work.'

They Crash the Tony Joints

A young man is telling a story to a man from out of town. 'You know there's a restaurant here a gang of us has patronized for some time, a little like "Twenty One" in New York, the same kind of food, the same atmosphere. Well, I'll be damned if four of them didn't come in there one evening and sit down at a table and ask for a bill of fare . . . The fellow who runs it, he has a special bill of fare for people he doesn't like, about twice the usual price. Well, these guys never batted an eyelash. They ordered up all the most expensive wines, the guy ran his finger down the card till he found what cost most and paid for it out of a pay check on one of the automotive concerns for a hundred and twentysix dollars, told the waiter to hurry because he had to go to work . . . but they never did go to work because they got to drinking . . . That's absenteeism for you.'

Detroit Hierarchy

I was sitting in an office in the administration building of one of the big automobile plants. It was a large quiet room filled with even bright light from two big windows. The man behind the large uncrowded desk had an athletic look under his easyfitting light gray suit. He was in his late thirties, perhaps. There was an air of great competence about him. He talked slowly and well. The question he was answering was whether anything could be done to promote more cooperation towards the war effort between management and the men who worked in the shops. 'Well, the first thing we have to admit is that the workers' morale isn't what it should be . . . not by a long shot. . . . There's too much distrust of management on the part of labor. They don't understand what's at stake. Absenteeism is terrific, fifty percent worse than in normal times. Just an example: one plant over here had always had pretty good labor relations . . . At Christmas they gave everybody a turkey dinner and the day off; but they asked the boys particularly to be back on the night shift . . . Only fifty men showed up out of thirteen hundred. There's too much loitering on the job . . . The power curves show a drop of half an hour before and after lunch, and the same thing when a shift goes on and off . . . If there's a shutdown on account of shortage of materials half the men go get jobs somewhere else.'

'Are the labor-management committees amounting to anything?'

'I'll have to frankly admit that they got off to a bad start. Labor came in with some pretty gaudy ideas. There was a feeling around management that the committees were a gift from the shiny-eared Newdealers. There's been too much of the attitude that anything that was good for management was bad for labor and vice versa. The union sent out too many wideopen talkers who turned up not to have any grip on their rank and file. There were delays and delays. It took us six months to decide whether the committees should meet on the company's time or on the workers' time. The union people couldn't understand why, if the salaried officials talked on the company's time, the men from the shop shouldn't do the same . . . Our idea was that they should give their time like for civilian defence . . . We finally gave in on that and now we pay them at their regular rates for their two hours' weekly meeting. Most of the meetings don't last that long.'

'How about suggestions for technical improvements in production?'

He frowned. 'We don't think there's much in it. Of course there always has been a useful suggestion from time to time from a man in the shop. But here's the sort of thing we have to face. An ambitious Jewish boy in one of our plants made a suggestion that was moderately practical and now he's hellbent he'll go to Washington and see the great White White. He's trying to put through a fullfledged plan for suggestions on production and make it retroactive just to serve his own ambition. He gets in our hair at every meeting. He's almost driven us nuts.'

'Do you think the committees have a future?'

'The best I can say is that we're gradually ironing out our differences. The topflight union leaders have been pretty reasonable . . . But the union is so new. They hardly had a chance to get started before they were put under the strain of the war effort. The difficulty is that the union members of the steering committee can't put over their decisions on the locals . . . Don't quote me on this for God's sake,' he went on almost in a whisper. 'But one of the great stumbling blocks in our way is the government's rigid definition of coercion under the Wagner Act. Management just can't speak its piece to the men and any union man can. We have no way of telling them our side of the story any more . . . Another drag on production is the union premise that every man on a similar job should do the same amount of work every day. The good men quit when they've done their stint. You know the everpresent fear the men have of working themselves out of a job.'

'How are the union members of the committees selected?'

'Some are appointed by the union executives and some are elected in the shop ... In our plant we've selected topflight officials to meet with the committees, usually one labor relations man, an operating man, and a man from the sales and promotion department ... In some plants they haven't done that. Now across the way here' — he pointed out the window at the outlines of huge blocks of concrete buildings barely visible through the blurring snow mist — 'they meet with the plant police.'

'Which do you think works out best on the labor end, appointment by the union or election in the shop?'

There wasn't a quaver of doubt in his voice. 'Appointment,' he said emphatically.

At the headquarters of another great satrapy of automobile production converted for war the public relations man was even less willing to be quoted. 'We are not enthusiastic about labor-management committees,' he said. 'Frankly we think they got off on the wrong foot. They have been used for labor politics.' That was that. I asked him if he had any ideas about improving relations between management and labor, at least for the duration of the war. 'That's not up my alley,' he said 'You ought to talk to the personnel manager, but he's not in his office today ... Now, speaking just for myself, of course, I feel the whole idea of industrial democracy is very interesting ...'

Night Life

This was a tall lanky man with a sharppointed black mustache. He wore a belted tweed jacket and kept saying all evening he wanted to go duckhunting. Here it was late in the fall and he hadn't gone duckhunting yet. He and his wife had taken me out festively to dinner at a rathskeller where the bread and the beer were good. When I mentioned the words 'industrial democracy' first, he gave a hoot of laughter and then he looked sad. He started talking quickly and sharply as if to get rid of the matter once for all: 'I think we are going to have fascism in this country and I'm trying to get used to the idea so that it won't hurt toc much ... Hell, let's have some more beer ... When I was a kid,' he added when the steins came, 'I fell for the New Freedom and making the world safe for Democracy and the Russian revolution and justice, liberty, selfdetermination ... the masses. . My God! I used to think I was a mighty terrible red, but I don't like the way the words sound any more ... I like the way farmers talk and old backwoods drunks in the Upper Peninsula of Michigan I go duckhunting with ... I guess I'm getting old. Maybe the taste for eternal things rather than transient things is a sign of old age. But I don't like the words any more ... They make me feel embarrassed. Darling,' he said to his wife, 'suppose we take him to' — he whispered in her ear. 'She deals with eternal things all right.'

'Do you think he'd like her?' the wife asked in a startled tone.

'Sure he'll like her. She's a good woman and she's somebody he can't class angle.'

After we'd finished our dinner we found ourselves with paperbags full of beer bottles under our arms lurching across the slush frozen unevenly between the stained snowpiles along a dark street of tumbledown redbrick houses. The grimy light that spilled out here and there through a hallway seemed to deepen the darkness. Not even the snow had any light in it. When we found the number in the middle of a set of old brick houses all in a row, the racket of a small dog yapping answered our knock.

After a while the door opened and we all stumbled into the tiny dim hall in a bunch and stood there blinking, ears tingling, and noses running after the searching cold of the street. The woman who had opened the door for us was leaning down trying to quiet a plump white foxterrier with a brown nose. When she straightened up, you could see that she was a skinny woman of no particular age with frizzy peroxide hair. Her hornrim spectacles gave her a schoolteachery look. Only in her frilled blouse with its oldfashioned peekaboo embroidery was there any touch of frivolity. As soon as she'd got the dog quiet, she began to shriek and carry

on over my friends. How long it was since they had been to see
her, how they oughtn't to have brought the beer, she had plenty
on ice. The foxterrier got to barking again and would keep
jumping up into the blue velour armchair so that nobody got to
sit in it, but eventually we all got our overcoats and mufflers and
overshoes off and settled ourselves in the narrow parlor with the
polished upright piano that filled most of it up and the shaded
standing lamps that had the look of having been won at carnivals
and the chromos in big gold frames on the walls, each with a glass
of beer in his hand. She sat down on the pianostool in the midst
of us showing all her teeth and swinging herself girlishly back and
forth on the stool as she smiled from one to the other.

How was she? She was fine. No, Ed was away. No, she
wasn't lonely. She had three lodgers, all of them warworkers,
lovely boys. No, she wasn't playing anywhere, housework took
up her time and walking the dog and writing to the soldier boys,
she was writing to twentyfive of 'em and you bet you they answered by the next mail, they were so lonely, the poor boys. Sure
the fellers wanted her back, but there weren't any really good
night clubs any more. If we'd excuse her French she was sick of
playing for a lot of doublecrossing bastards. Of course they were
all making big money now packed to the doors with warworkers,
but it wasn't like the old days. All these warworkers had so
much money and were in such a hurry to get drunk and nobody
cared if you lived or died. In the old days it had been more
friendly like, fellers knew how to sing and to have a good time.
Now she didn't want any piece of it. Of course they were after
her because good pianoplayers were scarce and as for the run of
entertainers they had now she didn't want to be catty, but, my
dear, they were terrible. 'If I had a dollar for all the nights I'd
played through till the tips of my fingers was numb.' Now when
Ed Fish was alive it was different, he was a squareshooter and
gave everybody a break, of course he had run a tough joint, a regu
lar honkytonk . . . For a second she hid her face behind the
flashing rings on her hands . . . But my, hadn't they had a good
time in those days? When he was shot she'd cried her eyes out.

Right through the temple they shot him. Never knew who done it, plenty guessed, talked about the Purple Gang . . . My gawd, what a brawl that night! Suddenly she put her hand on my friend's arm: 'You and me we went to the funeral and you wrote it up in the paper, do you remember?'

'That's when I was a cub reporter,' he said in an explanatory tone to his wife. 'Suppose you sing us a song, Girlie.'

She swung round on the stool and started playing Frankie and Johnnie. She played with a hard precise metallic touch. '*Frankie and Johnnie were lovers . . . Great Jesus, how they could love.*' She sang in a hard accurate voice. My friend joined in. As the song went on, we felt as if that tiny parlor on that dark street was spreading out to include all the dives and honkytonks of the Middle West; the gleam of drinks along the bar, the music of the shaker, the smell of drinks, the soprano sharpness of lemon peel twining round the deep bass notes of rye, the faces pink with beery cheer, the mouths yawning out songs; the brisk hardfaced girls to dance with, the scent of bleached hair and powder; the allpervading swirl and yammer of the jazz; the sobering cold of the night and the arclights outside, the unfamiliar stairs, the latchkey, the sudden strain of being alone with a strange woman, the sour taste of ashen streets before day. After she'd finished on 'best part of the man,' she swung around on her stool to face us.

'Ain't the words awful!' she said. Her eyes suddenly filled with tears. My friend hurried to open some more beer. He started out on another song. As the evening went on they sang all the bawdyhouse ballads of the last twentyfive years.

She couldn't keep from crying. Her eyes began to stream. At last she had to jump up and run out for another handkerchief. When she came back she was still choking. 'Let's lay off,' she said, dabbing her eyes. 'It's not me that's changed, it's the town's changed . . . These warworkers don't have any fun in 'em . . . This has always been a drinkin' hellraisin' kind of a town, but it's changed. This war work has changed it. The boys don't sing no more. The whole world's changed into something terrible '

The Workingman Has Something to Say

The streetcars clanged through the slush up and down the broad street outside. Clattering trucks splattered past. Through the fogged window the ghost of a ray of sunlight shone down past crinkly blue cigarette smoke on the round yellow varnished table and brightened the color of the beer in the glasses. At the table were a husky young Texan with a low serious voice, a tow-headed blueeyed young man with his badge on his leather jacket who worked in an airplane plant, and a brighteyed youngster who looked like a college boy who sat hunched into his overcoat smoking a pipe. I was asking them questions. Behind us a number of men in a row, most of them young men with war-workers' badges, were drinking their beer at the bar.

At the table my companions were saying that in their outfit management was making no effort at all to cooperate, the men had their own union committeemen trying to increase production and to cut down absences, but it was uphill work; the bosses wouldn't meet them halfway. One fellow had sat up nights for weeks working out a scheme on paper to streamline production in his particular department, he'd taken it in to the supervisor and when he'd turned his back to walk out of the office the supervisor had dropped it in the wastebasket without even looking at it. Sure, plenty guys had made suggestions, but what was the use, if they were put into effect the foreman got all the credit. The management didn't want labor to cooperate.

Then it was mighty hard to convince the men that if production did get going full tilt, it wouldn't mean that they were working themselves out of a job. There was the story of the plant that made guns; at first they turned out eight a day and the army officers thought it was wonderful, but before long they'd stepped it up to two hundred a day and the army officers began to holler that they had no carriages to put them on, so everybody got laid off. And the place where they made sixwheel trucks, they'd turned out so many trucks they filled up half the county and had to call a halt.

The gist of it was that the men couldn't get over the suspicion that the great automobile concerns were using the war emergency for their own purposes; when it was over they were the ones who would come out on top. Why else did they have so many foremen standing around doing nothing? In one place there was a foreman to every eighteen men. What the hell did they care? Uncle Sam was footing the bill. 'And Uncle Sam, brother, that means you and me.'

A young man behind me at the bar had been squirming uneasily on his stool. Suddenly he turned around. 'I'd like to say something if you don't mind.' 'Come ahead, sit down.' There were formal introductions and a chair was found for him and he brought over his beer.

'I guess I'm pretty dumb,' he said, 'but I think it's a lot of hooey. Out where I work the Old Man seems to worry more about fellows smoking than he does about winning the war. They send you home for three days the second time they catch you and then for two weeks . . . If I can be laid off for two weeks for a little thing like that, what the hell do I amount to? . . . Now don't get me wrong. I may be dumb, but I'm a pretty good grinder. I like to do a firstrate job. Today I about blew my top trying to get through the work as fast as they wanted. I work on a camshaft for an airplane motor. I know it's got to be right. Men's lives depend on it. It's not like an automobile that just breaks down. Over there they can't get that automobile out of their heads. If it isn't to the right thousandth of an inch, the foreman, he says, put a burr — that's a metal coating — on it and let her go. It'll pass the inspector and what the hell? I may be dumb, but I think of the guys who are going to use that plane. We're in a war, ain't we? I just about blow my top trying to get it within the right thousandth of an inch. I like to do a nice clean job . . . But the way they treat you up there it looks like they wanted to take all the selfrespect out of you. If the army or navy or the government was to take over our plant, I bet we'd have thirty percent more production in a month.'

'Then if we do think out an improvement the foreman won't

let it get around,' another man piped up. 'Down where I work a guy worked out a jig for welding, a little gadget that keeps the arc moving in a straight line. He could finish twenty pieces in the same time he had eight before. When visitors come around from other plants, the foreman makes him take it off, don't want nobody to know how he gets so much production . . . He don't know there's a war on. It 'ud do me good to see the government take over the whole damn business.'

We drank our beers and leaning into the shrill cold wind walked around the corner to the union local. There we sat for a while in the little whitewashed cubbyhole in the basement where they get out the newspaper of the local. A burly sixfooter with color-less skin and redrimmed eyes, big wrists grimed with ash, who had just come off an eight-hour shift in the foundry, was standing in the door. He was still in his workclothes. His voice was low and hesitant. It embarrassed him to speak up. 'Down where I work we elected our committeemen and waited around for months for the management to come down and sit with us. When we figured out we wouldn't get no cooperation nohow, we just went ahead on our own. The two things we've tried to cut down is absences and misuse of tools . . .' A wiry Irishman with a bony face and eyes like a cat interrupted: 'And they're tryin' to tell the country we ain't patriotic. We're as patriotic as anybody, we've got our sons and our brothers in the service just as much as they have. We know production will win this war just as much as they do. But what can you tell men who know about how they was usin' vital materials for fenders for old model cars, or the alumi-num ashtrays they made up at this place over there to give away for souvenirs at Christmas. Us men who are workin' in the shops, we know they're not meetin' us halfway . . . Why should manage-ment worry? we're sayin'. It's the U.S. Government that's payin' the bills. All they have to do is rake in the profit.'

'The fact is,' said the slowspoken Texan as we walked up the stairs, 'that out of ten thousand plants engaged in war production in this country, only eighteen hundred of them have even made a stab at labor-management committees, and we don't know how

many of those are just window-dressing or being used for some
kind of politics. In the automobile industry only three or four
are putting on any kind of a performance.'

In the office on the ground floor the president of the local genially offered me a cigar. 'Now wait a minute,' he said, grinning,
when I asked about labor-management committees. 'We got to
go slow on these things. This union's in its first pair of diapers
... We aren't ready to do a man's work yet.'

Driving me back into town in his car stacked to the ceiling with
union leaflets, the towheaded young man in the leather jacket
talked as he drove. 'We know we're not going to gain during this
period,' he said. 'Looks to me like our business was education
for democracy ... I wish you had time to come over to our educational department. We really could show you something there.
We're having a whale of a time doing it. I never had any idea
this kind of work could be so interesting. You can see results.
It's really putting democracy into practice.' His voice rose with
enthusiasm. 'I'd never imagined it could mean so much to a
feller.' 'Watch it,' growled his friend past the stem of his pipe as
we slid to a stop in the slush just behind the red taillights of the
car ahead.

Labor Officials

Another day, out in the handsomely designed neat brick building
that houses the headquarters of the automobile workers' union,
I went to see a tall young man with glasses in the statistical department to ask him if workers were really making such fantastic
wages in the converted automobile industry. According to his
figures the average wages in the industry had been $50.34 a week
for a typical month before conversion, and stood at $57.83 for a
typical month since. Meanwhile food prices had increased 33
percent and overall living expenses by 19 percent. According to
these figures wages are not quite holding their own. Even now
only a small proportion of automobile workers own their own
homes. Those who do are mostly tool and die makers whose trade
has always been highly skilled and highly paid.

Downstairs I found the Man with the Plans, smiling and red-haired, with plenty of enthusiasm in his quiet voice and a disarmingly youthful manner.

'Well, we've got a new one now . . .' he said, smiling cheerfully. 'We still think our plan for conversion would have meant a whole lot more production a whole lot quicker at less expense to the taxpayer, but what we want now is an industrial council to plan production on which labor shall be represented. Another demand we are putting forward is that labor shall be guaranteed a forty-eight-hour work week. We think that will force industry to go all out in planning continuous production. We think they can do it if they want to. If they can't we can help them. While they can lay men off whenever there's a stoppage in the flow of materials, they have no real incentive to put their hearts into getting the necessary materials laid in ahead. That would force real industry-wide planning. We think the problem now has to be tackled at the industry level.'

'And at the Washington level,' added the man behind the desk.

Bridging the Gap

The labor-management committee of an automobile plant now converted to making motors for war is meeting at a long oak table. At the head sits the chairman for management, a longnosed dark-skinned man with aviator's wings sewn on the jacket of his business suit. His eyes have an eagerly questioning look; his manner of speech is downright and to the point. Next him sits a mild-mannered grayeyed man with a little touch of Irish in his background. The third representative of management is absent today. At the other end of the table sit the three men from the union. One is a middleaged broadshouldered man with a roughly chiselled face and a hawk eye who looks as if he had spent his life in the machineshop. He's wearing blue denim workclothes. Next him is a moonfaced man with glasses who might be almost any kind of middlewestern businessman. He's from the shop too.

The third man is the youngest, a white collar man with a smooth sallow skin and a touch of Union Square about his way of talking. He's recording secretary of the local. Through the windows, closed against the winter cold, comes a faint distant humming from the factory.

The chairman is explaining patiently and carefully how their system originated and how it works. To begin with, this particular concern had a long record of good relations with its employees behind it. This plan to increase production by getting labor and management truly to pitch in and work together got under way some time before Donald Nelson suggested labor-management committees to industry as a whole. The president of the company started it off eight months ago with a dinner and the handing out of pledge cards to every man who worked in the plant. Every man who signed promised to do his best to increase production (or, as one of the management people put it, to give sixty minutes' work for sixty minutes' pay). On its side the company promised that increased production would bring no change in the timing for any particular job, so that the workers wouldn't feel they were working themselves into a permanent speedup. This present steering committee was appointed, three from management and three from the union. It had turned out to be a full-time job for all six men. Of the union men, two were paid by the company at their regular rates, and the third, since he was already an officer, was paid by the union. It was immediately agreed that nothing pertaining to grievances or bargaining should come up before it. The business of this committee was production.

They worked out a series of pins, one warworker pin for everybody who signed up with the program, and others in the form of awards of merit for particularly good work or for outstanding suggestions. There were no cash awards, but every care was taken that every man should get full credit by name for everything he did. At first the suggestions from the rank and file took mostly the form of posters, slogans to boost morale, verses to post on the bulletin boards, but in recent months there had been more and more mechanical suggestions. In fact there were so many suggestions that going over them was one of the committee's principal jobs.

Every suggestion was turned in on a numbered blank without any name attached. It was only when the number was posted on the bulletin board as accepted or rejected that the name of the man who had presented it became known. In the case of mechanical suggestions that seemed worth patenting, the worker merely gave the company shop rights and retained the right to patent it in his own name. In several cases the company was helping the men prepare their ideas for patenting. Up to now they had passed on nearly a hundred and forty thousand suggestions. Of these around thirteen hundred had been accepted and put into practice. It had been figured that around two million dollars in costs had been saved already. One suggestion alone was bringing about a saving of three hundred and seventy-five thousand dollars a year.

The man in blue denim spoke up: 'The first thing we think of when we're goin' over a suggestion is, will it work? Then, can it be put into operation right now? At the bottom of this whole business is that we want to get production increased by usin' our brains instead of our arms. Let the machine do the work.'

'That's briefly the story on an individual basis,' went on the chairman. 'Now for group competition: we run a continuous contest between departments. Every department has a schedule of production set that's continually being adjusted upward. If a department's up to the mark, we hang up a handsome rayon banner. If it falls down, even if it isn't that department's fault, might be due to lack of materials, say, we hang up a rough looking *Behind the 8 Ball* banner ... That worries them more than anything. We've had to put a tag on it explaining why. I'll tell you the boys don't like that eightball banner hanging over them. They are crazy to get rid of it.'

'How about absenteeism?'

'Doesn't worry us.'

'Loafing?'

'The others won't let a man loaf. They want to have that

goodlooking rayon banner next month . . . In fact we feel that this campaign's been a great success. One reason is that we keep before every man's eye exactly how he's contributing to win the war, through posters and displays and through our paper. We feel we've got the men's confidence and that we're all in this together. Work to win. In spite of the fact that we've had to take on a great many green hands, and put all our old staff like the raghangers — that's what they call the men who used to upholster the bodies — on production of motors, our efficiency has increased right along.'

'Well, this company's never had any labor trouble anyway. One reason is that our labor relations are handled right from the top,' said the other company representative.

'The reason for that,' brashly piped up the union secretary, 'is that this is an independent concern and that it has to compete with the limitless financial resources of the big three and so it can't indulge in the luxury of wholesale union smashing.' A somewhat chilly silence followed this remark.

'To sum up,' said the chairman, clearing his throat, 'I think we can say with some confidence that we have increased production and that there is a whole lot more understanding between management and labor than there was when this thing started. At least we know there's a war on and what part we are playing in it.'

'You're damn right,' said the man in blue denim.

Home on Wheels

It was a cold Sunday morning. We were sitting on top of the Sunday papers littered over the couch of the trailer, talking in low voices because the baby was asleep in the bunk at the other end. It was warm in the trailer. Everything was very still. Through the window you could see the aluminum ends of the other trailers in the row, some bare trees, a corner of a white farmhouse, and rolling hilly country beyond where ranks of appletrees glistening with ice stood up out of the crusted snow against a low gray sky. The husband had broad shoulders and black hair and broad cheekbones and wide even white teeth. He looked as if he had some French Canadian in his ancestry. He'd been studying at the State Normal School to be a teacher. Then he'd worked in Flint, and in a soybean factory. Since he'd married and the baby had come, he'd bought himself a trailer and had come down to do war work in the enormous bomber plant that had just been completed down the road. Thought he might go to summer school at the University nearby. Before gasoline and tires had gotten so scarce, he was saying, there had been some point to living in a trailer, but now that it was a permanent stationary residence, he wondered. Still around here a man was lucky if he had any place to live at all. It was particularly hard on a woman with a baby . . . no way of getting away, no place to put the baby where it would be out of earshot. It wasn't so bad for a man who went to work every day, but women were getting what they called trailerwacky. In summer it would be better. They were going to plant flowers in their three feet of front yard, might even grow some vegetables; but in winter you were cooped up in there. Of course there was the company of other women, but they were all getting kinder wacky too. Here they were at least five miles from the nearest town. No chance for his wife to get in to see movies or go shopping very often. Well, he guessed it might be worse.

Oh, at the plant? Well, there was no end to the small irritations over there. Nobody had the feeling that production was really going yet, still too much standing around. And they almost drove the men crazy about smoking. Looked like that was the only thing management really worried about over there, that and putting on a show when visitors came through. He guessed it was because the Old Man didn't believe in smoking. Then everybody was always in a stew about the food in the cafeteria. The workers had to pay for their own food, and they felt somebody was cleaning up. One man got a mouse in his bottle of milk. There were maggots in the sandwiches. Oh, well, things might be worse.

He explained he had intended to teach school, but now he was getting interested in unionism, guessed he might take up union organizing as a life work. He was beginning to understand how much the man in the shop needed a union.

The wife, a wellset blonde girl with a rather bleak look on her face, came back from the laundry across the yard. First she rushed to the gasoline stove to look at something that was cooking in a roasting pan. A smell of hot meat juice trickled out. The baby who had started to yell was brought out and introduced, a clean, healthylooking infant. Of course, the wife said, it was interesting getting to know the other people in the camp. No, not many of them were from out of the state, there were two girls from West Virginia. They came from all kinds of occupations, milkroutes, screendoor factories, lawoffices, photographers, insurance salesmen. It was interesting that way. Of course, a trailer was an easy place to keep clean, but after you had done your housework and your washing, what then? That was the problem. She got a lot of reading done. It was all right Sundays when he was home. The two of them looked at each other and smiled. The wife suddenly looked very pretty.

Servicing the Workers

'Well,' said the skinny enthusiastic young man, the editor of the union local's paper, who was showing me around, 'we'd better shove along. I've got to take in a meeting down at the hall.' With some reluctance, because it was cosy sitting in the trailer talking to this quietspoken young couple, we said goodbye and walked off across the crunching snow in the sharp winter wind towards his car. We drove past comfortablelooking farmhouses under trees, big red barns with white arches painted on their doors and cribs of yellow corn and orchards and fields where cornstalks still stood up forlornly through the snow. 'This is some of the richest farming country in the state,' my friend told me. 'Farmers are all in a stew for lack of hands . . . They're all oldtime black Republicans around here. It sure churned their stomachs when this plant was built and they heard a union was coming in . . . I got to get hold of some of these farmers and talk to them, see what they've got on their minds . . . We might be able to get together with them yet.'

At the top of the hill behind a handsome old brick house half-completed frame dormitories stretched as far as you could see. Beyond them were miles of twofamily khakicolored trailer cottages, ingenious contraptions put out by one of the trailer factories that can be moved in a truck and that unfold on both sides like a child's cardboard dolls' house. In the other direction you could see the squat chimneys and part of the immense low silhouette of the bomber plant. Further along towards the town, in a gridiron of tracks through the snow, stood a confusion of new dwellinghouses, houses caught half-finished by priorities, tumbledown shacks patched up with tin. On several lots people were living in the concrete basements that were all that had been finished of their houses, with a flat tarpaper roof over them and a stovepipe stuck up through the middle. My friend said that welfare authorities had found one of these basements half-full of water with three kids locked up in there with pigs and chickens. The Old Man had heard about it and built the fellow a house, though actually he was nothing but an old drunk. Now he had a job in the plant and made himself a nuisance and sassed the foremen, but nobody dared fire him because the Old Man had been interested in him.

We drove into the town through a broad highway flanked by the usual nondescript storefronts and servicestations. Down side streets we got glimpses of blocks of mellow old houses on snowy lawns set with big trees. The union local had its headquarters in what had been an automobile sales and service agency. The garage part had been turned into a meeting hall and gymnasium with a stage for shows. The meeting was under way. A rostrum had been set up on the stage and two union officials were answering the questions of a group of maintenance men from the plant. A hot argument was raging as to whether painters should be classified as skilled workers or not. Several hardbitten old housepainters were protesting that no man could learn to paint in less than four years; if they weren't skilled, who was? The executives were arguing that in an industrial plant painting was not skilled work. One man agreed with them: 'Sure the way they do it they give anybody a four-inch brush and a bucket of machine blue and let them paint themselves sick . . . Looks like every time they have a visitor they repaint the plant.'

One old housepainter returned to the attack by asking when this local was going to have elections. 'When do we get rid of the international? When do we get so that we can run our own affairs? We want to elect our own president.' The union representative pointed out that a union local as new as this was couldn't be put on its own feet until the men had gotten accustomed to the organization. 'Why, we haven't even got the addresses of all our members yet . . . The company has the addresses but they won't give them up.'

My friend and I went across the street to get a bite of lunch. 'You see what it's like,' he said as we sat down at the counter of an overgrown sodafountain that was being operated by one lone girl. On the walls were signs advertising dainties named to fit the times: Blackout Sundae, Commando (Warworkers, get your Vitamins the Delicious Way), Flying Fortress Sundae, Morale Builder, Paratroops Sundae (Goes Down Easy). 'You see how it is . . . We've got a multitude of people gathered from the four corners of the *Chicago Tribune* belt — farmboys who think we're all racketeers — and we've got to make a union local out of them. And more pouring in every day. But it's a union that can't operate in any of the usual ways. Wages and all that are set. We've got to service these workers in education, housing, welfare, recreation . . . I came out here to educate these workers in unionism and, hell, I'm a social worker.'

'What do they do for recreation? Do they go to dances?'

'Believe you me, they are too damn tired to dance. The girls are too tired after they've done their housework. That's the greatest drag on our educational work, fatigue . . . Several dancehalls opened in town, but they've closed up . . . No customers. Our dances at the union hall are fairly successful because we serve beer. We've put on some boxing matches that were a hit.'

We gnawed on our sandwiches for a while.

'But look at the problem,' he said. 'Here's a little college town that had three or four small factories in the middle of a farming country and suddenly a city is dumped out on top of it, a city without housing . . . Some problem. But it's an opportunity too. It's an opportunity for the union to work with the rest of the community. We've made a dent already. We work with the community fund. We put on entertainments for the soldiers like U.S.O. There are two union members on the county rationing board. We're trying to do a public-relations job with the small businessmen. Already they've got a labor section of the Rotary Club.' I couldn't help laughing. He choked on the last corner of his sandwich. 'You go talk to them and see what they say.'

What They Say in Ypsilanti

I went to see the secretary of the Board of Commerce. He was a small man in a leather jacket smoking a cigar. Well, on the whole, he said, it had been worse in anticipation than it had actually turned out. While the factory was building, they had been overrun with surveys and investigations. For months people from Washington, social workers, all kinds of people had poured into town telling them how awful conditions were going to be when the bomber plant opened. Well, there were health problems, security problems, juvenile delinquency problems, children left alone all day — we call them doorkey kids — overcrowded schools, no priorities to enlarge them; but it hasn't been catastrophic. One bad thing was that the plant was getting as many quitslips as there were hires a day because people couldn't stand the living conditions. Perhaps that would change when the dormitories were opened. The point of view of the town was very simple. He thought he could speak for most of the leading citizens in that . . . This town had had a certain character as a quiet college town with pretty good schools and opportunities for young people to get jobs when they got out of school in the few small industries. He believed that what kept a town going was a situation where young people did not have to go away from home, but

could marry and settle down there. People who lived there liked
it that way. They didn't want to lose their individuality. They'd
had a war boom once before and had regretted it. They didn't
want to be smothered under bonded debt for utilities they'd never
need once this thing was over . . . There'd been the dream of the
Bomber City, well, that had been only a dream. He could assure
me that the town had never been opposed to it. The county
board of supervisors had been opposed because they were afraid it
would upset the political balance, bring a lot of Democrats and
union members into a straight Republican county, and certain
realestate interests had been opposed and, he understood, the
management at the plant had been opposed. Anyway, the
scheme for permanent housing had been ditched and now they
were getting temporary housing . . . The union too had been
worse in prospect than in actuality. In fact, the union leaders
had aroused a certain amount of sympathy in the town by their
willingness to cooperate in solving local problems. The sledge-
hammer tactics of earlier days had been laid aside. A different
element seemed to be in control. 'Well, all we can do is the best
we can . . . I think people all over the country will understand
the difficulties a small town has to face in a situation like this.'

My friend, the editor of the union paper, came in to pick me up.
He had a suggestion to make to the Board of Commerce that they
get some of the leading businessmen together with some of the
union officials for a smoker. Maybe they could get together and
talk frankly and spill what they had on their minds, clear up misunderstandings. 'I think that's a very good idea,' said the secretary of the Board of Commerce. 'We'll do it.'

When we came out of the office a white mist had blotted out
everything but the snowy ruts of the road. We drove out to the
edge of town to call on a pleasantfaced grayhaired man who for
years had run a small plant that made saws and hammers and
small hardware. He was sitting alone in the front room of a small
neatly varnished house that could well have been photographed
as the typical American home, the *Saturday Evening Post* ideal
in the good old days of Lorimer and Brisbane. He asked us to sit

down and began talking about the various fates that had in recent years overtaken this small town he lived in and loved. The early twenties had seen the last of the war boom and stagnation. Then a big manufacturer who had a theory that we should decentralize industry, so that the workers could live on the land and own their own homes, had set up a plant. A sound idea. Speaking for himself he believed in people owning their own homes, but the trouble was that realestate prices had become more and more inflated — a boom almost as bad as Florida at one time — and the worker had to spend all his six dollars a day making payments on his house, and the depression had come and they hadn't done so well. While this war was brewing and the plans for the Bomber Plant were in their early stages everything had been overshadowed by the controversy over the Bomber City, the dream of the Bomber City that was to have been a modern streamlined carefully planned industrial city. Various forces had blocked it so now they had the reality — trailers, temporary dormitories, a population of nomads. Well, we'd see what came of it. He hated to see his hometown flattened out. Small manufacturing plants, for one thing, were having a rocky time of it; if they got a war contract they had to bid for it, instead of negotiating it on a cost-plus basis like the big fellows did. Their workmen were all drained away. They didn't have the engineers the big fellows were able to hire to make the designs ... that was the worst trouble ... it was the brains that were lacking. The big fellows had hired all the brains away from them.

He spoke without bitterness. 'Still,' he said again, 'I like the idea of a man owning his own home, building it himself if need be, not so far away from his job so that he can't walk to work, not so far from the school so that his children can't walk to school. If you live in a town you don't need all these cars. The man who's struggled and saved to build and own his own home, he's pretty sure to be a good citizen. I don't see how we can do without him.'

Organizer

Late that night we sat talking in front of a fire of big lumps of soft coal in my friend's cottage in an apple orchard up on a snowy hill above Ann Arbor. His wife, who had been ill, lay on a couch, not saying much. A gray angora kitten flitted across our feet from one side of the fireplace to the other. The editor of the local weekly paper, a longlegged longfaced man in tweeds, who wore striped socks, had been talking about prejudices and how hard they were to eradicate and the need for religion in the world. 'My religion,' my friend said simply, 'is the union.'

He got to his feet as if he had a spring in him and stretched and began to talk in a voice full of warmth and feeling about the plans he had for the work he was doing. As well as being editor of the paper he was educational director for the local. He felt in this situation there was nothing to do but branch out. He wanted to get professors from the state university to give evening courses, a sort of university in miniature. Then a bunch of them around the local were getting kinder stagestruck, he said, and wanted to get up a musical show. There was all kinds of talent in the plant. There was even a chance they might get a symphony orchestra started. Square dancing was going big. There ought to be plenty of bowling and skiing and skating. Because people worked in a bomber plant was no reason why they should forget they were alive.

He dropped back into his chair again and stretched out his legs and stared into the fire. Up on the hill here way out of town, in the middle of the winter cold there wasn't a sound. There was that feeling you sometimes get in the Middle West that you are alone on the American continent, that there's nothing but the American continent in the whole world. Night blueblack like ink oozed against the windows and was sopped up in the pale glow of the snow. The firelight flicked yellow in the long narrow room. He went on talking, looking with glistening eyes into the fire. 'This isn't exactly unionism . . . or is it? We've got to do something new and broader . . . I've worked around in automobile

plants a good deal ... I've worked on a farm ... I don't care
much for money or possessions and we haven't any children. I've
figured I'd devote my life ... well ... to something like this.
Of course maybe the army'll get me and that'll be another story.
Times change, the union has got to be something else again, something like democracy ... There's some kind of a pattern in the
things we've seen today ... we're groping our way through it.'

Detroit, Michigan, January, 1943

BEHIND SCRAWNY TREES that have put forth a fuzz of green into the shrill spring wind the yellow brick courthouse has a dustbitten look in the middle of the square of low blank empty storefronts. A few cars marked red with splashes of dried mud are parked around it. The sidewalks are empty. Only at the corner by the drugstore where the bus stops is there any sign of life. There two skinny old men and a redfaced sailor are sitting on a bench in the sun. A colored girl in a bright blue outfit standing out in the street with a new cardboard suitcase in her hand is talking back over her shoulder to the old men on the bench asking if sure enough the bus for Little River stops here. They assure her that it is the northbound bus and that it will be along directly. The whites of her eyes roll anxiously. Already the bluegray bus with the white stripe comes blundering round the courthouse. The prospective white passengers have been sitting in a row at the sodafountain drinking cokes. They file out of the drugstore and crowd to the curb. There are three pretty girls, some farmboys in khaki, and an elderly woman with an old-fashioned gladstone bag. The sailor joins them hitching his pants as he comes. When the door of the bus opens nobody gets out. The passengers climb in, the colored girl last. The bus rumbles on. The two old men get up from their bench, stretch a little and hobble stiffly across the street. They stop for a moment to look in the window of the corner lunchroom opposite.

JOE'S COUNTRY LUNCH,
THE HOME OF GOOD EATS

is closed and vacant. Through smeary plateglass they can see the chairs upended on the tables. In the glass door a flyspecked sign, hastily handlettered in blue, reads:

Maybe you dont know there's a war on.
Have gone to see what it's all about.
Meanwhile good luck and best wishes
until we all come home,
signed,

JOE

CHAPTER 4

Bulldozers on the Old Plantation

U NDER LEVEL CLOUDS of dust the bulldozers are at work. Towed behind yellow tractors roadscrapers are levelling off pasture land. With a roar of motors mechanical shovels are chewing down red hills that a short time ago were woodlots of longleaf pines. From cement mixers lines of trucks move slowly across the rutted clay. When they want to wreck a farmhouse or an old barn of hewn logs they drive a tractor through it. Then they set a match to the pile of splintered boards and lath and shingle. As the work goes on the embers and fallen bricks of the chimney and scorched plaster and bent pieces of blackened beds and old tin cups and doorknobs and bits of china and rags from old quilts and bed-spreads are ground into the clay under the treads of the tractors. In two weeks a back country settlement with its shacks and barns and outhouses and horsetroughs and fences, all the frail machinery of production built up over the years by the plans and hopes and failures of generations of countrypeople will have vanished utterly and instead, among the freshcut pine stakes of the surveyors, you will see in the making the outlines of the long runways of an airfield, or the low farscattered sheds of a powder plant or the white concrete and glass tile oblongs of a war factory.

The Great Migration

Some families in the South have had to move on two weeks' notice, off land they had worked from grandfather to father to son.

[67]

Some have seen their crops destroyed in the field before they had
a chance to harvest them. There has been no resistance, not even
much complaint. People have felt that the defence of the nation
came first, that the complete uprooting of their lives was a small
price to pay for winning the war. Only a few of them have gone
to court to contest the prices offered in condemnation. Surprising numbers of them have seemed almost willing to leave their
farms and to make a stab at some other way of life.

After all, we are still a people of settlers. Our hold on our continent is only skin deep. Particularly in the South the people who
live in the back counties still have the frontier tradition. They
are a people who fell into a trance in their cranky shacks and
hastily knocked together cabins a century ago and who somehow
forgot which way they were headed in the trek westward towards
richer land and greener valleys. So they have sat there in the
back counties chewing and dipping tobacco and stagnating and
starving. They own so little, a few old iron beds, lamps with
broken shades, dented stewpans from the five-and-ten, some worn-
out chairs and tables, an old trunk full of threadbare clothes.
They pile the stuff on a truck or a wagon, shake the cornshucks
out of the bedticking, pile in a crate of fowls and a brood of flaxen-
haired children with smeared mouths and puffy eyes, and they
are off to take a job in a war plant or to try working on shares on
some other owner's land.

If you run into the lanky father of one of these families squat-
ting on his heels outside an employment agency, perhaps he'll tell
you with a feeling of chagrin and hurt pride, as if he'd been
swindled by a near relative, how little Uncle Sam paid him for his
farm and how long the folks in Washington are taking to pay him
what they owe him; perhaps he'll ask how do they suppose a poor
man who has a family to support is going to live in the meantime,
but he won't give you the feeling that there is anything very
strange or terrible in his destiny. His kin may have been there for
a hundred years but they were only settlers resting up. He's glad
to have a chance to be on the move again.

They Turn the Backwoods Inside Out

The whitehaired man with a round pink face full of small radiating creases who's rocking gently in the little space with a desk in it behind the counter in the back of his brother's country store used to own a thousand acres of land. Well, he guesses he had a hundred head of niggers on it, most of 'em from families that had been there since slavery days. His great-grandfather moved west into this country in the early eighteen-hundreds from South Carolina, bringing his stock and his negroes and his household goods with him in oxcarts. So far as he is concerned, he says, he is all right. The government hasn't paid him for his land taken for a powder plant but he reckons they will get around to it in time. He's an old man and the place has been too big for him to handle anyway. He would be a whole lot better off with a couple of hundred acres he was going to buy off one of his kinfolks. Seeing those niggers have to leave when he broke up the place had been the worst thing about it. Most of 'em had never been further than the county seat Saturday afternoons in their lives. It would be hard on them being turned loose like that. They'd always been so dependent. Right now most of the men were making four dollars a day as laborers on construction jobs. 'But what in the world are they going to do when they get turned off? . . . I'm not going to be in a position to look after them.'

Squatter Comes to Town

In the dusty hall at the foot of the narrow stairs that lead up to the relocation office stands a small sprylooking yellow man. His leathery cheeks are covered with white stubble. His white head is bent, and the yellow hand, gnarled as a cypress root, that holds his stained old widebrimmed gray hat against his knees is shaking. He has a rather cultivated oldtime Southern voice. He says he has lived alone for fortyseven years out in a shack in the piney woods. He boxed trees and dipped gum a little, but mostly he hunted and fished. No, he dont want to give his name. He was part Indian, he said. No, he dont want to give his age. He's getting along but he aint too old to work. The government man come and told him he'd have to move out. The army was taking the area over for manoeuvres. The government man said he could get his expenses paid. He has come in to get twenty dollars from the relocation office to move his things. He guesses he'll move into the city and get work. He dont like to ask for the money. He's never asked anybody for anything in his life, but he guesses that his huntin' an' fishin' days are over now an' he'll have to settle down an' get him steady work.

A Government Agency Tries to Stem the Tide

The relocation agent was driving me out past the steaming gray buildings of the chemical factories, over the hill that gave us, as the road looped, a backward view of the whole busy little north-ern Alabama industrial town with its trainyards and warehouses and the great pile of the steel mill and the long corrugated iron sheds of the pipe works lying in the bowlshaped valley under a ceiling of soft coal smoke. We passed a few tourist cabins turned into permanent residences and a last row of temporary shacks for chemical industry workers and turned onto a country road through a bleak shallow valley between scrubby pinewoods. Counting all the war dislocations in together, the agent was tell-ing me six hundred and ninetynine families had had to move off farms in this county alone. Of these Farm Security Administra-tion had helped five hundred and twentythree. Of these only a hundred and fiftyseven had gone back on farms. So far as he knew those figures were about average for the dislocated areas in the Southeast.

Of the families Farm Security had helped thirtyfour had been set up in dairying (he hoped to raise that figure to ninetysix before long), twentyseven in the chicken business, fifteen in beef cattle and the rest were raising cotton as they were accustomed to. Seemed a drop in the bucket, didn't it? But you had to begin slowly in a thing like this. If the experiment worked, it would be easy enough to multiply the number of farms.

The agent was a ruddyfaced young man immensely absorbed in what he was doing. He stopped the car on the side of the road and pointed proudly to a onestory white house on a little knoll of red clay barely fuzzed with new green grass. 'This is the first of our dairy farms. These places are already making cash money every two weeks selling milk to the army camp through the cooling plant. Let's take a look.'

Across the road beyond the new barbed wire fence oats were sprouting in even rows in the red land. 'That'll be our permanent pasture.'

The house was clean and new with screened windows and a screened porch. The milking shed with its concrete floor was clean and new. The small cows, by a Jersey bull out of local scrub stock, looked clean and new. Only the farmer and his wife, a lanky weatherbeaten pair, the man in overalls, the woman in Mother Hubbard and poke bonnet, had the oldtime backcountry look. Their clothes were clean though patched like crazyquilts, they were keeping the place clean all right, but they still looked ill at ease as if they hadn't settled down yet to feel this was really their home. The man kept talking about his waterpump in a worried way, kept saying he was afraid it was going to break down. His wife was complaining about the faucet in the sink in the milking shed.

'It's not his pump that's worrying him,' the agent said, grinning as he drove off. 'It's the loan he had to make to buy the cows. He's accustomed to making a crop loan of a couple of hundred dollars and twelve hundred seems a terrible lot. When I tell him that he's selling a hundred dollars worth of milk every two weeks the figures just don't sink in. He's doing fine but he can't believe it . . . Of course the high price of feed isn't doing us any good. About half of what we make on the milk goes into feed. Even so we are making out. The project's making out and the dairymen are making out.'

in another county there were colored people living in the small new low white houses. At the place where we stopped the mother and father had gone to town because it was Saturday afternoon.

We looked at the young chicks and the hogs and the neat hills of earth the man's sweet potatoes were stored in. 'This feller's going to be all right,' the agent said. 'There's one across the railroad tracks that isn't turning out so good, spends all his time working off his farm.'

A little barefooted black girl in a clean pink dress had been following us around timidly. 'How much preserving did your mother do last year?' the agent asked. 'Let's see them . . . Oh yes, canning is part of the program. Every client has a pressure kettle and is shown how to use it.'

The little girl was too scared to open her mouth but she ran on the tips of her toes to the kitchen door and opened it and beckoned us in. The kitchen looked as if it had just been scrubbed that morning. With a look of reverence as if she were showing off some sacred magical object in a niche the little girl pulled open the door of the closet opposite the back door. From floor to ceiling clear shining jars of corn and beans and tomatoes and okra packed every carefully, scrubbed shelf. They looked like the brightcolored vegetables you see winning prizes at country fairs.

'They look all right,' said the agent. He couldn't help puffing out his chest, you could see, as he showed them off. 'That means they've been eating something more than white meat and sweet potatoes this winter. That means a balanced diet.'

As we drove back down the scrawny back road where negro families lived in identically the same demountable white houses that were put up in other regions for the whites I couldn't help thinking that maybe in the electric brooders for chicks, in the electric pumps and the preserving kettles and the boilers for sterilizing the pails in the dairies and the vegetable patches and the clean hogpens there was the germ of a new way of life for the countryside.

'Is this sort of thing going to catch on?' I asked.

'Is Congress going to let us go ahead with it?' the agent asked me back.

Change in the Black Belt

When we drove out of town the hoarfrost still sugared the henna-colored sagegrass along the sides of the road and lay in a shining mist over the pallid green drifts of winter oats. The sun was rising dim as the yolk of a poached egg in the steaming sky. Crows perched on the scraggly bare limbs of locust trees and flapped cawing over undulant pasturelands where the red whitefaced cattle grazed in groups. The road curved out of the rolling land and cut straight across a level plain until it was lost in the frosty haze. At the beginning of the straightaway the Farm Security Man drove the car to the side of the road and brought it to a stop and made a broad sweep with his hand above the wheel. 'Now this is where the Black Belt begins,' he said. 'My people moved in here from Savannah way back in the last century with a wagon load of old English furniture and a barrel of French crockery and a couple of blooded horses and a bunch of niggers. They used to say nobody but a negro could work this heavy land. This was the empire of the cotton barons. Now it's all going into stockfarming and dairying, going back into the prairie it came from. The boll weevil started the process and the war has speeded it up.' He gave a short laugh. 'Looks like the war has speeded up every kind of process, good and bad, in this country.'

'That means less hands to work. What are you going to do with the people?'

'Of course we think resettlement's the answer, resettlement on family sized farms.'

'Why do you suppose there's so much opposition? Why is the Farm Bureau so dead set against it?'

He gave a little chuckle. 'I used to work for the Farm Bureau myself. I reckon some of it is institutional jealousy. Then they are scared of high wages.'

'I can understand why the communists should be against it. They are all for collectivization. But why hasn't it got more friends among the liberals?'

'I guess liberals are city people mostly ... Let's go talk to a

real successful farmer. This feller's a college graduate and a man
of really considerable learning. He runs a very successful farm.'
He started up the car again.

We found the college graduate just coming out of the door of his
henhouse pushing before him a shovelful of chicken droppings and
rusty feathers. He was a tall silveryhaired man with a narrow
head and long sharply marked features ruddy from the weather.
He was wearing overalls and an old sweater worn out at the elbows. 'You find us in a mess,' he said apologetically. 'We're
cleaning out the henhouse . . . But I've never seen a time yet
when this place was fit for visitors.'

We asked him what he thought of the Farm Bureau policies.
'To tell the truth,' he answered, 'I haven't had time to read up on
them . . . I'm probably a member. I believe somebody did come
around, and got five dollars off me. In general the farmer likes
the Farm Bureau because it's agin the government. Now, mind
you, I don't go with them all the way, but they are good practical
talkers and there's been so much inefficiency and red tape and
unnecessary regulation . . . I don't mean you, George, you know
that,' he said aside to the Farm Security Man. 'I think you boys
are doing a real good job, but all this war food program has been
so bungled up that I don't blame the farmers for following the men
who'll wade in and try to get 'em what they think they're entitled
to . . . People don't look far ahead in this country, they just see
what they've got in front of their noses . . . And the farmer he's
just too busy running his farm to keep up with trends . . . Want
to see the chickens?'

We walked through the long tarpaper building the shape of a
greenhouse that had an alley down the middle and layers and
layers of chickens on wire floors on either side. Near the entrance
the chicks were yellow and peeping fresh from the egg. Further
on they had pinfeathers and at the end they were clucking
broilers. The air was choking with the warm sour reek of crowded
fowls. 'They come in one end from the incubator and go out the
other to market,' said the college graduate. 'Works fine if you
don't slip up on something. I guess you have to do so much regu-

lating yourself running a farm that the farmers get sick of regulations. Right now we feel the whole system of regulations is a nuisance. We don't care whether the purpose is good or bad . . . Then too we are getting prosperous. A prosperous farmer's the most conservative man on earth. We were plenty sick for a while. Now we feel about ready to throw away our crutches. Just leave us alone. Get us good prices and let us produce, that's what we say.'

'What about the feller who still needs a crutch?'

'We'll hire him. By God, we've got work for him to do! I'm not so bad off as some for labor, but I could use three good men right now. My wife and I wouldn't have to break our backs cleaning out these henhouses if we could hire somebody to do it . . . Goodby.' He packed us off hurriedly but genially. 'I got to get back to my business.'

'Well, this isn't exactly the moving picture idea of life on the old plantation, is it?' asked the Farm Security Man, laughing as we climbed back into his car.

In Baldwin County They Raise Truck

This small pursefaced brown man in an alpaca suit with graying hair and untidy eyebrows is a farmer from the black muck country. We sit in rocking chairs with a spittoon between us in the lobby of the small hotel. Through unwashed windows against which buzz a few early flies we can see the courthouse and the parked cars and the empty square of the county seat. 'You want to know why we aren't producing more food for 1943 . . . Well, all I know is what happened to me. I have a boy in the service an' a girl who's enlisted as an army nurse an' even if we hadn't, the old woman an' I would have wanted to do the best we could for the country . . . in a time like this. Well, I raised thirty acres of beans last year and I figured I could raise a hundred this year with my tractor an' one extry hand. Well, I got my land plowed up all right but my new hand was so noaccount he stripped me a gear on the tractor, an' I was drivin' all over the country like a crazy man tryin' to get me that extry part, couldn't get no satisfaction nowhere. I got tired of waitin' for that part an' went into town an' bought me six head of mules at two hundred and twentyfive dollars a head. That's a pretty big outlay for a feller like me. It jumped my labor cost right up too, but my old woman says I'm right stubborn when I get started. I was bound all hell an' high water wasn't goin' to keep me from gettin' those beans planted. I got 'em planted all right and had a right good stand but be damned if this here late frost didn't come an' freeze 'em down. I was so worried about the expense an' not gettin' that part for my tractor an' all, I swear I took sick an' went to bed. I sent the old woman into town to buy some more seed to replant an' damn if some bureau in Washington hadn't frozen the seed. They unfroze it later on but it was too late for our season down here. Now about all that's left for me to plant is corn and I'll never get my money back; but that ain't the worse of it; we've lost a whole season's crop that might have produced food folks could eat. I swear if they don't quit hogtyin' us with priorities an' restrictions an' regulations the only thing us truckfarmers'll be able to do is close up an' go to work at something else. How are we goin' to produce crops if we can't get spare parts for our farm machinery?'

When I crossed the street in the windy glare of the early spring noon, there was nobody stirring, nothing on the street but a few cars parked in front of the dustylooking yellow courthouse. A yellow dog was carefully scratching himself with his hind leg on the postoffice steps. The county agent's office was in the basement. In there a few men in shirtsleeves drowsed behind desks. When I asked whether they'd have the labor down here to harvest their early crop a sandyhaired young man threw himself back in his swivel chair and stared for a moment at his feet thoughtfully crossed on the corner of his desk before he answered. To be sure they had lost right much population, he said in a slow drawl. What the army was taking wasn't a drop in the bucket to the drain into war industry. Labor was the worst problem they had. Not a tractor driver to be had in the county. Uncertainty about prices and the scarcity of seed potatoes were worries too. The

cash crop in this section was early potatoes. Well, last year the
farmers had gotten stung. They had lost money. The price
hadn't been right and there had been no labor to pick the potatoes
up. Well, this year there had been about two thirds of a normal
crop planted . . .

'Isn't the ceiling price all right?'

He swung his feet around and sat bolt upright. Price was all
right, but it had been set too late to affect the early crop. If a
farmer's been stung once on a crop you don't find him burning
his fingers again right away. A lot of them couldn't get the labor
to get a crop in. This was a region of small holdings, many families of Swedish, German, Bohemian origin who had come down
here from the Middle West and built up truck farms during the
last twentyfive years. Well, most of these families had one or two
members working in war industries: patriotism, a way of making
quick money to pay off mortgages and storebills, follow the crowd,
all sorts of reasons that meant less hands to work the small farms
. . . Then — he stretched out his arms and thoughtfully started
rolling up his shirtsleeves — there was a thing about the negro
that people in the North didn't understand. He wasn't used to
much money, so if one member of a family was making enough to
buy the groceries the rest of 'em just sat around. There was lots
of 'em in the county that could work if they wanted to but why
should they? They were sitting pretty. Down here, people, black
and white, were going to be fairly prosperous, but that didn't
mean we were going to get extra production.

The young man had picked up a pencil and was leaning over his
desk making doodles on a pad of yellow paper. Government
agencies were working on the problem of getting in labor all right,
he said. Right here the first difficulty was housing. This county
was so near a string of shipbuilding centers along the Gulf coast
that every available house was filled by workers who commuted
into the towns. Had I noticed there wasn't a soul on the streets?
All gone to the shipyard. Farm Security was going to help beat
that situation by bringing in a movable camp. After all, potatoes
weren't the only crop. There would be sweet potatoes, green

corn, okra, cucumbers, tomatoes coming along; strawberries, they wouldn't be much help this year. He made a sour face. 'But you can't get around the fact that there are going to be hundreds of acres idle when we need surplus food more than any other time in history.'

'Do you suppose it would help if farm labor got better wages?'

'Might help some, but what worries the farmer is if his hired labor gets used to making industrial wages they won't want to work for less when this is all over.'

The office of Farm Security was over an implement store on the other side of the courthouse. When I walked in the door a sixfoot lanternjawed backwoodsman in stained overalls with a quid of tobacco as big as an apple in his cheek stood leaning over the desk counting out ten-dollar bills while the administrator made out a receipt.

'Well, that jest about clars me up,' he said as he slapped down the last greenback on the pile on the desk. He lifted the window a little with a long leathery flipper and spat delicately out into the yellow branches of a willow tree just feathered with early green.

'Feel better?' asked the administrator.

'Right smart . . . Goodday, gentlemen . . . I'll be goin',' said the man gravely and stalked out of the office.

'To go by the speeches in Congress I've just seen something that never happens, a Farm Security client paying off his loan.'

'A very high percentage pay off their loans,' said the administrator sharply, 'higher all the time.'

He was a quiet studiouslooking man with a long closely cropped head. He wore a leather jacket and boots. He sat there at his desk for some time without speaking. Then he said suddenly, 'I'll tell you a funny thing,' and threw himself back in his chair and stared up at the peeling ceiling above his head. 'You know when we started this relocation work we picked our clients very carefully, made all sorts of investigations of their character and background to see if they'd be a good risk or not. Now we just take them as they come. Statistically the random clients work out as well or better than the handpicked clients.'

'What do you figure it means?'

'You tell me what it means.'

While I sat there trying to figure out an answer he straightened himself up at his desk and picked up a pencil in a businesslike way as if he were going to start writing with it. 'What it means to me is that the great majority of people will turn out all right if you give them the proper chance . . . I said the proper chance.' He paused again and smiled. 'Maybe that was the sort of thing the men who founded this country figured on.' He jumped to his feet in a hurry as if he were afraid he'd said too much. 'Suppose you and me go across the street and get us some dinner before they run out of everything,' he said in a voice suddenly warm and goodnatured.

The Farm Bureau Makes a Speech

Sitting in the outer office waiting to have a talk with a local Farm Bureau chieftain you are as likely as not to see through the half open door a man with a long black jaw under a dusty black felt hat moving back and forth in front of the desk and to hear his voice rattling excitedly. From time to time he slaps his fist into his open hand as he tells his story to the man behind the desk. He's explaining why he's through with farming. He's sold out his plantation to the government and to hell with it. 'One nigger'll get a job an' the whole crowd of 'em will live off that one an' won't raise a hand . . . all the men that's fit to work have gone to these defence jobs an' all you've got left is the old folks an' the children . . . Government's payin' 'em four times what they're worth. Who ever heard of payin' a nigger more than a dollar a day? It's running 'em plum crazy. They'll sit back in them little shacks, five or six of 'em up together like pigs an' that radio'll be bustin' out till they can't hear nothin' an' they wouldn't work for hell.' He is disgusted, the man will be roaring, he is through. If the government wants food, somebody else is going to have to raise it.

As the visitor stalks out a tall blackbrowed man gets up and leans over his desk and asks you to come in. He has the quiet forceful manner of a man who knows exactly what he wants. He is still grinning quietly to himself. Without referring to the other interview he begins to explain the four-point program for immediate action his organization is trying to put over in Washington. The first point is higher prices for food. He points out that in 1914 the average non-farm family paid 33 percent of its income for food and that in 1942 it had paid only 22 percent. Factory workers had paid 58 percent in the first year and 28 percent in the second. Meanwhile, farm wages were at 234 percent of the 1914 level. 'In a nutshell,' he says, 'that's why we are not getting the food.'

The second remedy is to give up the forty-hour week principle; that is to lower industrial wages. The third is to put an end to cost plus contracts that encouraged wastage of manpower in industry. The fourth is deferment of agricultural workers from the draft.

When I asked him what he thought ought to be done about so many families being put off the land, 'Better that way,' he said. 'We don't need 'em ... The good farmers among them will work out as hired hands and tenants and if they are thrifty they'll save up some money and buy better farms than they had before. Why can't they let it work out by natural law? All these coddling government agencies are trying to pauperize the farmer with a political intent ... I am beginning to think with a sinister political intent ... Working on the land, my dear sir, is a noble and respectable occupation. These Washington agencies carry on like a man who worked on a farm was some kind of a cripple who didn't know how to keep his own nose clean ... It takes a great deal more skill and intelligence and even education of a sort to become a successful farmer than it does to become a successful bureaucrat.'

But wasn't farming tending to become a mechanized large scale operation that needed big capital, I asked him weakly, and without the family farm as a base wouldn't the whole industry fall under the control of Wall Street?

He brushed that off: 'We'll meet that when it comes. What we are fighting now is mismanagement in Washington, for political ends.' There wasn't much answer to that. I gave up and walked out of the office with an armful of Farm Bureau literature and a copy of the latest scorcher that had been sent to the President of the United States.

There's Got to Be Some Plan

Next day I dumped the whole subject out on the desk of a man who looked a little like a college professor who ran a cooling plant. We'd been visiting his cows and his milking sheds and heard him say with some surprise that he wasn't having much trouble getting labor to work for him. Well, he always had paid a little more than the next man, felt he got better hands that way. A part was wearing out on the machine that washed his bottles. When we went back into his office, our nostrils full of the smell of cows and freshwashed concrete, he excused himself for a moment and called up a dealer to order the spare part. His visitors seemed amazed. 'Oh, you've been reading the papers,' he said. 'I'll get the part in a few days.'

Then we began to talk about dairy farming in his section of the hill country. The question I wanted to put was whether he thought anything could be done to stop the destruction of family-size farms and the establishment of largescale industrial setups in their place. We had agreed before that popular selfgovernment couldn't very well do without the small independent farmer as its balance wheel.

'Sure,' he said. 'Electrification can do it plus sensible management.'

'What about cooperatives?' I asked him.

'I don't care what you call your units so long as they are managed right,' he said impatiently.

On his own place, he said, his tenants worked a plan that differed a little from the Farm Security plan because after all (he smiled) he was running his farm to make money and not to set his tenants up in business . . . Still, the man who worked this particular farm right next to the cooling plant had come over from Georgia with a load of furniture and nothing in his jeans but an empty wallet five years ago and now he had five thousand dollars in the bank. Wasn't that building up the farm family and making a profit on it at that?

'Then why can't the small electrified farm with its preserving kettles and its sterilizing machinery and its electric brooders become a basic agricultural unit, a floor below which the standard of life in this country can't drop?'

'It probably could if people knew what was good for them.'

'Is the only basis of opposition to Farm Security that people don't know what's good for them?'

'Well, any organization makes mistakes . . . But I think it's a practical plan. There has got to be a plan or else we are in for a terrific mess when this is all over. The Farm Bureau boys have built up their organization on the theory that they are the only ones that know what's good for the farmer . . . I guess it's mostly politics in and out of Washington.'

'But how can they call a program to build up the family-size farm communistic?'

'Well, around here communism's anything we don't like. Isn't it that way everywhere else?'

Montgomery, Alabama, February, 1943

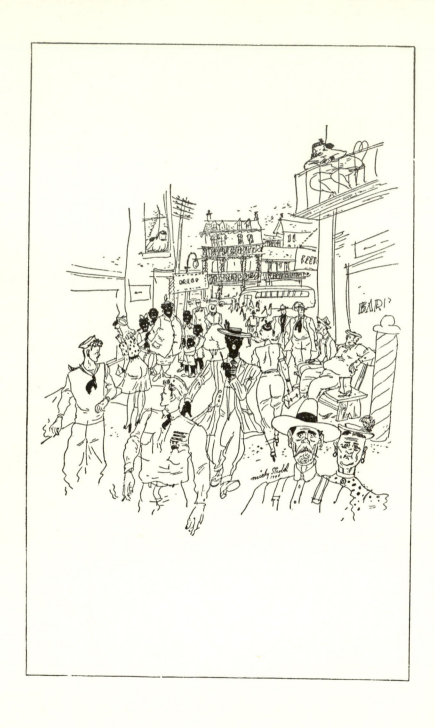

THE CARS WERE PARKED in a semicircle under the last of the great black liveoaks that led in a scraggly avenue from the high-road up to the house. It was a narrow old plantation house with symmetrical wings. The sun shone through tall uncurtained windows on freshly repainted floors and panelled fireplaces in unfurnished rooms. Outside the ancient broad weatherboards and the slender pillars of the porch were glossy with light yellow paint. The picnickers were grouped round a couple of rickety cardtables in a patch of sun between the parked cars and the porch steps. On the tables were plates of devilled eggs wrapped in waxed paper, and ham and beaten biscuit and piles of fried chicken covered with napkins. In a hamper on the ground were propped some thermos bottles full of hot coffee and cocktails. The younger people sat on the steps. The older ladies, bundled up in furs, were hunched in worn armchairs that had been dragged out from some of the colored people's houses. A few couples sat in the front seats of their cars. Young men in khaki drinking martinis out of paper cups roamed with the girls over the hennacolored dry sagegrass that grew sparsely out of the sandy ground between the trees. Some of the girls were picking daffodils.

The afternoon was hardly warm enough to sit still. The early spring sunlight was ruddy from the smoke of brushfires that gave a brown tinge to the pale violet sky. Behind the quiet voices of the young people you could hear continually the rumble of training planes circling over the airfields beyond the trees towards town.

'You see, my dear ...' The lame lady with silver hair pulled back tight over her narrow skull, who sits beside the cardtable with a touch of bourbon in a paper cup in her hand, is speaking. She is looking sharply around at the picnickers out of clear gray eyes, pointing with the crooked little finger of her free hand. 'You see.' She is pointing at a young woman in a yellow sweater who has just stooped to pick a daffodil. 'Every one of them pregnant ... I'd say four months that one. Isn't she pretty? I suppose it's a sign of wartime.'

'At least, Clara,' bubbles breathless a pansyfaced matron sitting in a mink coat thrown open to expose the massively embroidered yoke of her dress, 'I'm glad I can say they're all married.' She goes on eating her sandwich with small quick rabbit nibbles.

While we were drinking our coffee our hostess was saying, 'Nobody must forget to pay their respects to Aunt Lucy ... She's over a hundred years old.'

There were two cabins side by side down in the hollow by the fence back of the house. Beyond them broad glaucous pastures where groups of whitefaced cattle grazed stretched to the woods along the horizon. Following the deepworn path through the grass of the houselot tufty from overgrazing, we heard a bobwhite calling from the bare branches of the bushes along the fence and always from the distance came the purr of planes.

Aunt Lucy's cabin was stuffy but clean. In the back there was an iron bed with an old patched quilt on it and beside it a kitchen table piled with worn paperbacked books. There were calendars and a chromo of the Wreck of the Hesperus on the wall. In the middle of the floor on a rag rug Aunt Lucy sat rocking in a small overstuffed rocker.

Her granddaughter, a plump brown woman with a pink apron, had met us at the door. 'All the folks comes to see Aunt Lucy,' she had said, ushering us in. Our hostess' son had brought down half a tumbler of whiskey. 'Mother thought Aunt Lucy might want a little tonic,' he said.

'We was all mighty poorly this mornin',' the brown woman whispered, rolling up her eyes as she pushed the glass out of sight behind the books on the table.

The minute we had come in Aunt Lucy's eyes had fastened on the whiskey glass. As the granddaughter pushed it out of sight Aunt Lucy's eyes had followed it as far as they could without her turning her head, until all you could see in the deep sockets in her lined face the color of cocoa was the veined blueish-white of the eyeballs. Then, as we settled ourselves on the little rushbottomed chairs in front of her, the bright black pin points of her eyes moved back and twinkled in each of our faces in turn. She wore a red bandanna on her head, which completely covered her hair, and an oldfashioned knitted shawl crossed over her chest, and her twisted old hands were clasped in her lap. She sat rocking, looking us merrily in the face. The loose fold of skin over her wide mouth was still.

'Well, Aunt Lucy,' said our hostess' son. 'What's the good word today? This boy is learning to be a flyer.' He gave a dig with his elbow into the khaki sleeve of the redheaded young fellow next to him.

Suddenly Aunt Lucy's voice rose up out of her chest unexpectedly loud and deep. 'The Lord bless all these goodlookin' folks ... There's only good people comin' to see me today.'

The granddaughter leaned against the wall with her arms folded, looking down proudly at the old woman, when she noticed that I was looking at the books on the table beside the bed, religious works worn and dogeared, published most of them half a century ago. 'Aunt Lucy can still read books,' she whispered to me, 'it's a great comfort to her.'

The old woman was speaking again with her eyes cast up towards the ceiling. 'What message,' she was intoning in her deep whooping voice, 'can I give these handsome young folks this day?' She paused and rocked silently for a while. The rocking made a floorboard creak under the rug. Overhead there was the rumble of a plane that had circled nearer than usual. 'Indeed, the Lord has spared me beyond the lot of my brethern an' my sistern he set down in the good book, an' every day I bless the Lord. The Lord has been good to me an' mine.'

'Maybe you'd sing us a hymn, Aunt Lucy,' somebody asked.

'"Swing low, sweet chariot . . . waitin' fur to carry me home,"' She cleared the rattle out of her throat. 'Chile, I ain't got the breath in my body for singin'.'

'I ain't never seen' — her voice rose again from deep in her chest — 'such good people as has come to see me this day. Only good people come to see me. What's brought you all way out here to see an old woman more'n a hundred years old? Such good people!'

The young flyer with the red hair stammered a little when he spoke. 'It's the war, Aunt Lucy, brought me away from home. I came down here to try to learn to fly an airplane to help win the war.'

While he was speaking, the eyes, light blue and a little far apart under a broad forehead, of the sandyhaired girl who sat beside him were intent upon his lips. Before he had stopped speaking, the redheaded flyer's face had started to get red as if he felt he'd talked out of turn. The blush started on his neck at his khaki shirtcollar and kindled his ears and ran up into the roots of his hair. The girl began to blush too. As if to break the spell of embarrassment that had fallen on them, she cried out in a reckless tone, 'Today's a holiday . . . we've come on a picnic.'

The old woman wasn't looking at them. She was staring at the wall of the cabin over our heads.

'War,' her voice whooped. 'We don't hear nothin' but war . . . They don't do nothin' but hate an' kill one another an' use all the merciful bounties the good Lord has put into their hands to strike one another down. Lord, Lord, Lord, why do they do it? They can't seem to use the merciful works of the Lord any other way than for hatred an' murder an' beatin' each other down an' burnin' barns an' drivin' off stock an' draggin' their big guns across the standin' crops. They come here when Missa James was alive. They come down the road right here lookin' for Missa James. He'd gone off to hide his purtiest horses in the swamp, but they was drivin' off some right nice mules an' I run out of the house so young I wasn't scared of nobody an' I cotched that trooper's horse by the bridle an' I said, "Go long away from here . . . these ain't your horses, these ain't your mules. Missa James he raise 'em from a little teeny colt," an' he stop' in his tracks an' make like he reach for his sword hangin' from his saddle an' there was all his troopers on their horses wet an' sweatin'.' Her voice had sunk to a mumble. Suddenly it came back in a deep rattling whoop: 'Why do they do it? Why does the good Lord let 'em?'

'But, Aunt Lucy,' said the girl in a sharp voice. 'This time we're fighting to keep them from tearing things up any more.'

'Would you say a prayer for us, Aunt Lucy?' asked the red-headed flyer abruptly. As he sat listening with his eyes on the rough boards of the floor, the color had drained out of his face.

'Oh, yes,' echoed the granddaughter eagerly. 'She sho' says a beautiful prayer.'

'Lord,' the old woman's voice swelled so that the loose pane rattled in the window, 'make us good people. Make us good people in our hearts. Don't let us tear up everythin' there is fair an' lovely in this world. An' save us from hatred an' burnin' an' strikin' an' shootin'. Lord, make us good people an' save us though we have to walk through the valley of the shadow of death.'

The redheaded flyer got to his feet. 'Thank you, Aunt Lucy,' he said. 'It sure was a beautiful prayer.' He spoke hurriedly as if his throat were stiff. The girl got up too. As they turned to edge their way out of the cabin we could see that their eyes were wet.

'There's nothin' but good people come to see me today,' Aunt Lucy started again as she rocked and rocked. 'I can see in your faces you're good people ... I believe you gemmen came down here special with a little change in your pockets for poor old Aunt Lucy. I can see it in your faces that when you come out today you come out to do good.'

As we said goodbye and thank you, we dropped a couple of quarters in the lined pale palm of her hundredyearold hand.

CHAPTER 5

Gold Rush Down South

T HE BUS RUMBLES DOWN the sunny empty highway through the rusty valleys and the bare rainwashed fields and the scraggly woods and the hills the color of oakleaves that are the landscape of winter in the southeast states. Inside, the air is dense with packed bodies and stale cigarette smoke. There's a smell of babies and an occasional sick flavor from the exhaust. The seats are all full. Somewhere in the back a baby is squalling. A line of men and women stands swaying in the aisle. Behind me two men are talking about jobs in singsong voices pitched deep in their chests.

'What's it like down there?' one is asking the other.

'Ain't too bad if you kin stand that bunch of loudmouthed foremen . . . If you look crosseyed at one of them guards he'll reach out and yank off your badge and you're through and that's all there is to it.'

'Well, I've worked in about all of 'em.'

'Say, ain't I seen you somewheres before?'

'I dunno. Might have been on this bus. I been on this bus a thousand times.'

A Millworker Changes His Job

We're passing through a village, dusty storebuildings of yellow brick, some hens picking among the litter of old crackerboxes and cellophane and wrappings off baker's bread in front of the broken-down porch of an unpainted frame house with broken windows. A few tiny yellow stars of jasmine bloom on dusty bushes on either side of the steps. At the crossroads there is an empty filling-station with an old Model T with a tattered top standing by the bright yellow pump, and a soiled hound asleep on the concrete beside it.

The man in the seat beside me sits hunched up holding a cigarette in the stained fingers of a hand that hangs limp between his knees letting the ash drop on the scruffed toe of his fancy pointed shoe. He wears a thin sunfaded suit of some cottony material worn at the elbows and knees but his white shirt is clean. He has wavy brown hair and deepset eyes in a sallow slightly pock-marked face. Suddenly he begins to talk very low staring down at his cigarette. 'Went down an' got me a job down there, 'spector, 'spectin' ammunition before it goes on board ship . . . I got me a certificate that'll find me a job any time I want one . . . Been workin' in a cotton mill up home, not so bad . . . good people to work for, company gives you a nice house, sells you coal cheap, used to give you vacations down to the shore . . . all you had to pay was a dollar a day, before transportation got so tight; company's all right but there ain't no money in it. They don't pay no wages. My wife she works there too. I'm goin' to leave her home so that she kin keep the house. I wouldn't carry her down here where I'm goin'. I'm lucky to git a place to stay. A nephew of mine down there, he's goin' to board me for seven dollars a week. That's cheap but he kinda likes me. I'll git home once a month or fix it so my wife kin come down an' see me. Couldn't do it oftener. This trip wears a man out . . . Company's helped a lot of folks build up homes. They lend 'em the money for the materials an' some fellers build their houses theirselves . . . One of these days I'm goin' to build me a house. I always thought I'd like to build me a log house out in the woods. I'd buy me a piece of land an' cut down the trees to build the house with.'

We have left the lightcolored hilly country behind and for miles now have been grinding down long straight stretches through pinewoods. All you can see on each side of the road are the tall longleaf pines scarred by the slashing cuts the turpentine gatherers make. After a while strings of washing fluttering in the wind begin to appear among the pines, then brown tents with scaly old cars parked beside them, tarpaper shacks kneedeep in tin cans and old papers and cartons, occasional battered trailers at perilous angles. On the door of a corrugated iron barn far gone in decrepitude is a sign 'Housekeeping Rooms.' Back of a fillingstation a row of white tourist cabins festooned with laundry is lost behind dense ranks of trailers shining in the sun. The road dips down into a broad expanse of salt marshes and crosses a dyke along the edge of a broad brown bay. On every stump and snaggled log sticking up out of the shallow muddy water sits a brownishgray gull. 'A world of mullet out there,' says one of the men behind me to the other.

Startled by the roar of the bus, a white heron rises out of the dry reeds of the salt marsh and flies with slow wingflaps landward. Now, all along the horizon across the bay from out of a smudge of smoke begin to appear the tall derricks and the crossed.arms of cranes and the hoists and the great steel cradles of the shipyards. Along the sandspit in front of the yards as far as you can see, parked cars sparkle endlessly in the sun.

The man beside me is sitting up, looking out of the window with dilated nostrils. 'I didn't tell the company I was gittin' me this other job ... Thought I'd better see how I liked it first. They just think I'm off for a couple of days. I'll be makin' three times what I made up home. Might save some money this way ... for that log house.'

A Town Outgrows Itself

We are in the city now. The bus is swinging out of the traffic of the crowded main street round the low gray building of the busstation, and comes to a stop in the middle of a milling crowd: soldiers, sailors, stout women with bundled up babies, lanky backwoodsmen with hats tipped over their brows and a cheek full

of chewingtobacco, hatless young men in lightcolored sport shirts
open at the neck, countrymen with creased red necks and well-
washed overalls, cigarsmoking stocky men in business suits in
pastel shades, girls in bright dresses with carefully curled hair
piled up on their heads and highheeled shoes and bloodred finger-
nails, withered nutbrown old people with glasses, carrying rup-
tured suitcases, broadshouldered men in oilstained khaki with
shiny brown helmets on their heads, negroes in flappy jackets and
pegtop pants and little felt hats with turned-up brims, teenage
boys in jockey caps, here and there a flustered negro woman dragging behind her a string of white-eyed children. Gradually the
passengers are groping their way down the steep steps out of the
bus and melting into the crowd.

Out on the streets every other man seems to be in work clothes.
There are girls in twos and threes in slacks and overalls. Waiting
for the light at a crossing a pinkfaced youth who's dangling a
welder's helmet on a strap from the crook of his arm turns laughing to the man who hailed him. 'I jes' got tired an' quit.' Ragged
families from the hills and the piney woods stroll staring straight
ahead of them along the sidewalks towing flocks of little kids with
flaxen hair and dirty faces. In front of a window full of brightcolored rayon socks in erratic designs a young man with glasses
meets two girls in slacks. 'We missed you yesterday,' they say.
'I was sick. I didn't go in. Anyway, I've got me a new job . . .
more money.'

The mouldering old Gulf seaport with its ancient dusty elegance
of tall shuttered windows under mansard roofs and iron lace overgrown with vines, and scaling colonnades shaded by great trees,
looks trampled and battered like a city that's been taken by
storm. Sidewalks are crowded. Gutters are stacked with litter
that drifts back and forth in the brisk spring wind. Garbage cans
are overflowing. Frame houses on treeshaded streets bulge with
men in shirtsleeves who spill out onto the porches and trampled
grassplots and stand in knots at the streetcorners. There's still
talk of lodginghouses where they rent 'hot beds.' (Men work in
three shifts. Why shouldn't they sleep in three shifts?) Cues

wait outside of movies and lunchrooms. The trailer army has filled all the open lots with its regular ranks. In cluttered backyards people camp out in tents and chickenhouses and shelters tacked together out of packingcases.

In the outskirts in every direction you find acres and acres raw with new building, open fields skinned to the bare clay, elevations gashed with muddy roads and gnawed out by the powershovels and the bulldozers. There long lines of small houses, some decently planned on the 'American standard' model and some mere boxes with a square brick chimney on the center, miles of dormitories, great squares of temporary structures are knocked together from day to day by a mob of construction workers in a smell of paint and freshsawed pine lumber and tobacco juice and sweat. Along the river for miles has risen a confusion of new yards from which men, women, and boys ebb and flow three times a day. Here and there are whole city blocks piled with wreckage and junk as if ancient cranky warehouses and superannuated stores had caved in out of their own rottenness under the impact of the violence of the new effort. Over it all the Gulf mist, heavy with smoke of soft coal, hangs in streaks, and glittering the training planes endlessly circle above the airfields.

Riffraff

To be doing something towards winning the war, to be making some money, to learn a trade, men and women have been pouring into the city for more than a year now; tenants from dusty shacks set on stilts above the bare eroded earth in the midst of the cotton and the scraggly corn, small farmers and trappers from halfcultivated patches in the piney woods, millhands from the industrial towns in the northern part of the state, garage men, fillingstation attendants, storekeepers, drugclerks from crossroads settlements, longshore fishermen and oystermen, negroes off plantations who've never seen any town but the county seat on Saturday afternoon, white families who've lived all their lives off tobacco and 'white meat' and cornpone in cranky cabins forgotten in the hills

For them everything's new and wonderful. They can make more spot cash in a month than they saw before in half a year. They can buy radios, they can go to the pictures, they can go to beerparlors, bowl, shoot craps, bet on the ponies. Everywhere they rub elbows with foreigners from every state in the Union. Housekeeping in a trailer with electric light and running water is a dazzling luxury to a woman who's lived all her life in a cabin with half-inch chinks between the splintered boards of the floor. There are street cars and busses to take you anywhere you want to go. At night the streets are bright with electric light. Girls can go to beautyparlors, get their nails manicured, buy readymade dresses. In the backwoods a girl who's reached puberty feels she's a woman. She's never worried much about restraining her feelings when she had any. Is it any wonder that they can't stay home at dusk when the streets fill up with hungry boys in uniform?

'It's quite dreadful,' says the man with his collar around backwards, in answer to my question. He is a thinfaced rustylooking man in black with darkringed dark eyes who sits rocking in a rocking chair as he talks. 'We are quite exercised about the problems these newcomers raise for the city . . . Juvenile delinquency, illegitimate babies, venereal disease . . . they are what we call the riffraff. I've seen them in their homes when I was travelling about the state inspecting C.C.C. camps for the government. They live in an astonishing state of degradation, they have no ambition. They put in a few measly crops, hoe their corn a little, but they have no habits of regular work. Most of them would rather freeze than chop a little wood. 'Most of the time they just sit around taking snuff and smoking. You see little children four and five years old smoking stubs of cigars. It's *Tobacco Road* and what was that other book? . . . *Grapes of Wrath*. People say those books are overdrawn, but they are not . . . They aren't exaggerated a bit. No wonder there's absenteeism . . . They've never worked regularly in their lives . . . They live in a daze. Nothing affects them, they don't want anything. These awful trailer camps and filthy tent colonies, they seem dreadful to us, but they like it like that. They think it's fine. They don't know any different.'

'Don't you think malnutrition might have something to do with their state of mind?' He was strangely inattentive to my question. A smell of frying fish had begun to fill the bare front room of the rectory. Somewhere out back a little bell had tinkled. The man with his collar around backwards began to stir uneasily in his chair. 'I'm afraid I'm keeping you from your supper,' I said, getting to my feet. 'Yes,' he said hastily. I thanked him and said goodbye. As I was going out the door he added, 'Of course the people who come to my church, whom you were asking about, are foremen, skilled mechanics, good union men, they are a much better element. These other people are riffraff.'

Waiting for the bus at the streetcorner in front of one of the better trailer camps that has clean white gravel spread over the ground, and neat wooden platforms beside each shiny trailer for use as a front stoop, I get to talking to a young man in a leather jacket. He's just worked four hours overtime because the other fellow didn't get there to relieve him at his machine. He's tired. You can tell by his breath that he's just had a couple or three beers. He's beefing because of the state regulations limiting the sale of whiskey and cutting out juke boxes in beer parlors. When a man's tired, he says, he needs relaxation. Works better next day. What's the use of dancing if you can't have a drink? What's the use of drinking if you can't dance? If this sort of thing keeps up he's going to pick up and move some place where things are wide open. Meanwhile several busses so jammed with soldiers from the airfield there's no more room, have passed us by. Hell, he groans, might as well go get him another beer, and he trots back into the silent 'Dine and Dance' joint across the street.

The Feudal Mentality

The office of the local trade union weekly is full of coming and going. A burly young man in a lightcolored stetson hat sits talking from behind a typewriter. He talks emphatically using salty soapbox phrases. The Government Man is exploding in the middle of the floor. He's a small man with wiry hair and mustache. Something about his eyes and his throaty voice gives you the feeling that he's absolutely on the level. He talks like a bunch of Chinese firecrackers going off. They've given him the job single-handed of stopping the turnover of labor. He's trying to get the unions and management to pull together. He's trying to get the companies not to fire men on the whim of any foreman and guard, to get some order into their system of releases to workers who want to be released. All he gets is a dogfight.

'None of us'll ever get anywhere,' shouts the young man in the stetson hat, 'until the employers'll treat labor like an equal.'

'They won't see it,' says the Mediator, an oldtime labor leader with a lined face who sits hunched in a corner with his hat over his eyes. 'They still think that when they hire a man they are doing him a personal favor and that he ought to be grateful.'

'It's the oldtime feudal mentality.'

A heavyset man with a bull neck and a cast in his eye bursts into the room. He has on a sporty striped necktie and wears two big seal rings on his right hand and one on his left. He's the president of the new local. He's just signed up six hundred new men and he wants to get it written up in the paper.

'These days,' says a skinny man with a waspwaist who's an official of the roofers, 'that's the easiest thing we do ... Try to make good union men of 'em, that's another story.'

'Our boys take to it fine. Nowadays we get along without any rough stuff,' said the big man plunking himself down in a chair. 'At least not much.' He glances down at the big hands with the seal rings on them clenched on his knees.

'What we need in our movement is brains, brains at the top,' says the young man in the stetson. 'Last night I was reading over Gompers' speeches. Gompers had a good clear head. We've had no man with real brains since Gompers died.'

'They could use some the other side of the fence too,' spluttered the Government Man. 'But I've got to get back to work.' He popped out of the room as if shot from a gun.

'And now they've unloaded the race problem on us,' mumbled the Mediator. 'We were gettin' along all right until they stirred that up on us. We were givin' the colored folks the best break we could.'

'Ain't never no trouble,' said the roofer, 'unless somebody stirs it up.'

'Washington kicked off and the politicians down here are runnin' with the ball ... White supremacy's a gold mine for 'em.'

'As if we didn't have enough troubles organizin' this pile of raw muleskinners into decent union men and citizens,' cried out the man in the stetson hat, 'without having these longhaired wiseacres come down from Washington to stir up the race question ... You know as well as I do that there isn't a white man in the South who isn't willing to die for the principle of segregation.' He paused. All the men in the room silently nodded their heads. 'Hell, we were jogglin' along all right before they sprung that on us. Sure, we have colored men in the unions in the building trades; the bricklayers even had colored officers in some of their locals.'

'It's a thing you just have to go easy on,' spoke up the Mediator. 'Most white mechanics down here 'ud rather have a colored helper than a white helper, but when a colored man gets a notch up above them, they don't like it ... Ain't a white man in the South'll stand for it. We tried that once in reconstruction days ... I know of two of those niggers that fair practices board ordered upgraded who are dead niggers today. A piece of iron just fell on 'em.'

'If they'd only just concentrate on givin' the negro a square deal within his own sphere most of the liberalminded people in the South would go along.'

'There are small towns out here where all the young white men have gone to the army or war industry, and where the old men are all deputy sheriffs with guns slapped on their hips.' The Mediator was talking in his slow drawling voice. 'The people in those little towns are scared. If some day a drunken nigger made a pass at a white woman all hell 'ud break loose. Now there ain't nothin' goin' to happen, we know there ain't nothin' goin' to happen, but, mister, you tell your friends up North that this ain't no time to rock the boat.'

'We've got our friends in the industrial unions to thank for that,' said the young man in the stetson hat, spitting out his words savagely. 'They came down here when we had the whole coast organized solid and put in their oar. They beat us at an election in this one yard ... they got the negroes to vote for 'em, but they couldn't get 'em to join their union. What kind of labor politics is that? They've only got nine hundred members to this day, out of thousands. That's not majority rule ... That doesn't sound like democracy to me.'

A few days before in a mining town in the northern part of the state I'd had lunch with a young college man from North Carolina, who had given me in a slow serious voice the industrial union side of the race question. They knew it was a difficult matter, he'd said, but they had decided to face it squarely. At first the employers down here had hired negro labor to break the white unions, but now that the negroes were joining up the employers were trying to hire all white men. On the whole the negroes had stuck to their locals through hard times better than the whites. In locals where they'd faced the issue squarely ... equal rights for all ... there had been very little trouble, even in locals made up of country boys from the farms. He told me of one local right in the black belt where they had tried it without having any real trouble, but the strain on the organizer, who was a Southern boy, had been terrific. He'd gone to a hospital with a nervous breakdown. I laughed. He didn't. It wasn't easy, he went on unsmilingly, but prejudice was something that tended to die away if nobody stirred it up. The cure was firmness and courage — meet it head on.

I told him about a meeting I'd drifted into in the basement of a colored church in a war industry town in the North. It was a meeting to protest against the separate dormitory the government was erecting for colored people. Quietlooking elderly negroes were sitting on cane chairs round an oldfashioned coal stove listening to the booming oratory of a preacher from the city. In a voice stirring as a roll of drums he invoked the Four Freedoms and asked how this country could fight for democracy in the rest of the world while there was still discrimination and segregation for thirteen million of our citizens at home. A lawyer had talked about the Constitution and said that now was the time for negroes to rise up and insist that they would no longer be treated as secondclass citizens. If they were called upon to send their sons and brothers to die for their country they had the right to demand equal rights everywhere throughout the broad land. Very much stirred, the listeners had whispered fervent amens at every pause. A young labor organizer had gotten up and said that such injustices made him ashamed to be a white man.

I was asking whether, perhaps, if only as a matter of tactics, it would not be better to work for fair play, equal wages, equal living conditions, first. Wasn't trying to break up segregation that way an infringement of the liberty of white men who didn't want to mix with negroes? After all, white men had rights, too.

'We have found,' the young man said quietly, 'that to get fair play for poor whites we've got to fight for equal rights for poor negroes. Of course we have to use tact, a great deal of tact. But in the unions, at least, the question has to be met head on.'

Twentyfive Years Behind the Times

And all the while, by every bus and train the new people, white and black, pour into the city. As fast as a new block of housing is finished, it's jampacked. As soon as a new bus is put into service, it's weighed down with passengers. The schools are too full of children. The restaurants are too full of eaters. If you try to go to see a doctor, you find the waitingroom full and a long line of people straggling down the hall. There's no room in the hospitals for the women who are going to have babies. 'So far we've been lucky,' the health officers say with terror in their voices, 'not to have had an epidemic. But we've got our fingers crossed.'

Lines of men wait outside of every conceivable office. If you ge to see the mayor in the City Hall, you find him, a certain desperation under his bland exterior, desperately calling up Washington to try to pry loose some sewer pipe. The housing project has attended to the plumbing within its domain. The army has attended to these matters within its camps, but nobody has thought of how the new projects are to be linked up with the watermains and sewers of the city.

If you go to see the personnel director of one of the big yards — he used to be a football coach — you find him fuming because he can't get the old team spirit into his employees. 'What can you do when workingmen are making such big wages they don't give a damn?'

If you ask a labor man why management and labor can't get together to take some action about absenteeism and labor turnover, he snaps back at you: 'Management down here won't talk to labor. The men running these yards are twentyfive years behind the times.'

'I try to tell the president of one of these concerns,' says the Government Man, 'that he ought to set up a modern labor relations department and he just gives me a kind of oily grin and says, "Oh go 'long — you get it all out of a book."'

The Government Man's office is under continual siege. Today two very pretty girls in overalls with magnificent hairdos and long sharp red polished nails have been waiting all morning to tell their story. Meanwhile, they tell it to a sympathetic telephone girl. They are welders. They want a release from this company so that they can go somewhere else where they can get more money. The mean old company won't see it their way. Can't the government do something about it? A group of farmboys is complaining that the local police won't let them run their cars without getting local plates. They can't get local plates until they get paid at the end of the week. Without their cars they can't get to work. Can't the government do something about it? In the hall some very black negroes are hunched in a group leaning against the white marble sheathing of the wall

of the officebuilding. They are appealing to Caesar. At the
personnel office they've been told that if they quit their jobs
they'll have to leave town. They want Uncle Sam to say if it's
true. No, it's not true, not yet.

'It's incredible,' says the Government Man when his office is
finally clear. 'Labor turnover in this town has reached twentyfive percent a quarter. That means every man Jack of 'em
changed his job in a year. It's rugged individualism, all right.
What they do is come into town and get some training, then when
they've qualified for the lowest rate of skilled work they go and
get 'em a job somewhere else. They can say they've had experience and can get in at a higher rate. After they've worked
there a while, they move to some other outfit and get taken on
in a higher category still, and they don't know a damn thing
about the work because they spend all their time on the bus
travelling around. It's the same thing with the foremen and
executives. Before any one of them has a chance to learn his
work he's snatched off somewhere else. I can't keep anybody
in my office. Don't know anything about organizing industry,
but they all get big jobs in management. It's upgrading for fair.
It's very nice, but nobody stays any place long enough to learn
his job. It's a nightmare.'

And still . . . the office is in a tall building. We both happen
to look out the window at the same time. Across a welter of
sunblackened roofs we can see in the slanting afternoon sunlight
the rows of great cranes and the staging and the cradled hulls
and beyond, in the brown strip of river, packed rows of new
tankers, some splotched with yellow and red, some shining with
the light gray of their last coat of paint. In spite of turmoil and
confusion, ships are getting built, ships, ships, ships.

If I Could Save Me Up Some Money

The busdriver is a stout middleaged pleasant man who looks a
little like a country doctor. He's had some difficulty packing
his passengers and their chattels in. A stout frowstyhaired

woman, with three pastyfaced children and a lot of bundles, has gotten into the places belonging to two stout men in rayon shirts open at the throat, who start a loud complaint that those are their seats and they left books and magazines in them. As the woman struggled to get out into the crowded aisle, she says in a resigned tone, 'The baby's goin' to have a hemorrhage . . . I'm tryin' to git him to a doctor.' The husky men settle back into their seats regardless. The bags and the babies are finally stowed and the bus moves out of the station into the honking traffic of the street. When the last row of new houses and the last rubbish pile and the last trailer are left behind and we are speeding smoothly over a long straight road through the evenly spaced pines of the turpentine forest, the busdriver wipes his face with a handkerchief and turns to nobody in particular and says: 'See those drivers? They're the worst drivers in the world in that place . . . don't know if they're comin' or goin'.' I am sitting on the little step beside him squeezed into the narrow passage with my knees up to my chin. Beside me a thin-faced male child with large black eyes who looks ten but might be thirteen is solemnly inhaling a cigarette. It was his father, a ruggedfaced man in overalls, with the same features only larger, in the seat by the window who lit it for him. Talking under the driver's elbow I agree with him by replying that they are very bad drivers indeed. We get to talking. 'I declare that's the hellhole of creation,' he says. 'I always feel better when I get out of it.' A little farther along the road he points out a place where he saw a fox last night. 'He ran right out in front of me and was off hellbent for election up the highway with his brush straight out behind him.' I ask him about hunting in these parts. 'A little farther up the road there's a world of rabbits misty mornin's. Once they get started across the road they won't never turn back. I hate to run over them. Sometimes you can let 'em get past by just putting your foot on the brake ever so lightly . . . you wouldn't think it, but this bus drives as sweetly as any passenger car.' His voice becomes confidential. 'A little farther along after you cross the river I want you to notice a fine old place on the left, settin' up among some trees. That feller he's settin' pretty. He raises a couple o' hundred head of cattle on an island in the river, rich bottom land it is, real permanent pasture . . . no fences nor nothin' to worry about. That's what I'd like to do if I could save me up some money, buy me a couple of hundred acres and raise me some whitefaced cattle. Like that a man can feel independent.'

Mobile, Alabama, March, 1943

DRIVING THROUGH the valley lands in the spring you are hardly ever away from the smell of orange and grapefruit trees in bloom. Sometimes it's so strong you feel the touch of it like velvet, sometimes it's just an indefinable sugar in the air. Mixed with it is the pottery smell of dry earth freshly wet when your car passes a field the water has just been turned into, or the reek from a green patch where the Mexicans, men, women, and children dressed in ragged brown and blue, are swarming down the rows pulling and bunching onions, or the pungence of bruised foliage under the hot sun if it is tomatoes they are picking. In the open land crisscrossed with irrigation ditches between the citrus groves are immense fields of peas, beans, cabbage, young peppers not come to bearing yet. The lettuce is over. We are driving along an acreage of crinkly green potatoes that reaches to the horizon. Skimming so low they seem to be almost knocking the bloom off, two yellow biplanes cruise back and forth trailing a cloud of dry arsenate of lead behind them to dust the plants. When they reach the telegraph wires along the highroad they hop over them neatly, bank sharply and turn.

When the sun goes down frogs croak along the ditches. The air gets thin and cold and is streaked with reedy dampness when we cross a culvert. Freshlooking towns planted with palms spread out along the railroad line from clusters of fruit and vegetable shipping sheds and processing plants around the stations. The shopping streets have a look of jimcrack confusion with their tangled neon signs and their glaring storewindows, but the dwelling houses behind lawns sheltered between windbreaks of bamboo and feathery dark Australian pine are plain and square and white and look comfortable to live in.

We decide to stop at a yellow stucco hotel. When we park the car under the palms we find that the town is very silent. Our ears still roar from the long drive. There's no traffic in the broad two-lane street. There are palms in the hotel lobby. There's a pleasant waitress in the dining room. They actually have green vegetables on the menu.

When we come out of the stuffy hotel dining room the night smells of leaves and distant blooming citrus groves and gardens, with a dusty flavor of dry earth sopping up water. There is a moon. The palm trees are full of zizzing insects. There is a settled cultivated feeling about the little town with its quiet densely overgrown streets and its small white houses full of light nestled back among vegetation, a feeling of having been well lived in for generations you don't often get in a town north of the Rio Grande.

When I went into the newsstand to buy a late paper I remarked to the skinny man with a Hoosier way of talking, who was sitting behind the counter with his glasses on the tip of his nose, reading a magazine, that there was a whole lot happening in this valley.

'Everything's happened in this section since I've been here,' he drawled. 'I soldiered down here in the valley in 1917. Back up north I kept getting sick. Couldn't stand the winters. Doctors all shook their heads. Circulation's poor. I don't reckon I'd be alive today if I hadn't moved down here. It meant a new lease on life for me . . . I couldn't get this valley out of my head,

so I just picked up and come on back down here. There wasn't
no town at all. Scrub and mesquite, that was all ... We used
to manoeuvre in the scrub and mesquite where this town is now.
Some change, you say? Well, things ain't begun to happen down
here yet.'

'How long have you been here?'

'Well, I guess I've been here going on to fifteen years.'

CHAPTER 6

Valley in Bloom

Hhistory down here in the lower Rio Grande Valley begins with the shipping out of the first carload of mixed vegetables in 1905,' said the leatheryfaced young man with a steely blue flash in his eye. 'At least modern history does... The part I like's our ancient and mediaeval history but we won't go into that right now,' he added in a changing tone of voice. He yawned. 'If you want statistics...' he made a sour face. 'Last year we shipped out fiftysix million carloads ... I don't mean I don't think that isn't goddam wonderful but what I like's fishing and open country. It's ruining the country for me, all this stuff. I'll have to pick up and go live down in old Mexico ... Well, how did it happen? Four things: irrigation by pumping water out of the Rio Grande ... and it wasn't the federal government or Wall Street ... the local water districts raised the money right on the spot. This section has lifted itself by its own bootstraps ... Well, federal flood control did help some ... Then cheap and skilful Mexican labor ... Then desert soil that hasn't had a lot of rainfall to wash all the minerals out of it and a climate pretty near frostproof ... But if they'd asked me I'd rather have had the old ranching days when all they could ship out of a steer was the hide and the horns and the bones. You cut out a couple of steaks to fry for supper and left the rest for the coyotes. Ranching and farming are city fellers' occupations now. A retired dentist from Keokuk sits on his front porch and watches his grapefruit get ripe. A maintenance firm is doing the spraying and cultivating and will pick the crop and ship it for a commission. A business-man has his office in town and farms by telephone. You put in a crop and sell it to a middleman who gets him a jefe and a truckload of Mexicans and harvests it for you. That's why we don't want these government agencies taking away our Mexi-cans and scattering them all over the country . . . It's the farming of the future but I don't like it. You gamble on crops like you'd gamble on the stock market. Well, gambling's all right but the life is so sedentary. I like to get out of doors . . . Hell, that's the twelve o'clock whistle. Let's go out to the car and have a little drink of whiskey.'

Migrant Camp

The doves were thick along the roadsides. Big white and blue herons, long beaks poised like a spear, stood stiff and attentive along the sides of the irrigation ditches. Behind a thicket of feathery green across the ditch we saw a set of low buildings neatly set out in a series of horseshoe formations in green lawns planted with flowering shrubs. We drove in to see what the place was. It was one of the Farm Security Administration camps for migrants.

At the office we found the manager. He was a firm round-faced thickset man with a little the manner of a schoolteacher. Before showing us around the camp he pointed out a map of the region between the Appalachian chain and the Rocky Mountains from the Rio Grande up to the Canadian border, that hung on the wall of his office. 'You see,' he said, with a little the manner of starting a lecture, 'they start down here picking vegetables in the winter and they work up through the cotton section in spring and summer and get to the Panhandle of Texas in time for the wheat harvest. Then some of them go to Colorado for the sugar beets and others into the central Northwest and Michigan and Ohio. The Mexicans go with a jefe or patron who owns the truck and gets together several families. Often they go with the same patron every year, men, women, and children, they won't go any other way. The patron does all the bargaining and bosses the group ... That's the standard setup for migrant farm labor. Down here in back roads along the valley they have their little villages of brokendown shacks they come back to each year. The local growers look with a jealous eye at anything that'll disturb their Mexicans. They are part of the wealth of the country which the growers feel is theirs to exploit, like the soil and the climate ... if you talk to 'em about clearing up illiteracy and tuberculosis and venereal disease and making citizens out of these folks what it stacks up to from their point of view is high wages ... When I started up down here they were just about ready to ride me out of town on a rail ... They don't mind me so much now. You can get used to anything, I guess,' he smiled ruefully. 'But the picture is changing all the time. A curious thing is happening. We thought we were starting a camp for migrants and what we've got is a substandard housing project. About two thirds of our folks now are white Americans who've come down in the world. It was the style a couple of years ago to call them Okies. Well, when these folks find themselves in half way decent conditions they tend to stay put. We've got a kindergarten here to take care of the small children and the kids go to the local schools while the older people are at work ... Oh, they work in packing sheds and processing plants and picking fruit. A good many of them have their own cars. Others go in bunches in trucks like the Mexicans. What we seem to be building up here is a reservoir of skilled workers, not just hand-skilled like the Mexicans but folks who can run tractors and machinery and do carpentry and like that. These folks are working themselves respectable again.'

'Won't skilled men pay off better at high wages in the long run than oldfashioned lowwage handicraft labor?'

'That's been the experience in most places.'

'Then what's the kick?'

'When people don't know what's griping them they pick on something and call it bureaucracy or communism or the New Deal' . . . The manager gave a stoical kind of grin as if he felt the gripe in his midriff. 'What I say is do the best job you can with the materials at hand and people will come around to your side.'

We went out into the sunny day and the sweet spring air. The place was empty. The children were at school. The grown-ups were at work. We did pass one group of lanky men tinkering over a brokendown Model A Ford. We walked past rows and rows of corrugated iron barracks cut up into compartments with two windows and a door. The older buildings were better and had a more permanent look. Vines had grown over them. The new ones were grim. Evidently the standard now was that of a concentration camp. Must be stifling in summer and chilly in winter, we were thinking to ourselves. To live in that place surely wasn't being coddled. At least it was shelter. The stalls were kept clean. You would have all the sweep of the great plain sparkling and green with early crops on every side of you.

'We mustn't forget that changes hurt,' the manager was saying thoughtfully. 'One of the biggest changes to hit us down here is going to be in the handling of vegetables. Dehydrating processes are just about perfected. It'll mean we can ship dehydrated vegetables by plane to any place on earth direct . . . It's my hunch that the war and the need to feed the civilian populations of conquered countries is going to bring about a great development of dehydration . . . It'll take a lot of the gamble out of the crops for the growers . . . Dried vegetables will be cheap and easy to store. Be sure and take a look at the dehydrating plant down the road.' He detailed a set of intricate directions.

As we got into the car to drive off we complimented him on the neatness of the camp. 'Well, that's one thing I can do, keep the place neat,' he said a little sadly. 'We've had remarkably little trouble with keeping order . . . it is rarely we have to put a family out . . . but neatness' . . . as he spoke he stooped to

pick up an empty cigarette package off the gravel drive. 'I have
to start with myself and that makes the rest of 'em toe the mark.'

Dehydration

The road climbed up into the dry farming belt through broad
fields of bluegreen bearded barley. We turned off into a side
road and were back among irrigated grapefruit groves again,
heavy with the fragrance of blossoms and full of mockingbirds
and cardinals singing. We stopped at a building that turned
out to be a fruit-packing shed. A pleasant stubby woman told
us that the dehydrating plant was farther on but said that since
we were here we'd better step in to see the grapefruit being
packed.

She led us upstairs into a sort of balcony at one end of the big
shed from which we could look down through the streaky amber
light on the fruit bouncing and jostling along on the conveyors
like a great concourse of people hurrying for different trains in
a railroad station. In the course of their travels the grapefruit
were washed and waxed and graded and stamped and finally
came to rest on long tables on the lower floor where girls were
packing them into boxes. Just below us there was an automatic
table for sorting by sizes where the grapefruit jigged and bounced
prodigiously, like couples on a crowded dancefloor. It was a
little like looking down into an amusement park.

We drove on through the dark green groves until we came into
a section of flat irrigated meadows planted with ryegrass and
alfalfa. Blue rockpigeons flew up from the road ahead of us.
We drew up in front of two big metal cylinders under a shed that
let out a roaring sound. This was the dehydration plant.

In a corrugated tin office to one side we found a longfaced man
in his shirtsleeves. He was deep in working out a set of statistical
charts. Beside him on the desk lay a worn volume of Mills'
Statistical Method.

When he saw us looking in through the open door he got slowly
to his feet and came out, stretching himself as he came. He

answered our questions with an air of philosophic resignation. No, he wasn't dehydrating vegetables just at present, he was dehydrating ryegrass and alfalfa to be used in chicken feed, but the principle would be the same. He led us round to the front of the two roaring cylinders. There we stood watching a colored man forking freshcut green hay into a hopper out of a wagon. This was the flash process. The matter to be dehydrated was chopped and forced by a blower through an intensely hot chamber. The engineer had to shout to make himself heard over the roar of the blower. He opened a little trapdoor in the thick galvanized pipe and showed us the stuff flying upwards. We followed him up to the other end of the cylinder where it was cooler and where we could hear what he was saying. The paradoxical thing about it, he was explaining, was that in spite of the extreme heat the process was so fast that a little envelope of steam kept each separate particle comparatively cool so that the vitamins were not destroyed. Through the door at the end of each of the big cylinders we could see through the dazzling glow of the gas the hurrying dark particles out of which the water was being sucked. In another part of the shed the finished product poured out into bags in the form of a darkgreen powder. 'Of course,' he said, 'if we didn't have a lot of cheap natural gas this process wouldn't be financially practical.'

'Could you dry any vegetable by this method?'

'Why not?' he asked, frowning, as if the question had put him on the defensive. 'The principle's the same ... There's a whole lot of work to be done before it's perfected. It all takes slow patient work, plodding grimy work ... You people,' he added accusingly, 'read half a magazine article and you think all you need do is press a button and get the New Jerusalem. Sure, I've read about planeloads of dry vegetables unloading at the corner grocery and you put a little water on them and there you've got a bunch of carrots right out of the garden ... It's not so easy as that.'

I asked him what those statistics were he was working on when we disturbed him.

'Oh, it's pretty dull,' he said. 'I'm trying to work out the relation between water, fertilizer, and output on the crop of rye-grass. You can measure the water pretty accurately since we hardly ever have any rain. Water and fertilizer are the two costly items in this crop. Intralineal correlation won't give you the right result. You have to go to the second degree curve to get it.'

He added that we ought to go to a place about ten miles from there to see a plant where they were using the tunnel system.

We said we'd go right there. 'Well,' I said as we shook hands, 'it's a surprise to see a man farming with Mills' Statistical Method as a handbook.'

'You can't do without it,' he answered laughing.

We drove on in search of the second plant. Eventually we found it set up in the old stucco building of a defunct citrus exchange. The place had just had a fresh coat of paint. The machinery looked new. There was nobody on hand but the girl in the office and a sixteenyearold boy who said he was the son of the man who owned it. We were just turning away when he said wouldn't we let him show us around. He showed us all over exclaiming all the time that he wished his dad was there to explain things better. He knew the process by heart. He was evidently immensely thrilled with the whole proposition. This setup was using the tunnel process. Vegetables ranged on shallow trays were moved on a conveyor through a hot tunnel that took out about half the moisture. Then they were ranged for several hours in a chamber of very dry warm air. The boy said they were having good results from carrots and parsley. He showed us the dried green parsley packed in cellophane bags for shipment and sample carrots, beets, and potatoes looking somewhat mummified in a set of glass jars. We went away munching slices of dried carrot.

That night, in a neat new treeshaded little town we went to call on the man who, everyone had told us, knew most about dehydration in the whole valley. We found him a quietspoken little gray man, sitting by a shaded lamp in his living room with his wife after supper. They brought us out grapefruit to eat.

We asked him to tell us about the comparative merits of the flash and the hot tunnel systems. He said that what he was most interested in was a combination of both. The juice of the vegetable would be extracted by a press and reduced to crystals or to syrup according to its makeup, and the pulp would be shot through the flash system and reduced to a powder. Then they'd be put together at the time of cooking. That was the only way he knew of conserving the highest percentage of salts, vitamins, and everything else.

Wasn't the war, I asked him, giving a great impulse to dehydration of vegetables on account of the saving in space and weight for shipping by air? He nodded and made a wry face. He would have thought so too, he said, in fact for the twentyfive years he'd been working on this business of dehydration he'd been waiting for just such an emergency . . . But now a funny thing had happened. 'The price of vegetables has gone so high that you can ship anything you grow at a profit fresh; so there's no incentive for processing . . . Isn't that something?'

The Ceilings

To reach the office of the growers' association we had to walk between piles of vegetable boxes that smelt of raw wood, through a long corrugated-iron shed which opened on one side on a broad gravelled space where trucks unloaded and on the other on railroad tracks flashing in the sunlight. In the office a small jumpy gray man with just a touch of the racetrack about his green bow tie and checked suit sat at a bare desk between two telephones. When we walked in the door a tall sunburned man in khaki breeches and shirt with a broad dustcolored hat on the back of his head was lunging back and forth in front of the clerk and shouting, 'I'd like to have those darn counter jumpers down here to give them a piece of my mind.' When he noticed there were strangers in the room he took his hat off and went on in a quieter almost whining voice. 'But why won't they take the growing cost into account? Please tell me why. I tell you it's up to us growers to raise a holler . . . that's what we've got a representative in Washington for.'

'He called me up a little while ago,' said the man at the desk soothingly. 'He's around at the O.P.A. right now. Don't you worry, Jed.'

'I'll quit worryin' when I get every last load of that cabbage shipped out of here. Didn't they have a frost in the Florida black muck section? I'll quit worryin' when you get me those freightcars, Ed, and I get that stuff cleared out of here. Used to be all the grower had to worry about was frost and low water . . . Now we've got to worry about the government, too. Suppose they took it into their heads to freeze us again?' He went out with his big hat in his hand shaking his head and muttering to himself. 'I'm worried . . . I can't help it . . . I'm worried.'

The man between the telephones made a face after he'd gone. 'As if I didn't have enough to do without having to hold the growers' hands all day. That freezing order paralyzed the first part of the early vegetable market and now we're doin' business under terrific pressure as a result.'

'Don't the ceilings give the growers a profit?'

'Sure, and if you holler loud enough they'll adjust them for you in Washington. You can get anything if you just holler loud and long enough. If we'd had an assurance earlier of the ceilings we've got now we would have had a bigger crop. It'll be the biggest on record as it is. No, the growers don't need to worry. Cabbage used to be the sure-thing low-profit early crop down here because it could stand a freeze. Beans was the gamble. But now cabbage is a gold mine. I just had a long-distance call from San Diego, California, asking for cabbage. And there's not a potato on the Coast. Los Angeles is on the phone every minute. Imagine that! I used to spend half my time haggling over prices. Nobody ever even asks the price any more.'

'Growing any potatoes down here?'

'Shipped a hundred and thirty thousand carloads last year. We'll beat that this year. There's a real potato famine. They ate up a lot of seed potatoes up north last winter. Dealers are fighting for anything that looks like a potato.'

'So the growers aren't going to lose money?'

'Lose money! They are all bailed out already. In this country, at these prices, with this market, a man can bail himself out with one crop. We run two crops a year, three in some items.' . . . The buzzer rang on his desk, he picked up the receiver. 'That's Washington,' he whispered, 'that'll be long. I'm afraid you'll have to excuse me.'

Settlement and Resettlement

For a long time we had been driving up and down over arid land full of flat rocks where cattle grazed in the dust between feathery bright green mesquite bushes and flatleaved thorny desert plants. Then the road broke through a dense thicket of trees and crossed an irrigation ditch full of abundant muddy water, and we were back in the valley again, coming out on a broad irrigated plain of brightcolored fields. On a rise of land ahead of us rose a white fivestory building that looked like an expensive Florida resort hotel. A drive curved in towards it past a vivid green lawn that had a fine spray playing on it from a hose. There was no sign on the building so we went into the office to find out what it was.

It was one of Farm Security's collectives that congressmen so dread.

In the office they told us the story. This had been a clubhouse run by a land company during the days of the last great boom in irrigated valley land in this section. Investors from Chicago and Omaha and Kansas City would be brought down here by the real estate agents to visit citrus groves. The company would put them up in the clubhouse, fill them full of food and drink and illusions of retiring to spend their declining years among orange groves and murmuring waters, and sell them citrus land at two thousand dollars an acre. There was a paradisiacal scheme by which the company operated the groves for a commission. So all the homeseeker had to do was sit there in his twentyfive thousand dollar home through an eternal balmy afternoon, and let the grapefruit fall into his lap and the dollars flow gently into his bank.

Once they got into the clubhouse the agents never let the prospective buyers get out of their sight. They were doctors, dentists,
lawyers, and aging professional people mostly. The land agents
kept them in a trance. They never had a chance to look around
for themselves. They were kept carefully segregated from the
local inhabitants, who referred to them jeeringly as homesuckers.

That boom collapsed in nineteen-thirtythree, the homesuckers
couldn't complete their payments and lost their equity, the land
companies went broke, the banks went broke. The real wealth re-
mained there idle, the roads, the land, the citrus groves, the irrigation ditches, and amenable Mexican daylabor. Since then this
particular clubhouse had been in the hands of mortgage holders,
bankers and insurance companies and now Farm Security had
bought it with its attendant twentysix thousand acres to use as a
resettlement centre for small farmers driven off the land. If
Congress forced the Administration to sell out, what would become of it? 'Lord knows,' said the administrator. 'In these
parts wonders never cease,' and he handsomely invited us to lunch.

After lunch an elderly man, who stood very straight in his
boots, six foot six and more under his dusty broadbrimmed hat,
showed us around the place. He came from the Panhandle of
Texas and had been ranching and farming all his life.

'There are two things you can do,' he said. 'You can sell land
or you can build up the country. They used this place to sell
land, in the worst way . . . now we are trying to use it to build up
the country.'

Around the building he showed us proudly the various varieties
of papaya trees he'd grown from seed he'd crossed himself. Then
he drove around the experimental farm where the fields were con-
tourplowed into strips where he was trying out rye and barley and
hotweather legumes.

'The rows ain't straight, see?' he said. 'The aim of contour-
plowing is to make running water walk . . . I have the hardest
time gettin' some of these fellers to try it. It near breaks their
hearts not being able to make straight rows. I never argue with
'em. I just tell 'em to go ahead and do it in their own way. One

feller I did ask if he was farmin' for straight rows or if he was farmin' for crops.'

We were standing in front of a magnificent stand of pale blue flowering flax that stretched waving in the wind as far as you could see across the flat land. 'I brought that seed down from the Dakotas... I never argue with anybody,' he said. 'I just try things out an' let 'em see how they work. When we used to have all the room in the world in this country it didn't matter what any one man did. He could go off on the range and get drunk and do any damn thing he liked in his own way. There was still plenty of room. If you wanted to put on a phoney land boom you hurt nobody but yourself and a few suckers. It was devil take the hindmost. What I try to tell people now is that we can't be free that way any more in this country. There ain't the margin for error. We've got to learn to cooperate ... in farming like in everything else ... But don't never argue with them, I say. Just find a chance to try it out and let 'em see the results in yield to the acre.'

Brownsville, Texas, April, 1943

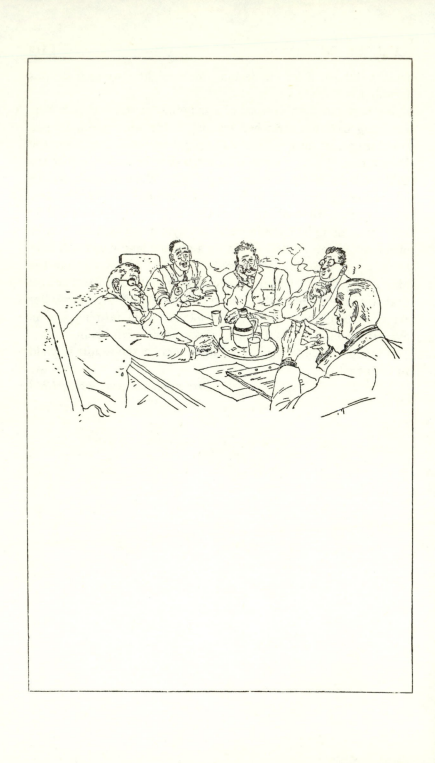

THE BUS LET ME OFF at the corner of two broad avenues
On each side of the street there were cemeteries. Through the tall
iron palings behind me I could make out dimly, in the glimmer
from the streetlights through the misty spring evening, oblong
tombs set above the ground, Ionic porches of vaults, vague shapes
of weeping angels in marble, urns, broken columns. Occasionally
a plane with red and green lights purred softly across the clear
space of sky overhead where a scattering of stars showed. After a
while a car stopped and the door opened. A young man in a blue
uniform was at the wheel. 'This is a nice place to keep a man
waiting,' I said.

He laughed. 'Aw, the whole town was a cemetery before he
got started . . . Come ahead. Hop in.'

'Imagine finding you working for Uncle Sam. What is it? The
Coast Guard or the Navy?'

'I'm sworn into somepen' but I work for the boss . . . I'm goin'
to show you somepen' tonight you never saw in your life.'

He explained he'd left his drugstore job and been out here a
year now. He'd seen the place grow up from nothing.

We were driving past a floodlit lumber yard. 'This is the
greatest collection of seasoned tropical woods in the world. Sure,
he uses all kinds in his boats. He's still experimentin' with differ-

ent kinds of plywood. If this ever got on fire . . . my, my . . .' He parked the car back of a long white building full of light. 'This is where he builds the boats,' he said. He pinned a badge on my coat as he ushered me in past the guards. We climbed up a narrow wooden stairway. 'PT boats,' he whispered in my ear. From the top we could look down into the inside of an immensely long broad barnlike building that shrilled with saws and sandblast noises punctuated by the ratatat of pneumatic hammers. The air was full of the pungence of steamed wood and the smell of fresh shavings. Along one side of the floor below you could see the boats grow out of keels and ribs into complete skeletons. On the other the smoothly contoured surface spread over the framework until the hulls were complete. In the middle the finished boats were being fitted and painted navy gray as they advanced towards the railroad track that led out of the far end of the shop. Brightly floodlighted, the features of men's faces and the muscles of bare arms stood out sharply as they worked among the moulded shapes of the boats that stood out in high relief in the glare against the dark. 'Ain't that somepen'?' he said. 'I never get tired of seeing this. It never stops . . . Get me? . . . I knock off an' go home to bed with my wife. I have my day off an' get stinkin' or lose a wad of dough at the races but all the time it's movin' . . . Those boats are comin' together part by part an' they're bein' smoothed an' shaped an' fitted an' painted an' the crane lifts 'em out on a gondola an' the shuntin' engine forms 'em into trains an' they go on out to all the wars in the world. I guess I'm simpleminded but I never had nothin' to do with production before. It sure gets you. I didn't used to know what the word meant.'

We were out in the dark again. We climbed back into his car. 'Now I'm goin' to show you somepen' you never saw in your life,' he whispered. 'Maybe I oughtn't to but a man has to use his own judgment about these things. After all, you ain't an enemy alien.' We drove across a canal where the streetlights shone reflected in the black water, then along a palmbordered avenue past rows of small weatherworn white houses isolated among gardens into a park full of the great shadowy blurred shapes of liveoaks, across another canal, round a great building full of steam and the sound of hammering, spilling the fluttering glare of welding arcs out into the night from every window. 'That's where he builds his steel boats,' he said with a sideways tilt to his head.

'What kind of boats?'

'You'll see in a minute.' He drove around a block and came out on a dirt road that followed along the canal again. Everything was dark except for an occasional glimmer in the water of a spot of light reflected from the town. 'There they are,' he said, stopping the car sharply.

'What?'

In the car's headlights we could see dark narrow scowlike shapes. The canal was full of them. He started the motor up again and drove along in low pointing with one hand out the window. They were tied up, rank on rank along the opposite bank. As far as the road went they filled the canal, stretching into the inky mist under the blue glimmer from the stars overhead. 'Don't you know what they are?' His voice rose. 'Those are invasion barges.'

CHAPTER 7

New Industries Make New Men

T HERE'S A TINGLE OF ELECTRICITY about the air of the United States Employment Office in this great wide scattered gulfcoast city of Houston. Under the humdrum surface of bureaucratic boredom, of people waiting their turn and girls answering telephones and office routine and searching in indexes and tabulation of qualifications on filing cards there's a feeling of decisions and departures. This is the place where the future course of many a man's life is decided.

The office fills the whole lower floor of a large frame building with windows opening out on three sides onto parked cars glistening in the sun and stretches of glaring asphalt across wide sunbeaten streets. The dark central part where the interviews take place under hanging electric-light bulbs consists of a platoon of desks cut off from the outer section by a broad counter. It is early in the morning but already a mixed crowd of old men, young men, women, boys is waiting in lines at the various windows set up on the counter. Rows of people sit on the benches in the back of the room. A number of elderly men have turned up, and surprisingly many middleaged women. There are young kids still in highschool who have taken courses in metal-working, women whose husbands and sons have gone to the war who feel they must do something to help, grayhaired men who have wrenched themselves loose from the habits of a lifetime and gone to school again in the machineshops. There are a few hardbitten lanky lanternjawed characters from the oil fields. By themselves at one end in dusty overalls stands a group of very black negroes out of the backcountry.

I've been sitting at one of the desks talking to the personnel manager for one of the shipyards, a burly redfaced man with black hair slicked back on his head. His eyes follow my eyes across the bank of faces. 'Soon we'll be scraping the bottom of the barrel,' he says in a rasping voice. 'Up to now we've done pretty well.'

'How many of your employees ever worked in a shipyard before?'

He said ten percent at the outside. That went for foremen, supervisors, vice presidents, right on up to the top. They came from lumbering and the oilfields and the farms and the garages, some few from the machine-tool industry. The main core was made up of construction workers. Building ships was construction, wasn't it?

'There were a lot of crews building dams up here in the state. They built a lot of big dams in this flood control and rural electrification scheme. Luckily they were just winding up when it got to be time to pitch in and build us some new shipyards. The same fellers who built the shipyards went to work to build the ships . . . and the dams they'd just built gave us the power to work with . . . It's all construction work.' He paused and leaned back in his chair, scrutinizing the faces along the counter through narrowed eyes. 'I used to work here,' he said suddenly, looking back at me grinning. 'A lot of the personnel managers in the new industries around this town were hired right out of this office. Among other things the U.S.E.S. has proved to be a regular training school for personnel managers.'

The short active young man with glasses who had arranged the interview for me was hovering over the desk. 'Sorry to break it off,' he said, 'but I've got another man waiting for you over there.'

'I was just telling him I was one of the graduates of this institution,' said the burly man.

They both laughed. 'Yes, we've had a lot of trouble that way around here,' said the young man with glasses.

'But we all seem to come back. Gone are the days when the personnel manager used to sit in his office and watch the men line up to beg for a job,' said the burly man.

'Yes, sir, he has to come down here and hustle for his hands.'

The new man was standing against a window. He was thin and welldressed and had a kind of a poloplaying look. His firm produced machine parts. He said his labor force was about twothirds of what it should be; all the local sources were just about dried up; he'd been experimenting with paroled men and exconvicts and he had had very good luck with them. So far not a single one had gone bad on him. They put them through a training course like everybody else, of course they kept a fairly close watch on them, but so far the results had been one hundred percent. One other department of the training system was just getting into operation. Casualties discharged from the armed services. They had a man from the Solomon Islands and a man from New Guinea. In the long run they expected that to be the most important part.

Salaried Man

My friend with the glasses was back again. 'Speaking of casualties . . . This is one of the casualties of the freezing of wages,' he said and introduced me to a ruddy pleasantlooking young man in a frayed shirt held in at the neck by a necktie worn to a string. 'I sure am,' he said laughing ruefully. 'Cement's at the bottom of the heap. My job's hiring labor for a cement factory. We just have to take the maimed and the halt and the blind if we can get 'em. Last winter we lost forty out of a hundred men in one month . . . went off for higher wages, nothin' else in the world. If it weren't for about fifty faithful employees who stick with us we'd have to go out of business. And rents and groceries are goin' up every day. Right now I make just seventyfive dollars less a month than it costs me to live. And they ask me to buy War Bonds!'

Old Lives Made New

The man in charge of the employment office sat at his piledup desk in the glassedin office in the corner and talked about his work, the tracing of clearances for job transfers, the effort to obtain straight records on qualifications and past experience. One thing he could say was that there was no waiting around any more. When a man wanted a job he knew where to come, in fact, if he didn't want to work he'd better keep away. The personnel men were down there waiting for him. They were even taking them with hernias now if they wore trusses. The office was doing its best to try to steer farm workers back to farm work, but it wasn't any too easy. The tough problem was defining just what a farm worker was. There were some right pathetic cases of old people who were just on the borderline between being able to work and being unemployable.

'There's one right now.' He pointed out through the half open door of his office at a grayhaired man with broad shoulders and a gray felt hat on the back of his head who had just come up to the counter and was leaning over asking the reception girl a question. I slipped out of the office and sidled up beside him. He was unfolding a certificate from an industrial school to the effect that he had successfully completed a course in machine milling. He was sixty years old, he was saying with some pride. He'd been a salesman all his life, sold everything from washing machines to chewing gum, but there was no call for that sort of thing now. He'd raised a family but he hadn't managed to lay much money by. Now he wanted to pitch in and do some real useful work. No, he didn't want a whitecollar job or a job as checker or expediter. No, sir, he wanted to run a milling machine. His gray business suit was creased and worn. He had lost a button off his vest. The points of his starched collar didn't meet very well under his sagging chin. He had a pair of glasses that he kept putting on and taking off as he talked. As he turned away from the window to take his certificate to the other end of the counter you could see, in the horizontal light from the window, the tired skin around his

intent gray eyes, the anxious twitching of his mouth. He walked
with a firm dogged step, his head a little bowed, and the certificate
held out in front of him.

Light Metals

The magnesium plant is a few miles out from town. You drive
out between roadsides blooming with every conceivable kind of
wild flower, blanketflowers, paintbrushes, bluebonnets, coreopsis,
big white prickly poppies with yellow centers. The flowers frame
broad bluegreen pastures under a bright robin's egg sky full of
small bright clouds. As soon as you begin to see against a creamy
bench of hills the low creamcolored silhouette of the buildings, the
tall brick stack, the curious aluminum-painted outlines of what
looks like something in an amusement park that later turns out to
be the kiln, you know that the place is spanking new. The bright
fences are new. The very ground looks new as you drive over
freshcrushed creamcolored rock into the parking lot.

The low shoebox-shaped administration building with its
windows shaded by venetian blinds is as neat inside as it is outside. You have a feeling that instead of a foundry you are being
taken through a perfume factory. It's a surprise to find that the
boss sitting behind the desk in the main office is a big strapping
football player from Chicago. He talks in a low almost hesitant
voice, a small voice for such a large man. He explains to us why
the plant came to be in that particular place.

The first reason was the great amount of current generated by
the new dams, the same dams the construction workers came
from who went to work to build shipyards along the coast, and
when the yards were built, the ships themselves. Second, the
surveys of the local university's department of economic geology
had brought out the fact that many of the quarries they had used
for stone for the dams contained dolomite, a kind of rock which
when burned in a kiln becomes the basis for conversion into magnesium. Third, the town nearby had housing for the workers and
metallurgists who would have to be brought in. No wonder the

place looked new. He puffed his chest out a little when he told us that the first metal was poured only six months ago, and that the ground was broken for the site exactly a year before that.

The company that is running the plant for the government, the football player explained, had been for years in the chemical business producing phosphates. Their engineers had been puzzled to know what to do with a waste product called magnesium chloride. This is now the basic component of a sort of chemical soup they call cellfeed which electrolysis converts into metallic magnesium. This basic slop can be produced from brine or seawater, as in the original plant at the brine wells in Michigan, or from a number of other substances such as brucite and dolomite. The list is increasing. A year ago, he said, the only process available was the brine and seawater process. Now short cuts have been found. Already more magnesium is being made in this country than there was aluminum made before the war, and if you reckon its price by volume it is already as cheap as aluminum. 'In fact,' he said, allowing himself to smile for the first time, 'the whole magnesium program is well ahead of schedule.'

'Where did you get your employees?'

'Well, we advertised in technical journals for technicians. At that time there was still a considerable backlog of technicians being let out of nonwar industries that were closing down. Then we sent men from round here up to Michigan for training. That plant up there is the grandfather of all the magnesium plants in the country. That's where they worked out the basic process. Some of 'em had had some electrical experience. Some of them were just clerks or bellhops or off laundry wagons ... about anything you can think of. No, we don't have any absenteeism, I don't know why.'

'Could it be that there's a certain amount of excitement in working at something absolutely spanking brandnew?' I asked him.

He paused for a moment and then went on without answering my question. Magnesium evidently wasn't particularly new to him. 'We have a full set of labor-management committees ..

they work all right, they attend to gas rationing, sharing cars and things like that . . . One thing we can't get the men to do is take the busses . . . take 'em about a half an hour longer to get home and they just can't see it . . .' He paused again: 'Well, now we've got a union. They voted for the A.F. of L. union just the other day.' He wrinkled up his mouth.

He heaved his big bulk up from his desk. 'Suppose we take a look at it.'

We drove down a road between laboratories and machineshops and came to a stop near some piles of pinkish rock. There were no workmen in sight. The long inclined tube of the kiln was rotating slowly on itself. It was in that kiln that they burned the dolomite to separate it from its magnesium content. Byproducts from this process that would be useful whenever they got time enough to handle them would be gypsum and white lime, he told us. Next we walked past an orderly forest of black retorts linked by great black pitchcolored pipes. The football player made a gesture with his thumb in that direction. 'That's the peskiest thing to keep in order in the whole plant. That's where the stuff is treated with hydrochloric acid . . . It's always getting out of order.'

'How about magnesium after the war?' my friend was asking.

Already we were walking up some iron stairs into a great black cylindrical room with a tar floor that was full of the roar of electric furnaces around the walks. 'Now,' the football player whispered in our ears, 'the cellfeed is ready for electrolysis.'

This is where in a series of cast steel cells under a roaring niagara of electric power the metal is actually produced. The alchemist's dream. We came out breathless.

As we were climbing down the iron stairs again my friend from the town repeated his question about the chances for magnesium after the war. The football player stopped in his tracks and turned to us with a confident drawl. 'They ought to be pretty good. It's a metal that doesn't fatigue.' He let us have a half-inch of smile. 'Somebody listed the most important industries after the war in the order of their probable importance.'

'Yes, I think I read it: transportation, that is planes, came first. Then light metals, magnesium and aluminum. Then plastics. Then communications, radio and television.'

'I don't think we need worry about magnesium. Why, for engineblocks alone . . .'

So far, except for an occasional truck along the roads, the great plant had seemed as empty of people as a painting by Chirico. We crossed the railroad tracks and found a crew of men loading the bright neatlooking bars into a freight car. In the building where they mixed the alloys there were more men at work. Two men with isinglass guards over their faces were stirring a gray powder with longhandled ladles into each of the round vats of molten metal. When the ladles came to the surface they set off starshaped silvery flashes. 'I think this batch is probably incendiary metal . . . That's a special alloy . . . about half our production is going into that right now,' said the football player. He gave another half smile. 'Well, there is a war on,' his words trailed off a little.

The last place we visited was the control room. We had to leave our watches with the elderly negro who was puttering around downstairs to keep them from being magnetized. It was a large windowless brick room with great switchboards along the walls. A lean sharpchinned middleaged man with his hat on the back of his head was in charge all by himself. He came forward and smiled and nodded. 'We have to be a little careful what we do up here,' the football player was explaining. 'We could blow out this hydroelectric station over there at the dam pretty easy.'

'So this is the most important job in the place?' we asked as we went down the stairs again.

'It's one of them; he controls all the juice.'

'Well, this fellow who's in charge right now — what was he doing before he took a job with you?'

'I'm not quite sure. He might have been an electrician in a theatre or something like that. Pretty small potatoes.'

'And now he's a great man.'

The football player nodded gravely.

When we were ready to leave he walked over to the car with us and stood bareheaded in the flailing sunlight beside the open car door. There was something more he wanted to say.

'How's the union working out?' my friend asked him again.

'All right, I guess,' he said in a hurried preoccupied tone. 'Don't quote me either way. Only . . . let's look at it this way. Up to 1929 or so the big business boys were in the saddle. They drove the old horse pretty hard, see? They went too far. Now we don't want to see labor make the same mistakes . . . we may be wrong but with this Administration we think they've got the upper hand. They'll take a licking just like business did if they make the same mistakes.' He rolled up his eyes. 'I'd hate to see that.'

An Old Man Gets a Job

We were walking through a small machineshop on the bank of a stream. They were enlarging the big central shed. Round the edges of the old rusty stockpiles still hooded in canvas, stood new machines about to be installed. The open end of the rustcolored shed was shot through with green light from the bright trees along the riverbank. The river was a light caramel color. The creamy rocks of the shallows beyond seemed to be set in violet, the sun was so bright on them. We had been sitting on the edge of the desk in the dark office looking at photographs of a contraption this concern was about to put into quantity production. It was a horizontal spinning disk saw adjustable to any level that could be attached to the front of a tractor to clear trees. For trees under five inches the tractor didn't even need to stop. It was a contraption a young inventor had been struggling with for many years. Various concerns had taken it up and dropped it, but at last it was coming into its own. Many of the machines had proved satisfactory clearing dam sites in the west and in roadbuilding, anywhere where trees needed to be cleared without being grubbed up by the roots. Now the army was interested. It was going into production in a large way. 'It's funny,' one of us had said. 'We used to just kinder tolerate inventors in this country, and now it's beginning to seep into people's minds that our mechanical ingenuity is the only thing that's going to save our necks.'

'Yes, sir, in this war all the courage in the world won't help us if we don't keep our machines ahead of the other feller's. We have a slight edge on the Germans and the Japanese now, maybe. When we are twentyfive years ahead of them we will have won our peace.'

Blinking, we had come out into the strong light at the end of the new shed. The manager, who was a quiet cosy man in a blue shirt, with narrow spectacles on his nose, was taking us to see some precision parts he was making in a smaller shop to one side. He lifted one of the heavy pieces of metal up proudly and pointed to its smoothly ground inner surfaces. 'They said this couldn't be done west of the Mississippi River,' he said. Then he started to talk about labor.

'But, my, it's hard for us to hold on to our skilled men. We can't raise our wages and this town has been designated as having a surplus of skilled labor ... The government is absolutely all wet. I don't mean to criticize them. They are wrong, that's all. There's nothing left here but boys with twelve weeks' training. In getting out this stuff we have operations that demand twentyfive years' experience ... Well we make out the best we can. I even took on a man sixty years old with no previous experience. He'd taken a course in milling, but I thought I'd better put him on a shaper to try him out.'

I followed his glance across the shop and there at a whirring metalworking machine in a line of other whirring metalworking machines was the grayhaired man who'd so doggedly been waiting that day in the employment office. His glasses were pushed up on his forehead. His business suit had gone and he had on a new pair of blue overalls.

The Boatbuilder

It's one of those days in the early Southern spring when the world seems made of jasmine and wistaria. We have just had a couple of first-rate sazarac cocktails followed by a first-rate lunch. As we drive out of town under a pale blue sky full of fluffy clouds faintly tinted with yellow and pink, we smoke our cigars and feel in the air the immense gentle insistent explosion of new growth. The houses along the road, their white paint weathered to lavender, pirouette in their palmshaded gardens as we pass, showing off weatherbeaten little details of extravagant columned porches and pediments and dormers ornamented in merrygoround style. The people along the sidewalks have an entertaining and congenial look. Vines tumbling over scaling stucco walls show off a whole notion counter of novelties in leaves and flowers. At an intersection of two broad empty avenues fringed with palms, Tanagra ladies green and rusty in the sun hold up an old iron fountain.

The man who's driving me out to the plant, where they build PT boats and landing barges, does public relations for the boatbuilder. He's a quiet mellow man with little ballyhoo to his manner. Only gradually he starts to talk.

'There are more angles to the work they are doing out there than just landing barges and motor torpedo boats,' he is saying. What he likes is the constantly new horizons for the future. The original boat, the before the war model, was designed for river work; the hull was pearshaped in the bow and scooped out along the keel under the stern. Later this afternoon we would see a movie of one of those boats jumping right over a sandbar. It could run the bow up on a beach and back off by its own power. Well, the plan was to use these boats in South America, a modification of the landing barges specially built for carrying trucks like a ferry. For the first time the tropical rivers would become real arteries. These boats had such shallow draft they could go anywhere. Where there were falls and rapids too swift to navigate, roads could be built and the trucks driven up to the next open stretch where another boat could be waiting. No need for bridges. Trucks could be driven far up into the interior without handling the freight. The darn things wriggled over shallows like an alligator. They could run right up on the bank so they would not need any wharves. They could be put to use right away as soon as we stopped producing for war. It would open a new era of transportation along the great tropical rivers.

As he talks the blue afternoon swells to include the whole immensity of the Amazon basin suddenly open to trade and traffic. Already — the man in the back seat puts in a word — these boats have made themselves useful in the great African river routes that had to be opened up to get supplies to Egypt for the Eighth Army while the Italians still had the Mediterranean bottled up. The volume of goods that crossed Africa by river is still a military secret

In front of a small shining white building beside a canal Public Relations brakes the car. This is where the plywood man is working, he explains. He was one of the pioneers of plane construction, a great inventor. Now he's working in plywood, he whispers in my ear as we go in.

Inside, the room is bright and full of sunlight. A skinny thinfaced grayhaired man with a hardbitten New England look is leaning over a strip of polished veneer on a drafting table. He looks up startled with suspicion in every line of his face. 'You'd better put your watches in the far end of the room if you don't want them magnetized. The magnetic press is on,' he says sharply. A stout grinning young man in shirtsleeves and an apron collects our watches and takes them away into an adjoining room. Meanwhile Public Relations is talking smoothly to the inventor. He almost smiles when the guests are told that the magnetic press is one of the most powerful in the country. He unbends enough to let us hold a magnet over its smooth sullen iron surface to feel the pull of the lines of force of the magnetic field. Then he brings out samples of plywood compressed out of various woods laminated and woven together and highly polished. Stronger than any metal, we are told. Can be produced in continuous tubing for pipelines and all sorts of work where you need a nonconductor that won't corrode. When somebody says the weave reminds him of the hickory baskets they make up in Vermont, the inventor's face sours again. 'The entire process is new,' he says tartly.

We climb back into the machine, talking of plywood, of the

great flying boxcars that are soon going to be produced in quantity. We drive on out into the country to see the freshdrained swamp where the Boatbuilder's shipyard was to have been. What stopped it? Politics? The old shipbuilding concerns? In any case it would mean many million dollars' loss to the taxpayer. Yellow tractors and bulldozers move back and forth over a vast stretch of made land. No sign of buildings yet. The Boatbuilder was converting the unfinished shipyard into a vast plant for building plywood transport planes; flying boxcars, Public Relations liked to call them. He hoped to keep the loss down to a million. What the Boatbuilder was looking forward to when this first order was finished, was building something entirely new, a great flying wing transport that would beat the field in carrying capacity. As we drove out along the brown canal shimmering with blue light after leaving the plywood laboratory, Public Relations had pointed out a symmetrical white house between two symmetrical groups of palms where another famous airplane designer the Boatbuilder induced to come down here was working on the model of a flying wing right now.

At last we drive into the parking space beside the dramatically designed façade of the office building of the central plant. The lobby is full of people. Girls, young men, old people, sit on benches waiting with application blanks in their hands for an interview with the personnel manager. We get our passes at a desk and go up in a monelmetal elevator and are ushered into a boardroom. There we sit around the table to watch a film of the various types of boats performing in all sorts of seas all sorts of gyrations, jumping over logs and snags and sandbars, poking their noses up on muddy shores and sandy shores. Backing off again. Turning on a dime. There's a final picture of a boat making a landing on a sheer breakwater in a brisk sea. After the brilliance of the afternoon the gray moving pictures look thin and ghostlike.

During the last few minutes of the picture distracting roars have been coming from the adjoining office. Hurlyburly. Shouts and storms of laughter. The Boatbuilder himself is back in his office.

Still blinking from the flicker of the moving pictures we are ushered through a door into an office that's all windows, and there he is. He is a big broadbeamed sweating man wearing a lavender shirt and an explosive necktie. He is leaning back smiling in a big chair behind his desk. He has the big movable mug of a stump speaker, bright fluent eyes under big lids, sharply pencilled dark eyebrows and a well modelled forehead. His broad mouth and the big active folds of his jowl are never still. There's a little crisp curl and a touch of dark red to his thin parted hair. The pink of his skin and the white of his teeth give him the air of a man with a good appetite and a good digestion for food, drink, work, all kinds of things. He treats people with a bullying cajoling joshing manner half affectionate and half abusive. He keeps going off into puns and jokes and stories in dialect. Everything is immensely dramatized. There he is flushed and roaring from his last crack sitting at his desk surrounded by models of boats and planes. There's a group of men sitting around him spluttering and nodding and bellowing when he laughs.

On one side is a whitehaired man with the air of an Irish judge, a boyhood friend who has just turned up and is being entertained. With him the Boatbuilder keeps up a long ramble of reminiscences about the days when they were kids in school together. They keep tossing fortyyearold quips and recollections back and forth. Now and then they just lean back in their chairs and look at each other with moist appraising eyes and laugh. Life hasn't treated them so badly. They are having a whale of a good time yet. Meanwhile, with a man from the shop the Boatbuilder is carrying on a discussion about some trusses. He's passing the time of day with Public Relations. He's giving his visitors the feeling he's interested in them and asking them searching questions.

The five o'clock whistle has just blown. He asks the company if that isn't a good excuse for a drink. A man in a dark suit has brought out small whiskey glasses. His alert eyes run around the room to see that everybody has one before he tosses one off himself. Then he sets the crowd off into a gale with an endman minstrel story. All at once in spurts like tropical showers he begins to talk savagely about his last trip to Washington. The one thing those bohunks never thought of was what was good for the people of this country. It was all how would it affect the labor interests or the steel interests or the aluminum interests, it never was how something would affect the people as a whole, you and me and the elevator boy. No, he wasn't against labor unions or big corporations. But he was for America. The only people not represented in Washington were the people of the United States. He was a Democrat, thank God, but why in hell wouldn't the Democrats grow up? He believed in the people but the people ought to get wise to the kind of world they were living in. It was time the people's representatives learned something about industry. He'd told 'em off good and plenty. He'd been explaining to a group of congressmen . . .

'Is it worth while . . .' somebody interrupts flippantly. 'Trying to explain to a congressman?'

The Boatbuilder snaps at the first half of the question. 'Worth while?' He blows up like kerosene poured in a hot stove. 'Worth while? Hell, yes! If you had a blowtorch applied to your tail you wouldn't be asking me if it was worth while to move, would you? Worth while? Everything is worth while that will help win this war. Worth while? You'll be asking next if it was worth while for the Wrights to try to fly a plane or for the Diesel engine to be invented or for us down here to split a gut working ourselves in a lather over the war effort. Sure, it's worth while to do every damn thing possible under heaven.'

The Boatbuilder's voice rises in a scolding whine, punctuated by explosions. Telling people off is one of his specialties. The men grouped around his desk sit frozen in noncommittal attitudes. Nobody raises his voice to say yea or nay. As suddenly as it comes on the fit passes and his big face dimples with smiles as he urges another drink on his friends and embarks on another Sweet Adeline Sally in Our Alley old college songbook ramble of reminiscence with the old boyhood friend.

'Washington wasn't any subject to bring up,' somebody whispers in somebody else's ear.

New Orleans, Louisiana, Spring, 1943

OUT OF THE WINDOW of the bus grinding up Route One from the South late in a summer afternoon you get a first glimpse from the top of a rise of Washington City far ahead sweltering in haze in a broad shallow basin in the hills. The tall dome of the Capitol bulges with rosy light out of streaks of mist above the coppery sheen of a broad reach of river. Beside the dome the sharp needle of the Monument cuts the horizon, and beyond, indistinct roofs in steps and pale broad masses of masonry merge into the cluttered misty hills. A few minutes later the bus is purring through a brick street of colonial houses out of old engravings. Then from the road behind the railroad yards a prospect opens again for a moment, beyond particolored freight trains and locomotives puffing tall white pillars of smoke, of the domes and the sprawling oblongs of the buildings on Capitol Hill with their western windows all aflame with reflected sunset. Across them transport planes with red and green navigation lights already lit are circling for a landing at the National Airport. Crossing the bridge you see to the left the immense low new jaillike Pentagon, and flashing through the trees in the Park on the opposite bank the white colonnades of the memorials to the great presidents slowly spin as you go past. When the bus comes out on the Mall the columned palisades of the government departments spread out ahead of you in either direction. The bus jolts slowly through the dense traffic, enters the district of shop windows and electric light signs and swerves round a corner in front of a tall church and comes to a sudden halt under the concrete roof of the station.

You scramble stiffly down into a packed mass of people damp and pale from the heat. There are young men in their shirt-sleeves, soldiers and sailors, girls in slacks or in light summer dresses, negroes in bright oddcolored clothes. The crowd moves deliberately, more like a crowd in Mobile than a crowd in New York.

You walk out of the dead coolness of breathed out air into the warm leafy gloaming. Broad green leaves muffle the street lights. There's a sense of a crowd in a forest, of dense traffic in a shadowy park.

On the grassy triangle at the intersection of broad streets opposite are vague human forms: young men and women stretched out on newspapers on the grass, sprawled sailors in blues and whites, soldiers in light khaki asleep with their heads on their overnight bags. A negro in a pink sport shirt is sitting up cross-legged playing a harmonica. Under the street light at the corner a young girl in neat overalls with her ashblonde hair in a pompadour is sitting on an upended suitcase making up her face. She is smoothing lipstick on her pouted lips. Her eyes under plucked brows are intent on the little round mirror she holds between the tapered red nails of her left hand.

CHAPTER 8

The Tar Baby

A MAN WITH A BRIEFCASE under his arm flags a taxi at the corner. The driver stops the cab to let him in.

'Going down towards Commerce?' he asked.

'I'm taking this gentleman to Social Security,' says the taxi-driver.

The man already in the cab raises his eyes off a pile of smudgy mimeographed releases he is reading.

'Why, if it isn't . . .!' He lets the words out with his breath. The man with the briefcase grabs his hand. 'Well, I certainly didn't know you were here.' He starts shuffling his papers back into order.

'How do you like it?' asks the man with the briefcase.

The other man gives a long groan and stuffs the mimeographed sheets back in their envelopes.

'I just been here two weeks. It does seem kind of a muddle,' says the new passenger, brightly.

At last the other man finds words. They come in a hurry. 'Muddle? Christ, it's the tar baby. You know the tar baby . . . You try to give it a kick and your foot gets stuck and you try to give it a punch and your fist gets stuck and you try to back off and butt it with your head and your head gets stuck.'

The car has drawn up at the curb in front of a great graywhite building that fills block after block endlessly reduplicating its pediments and columned porches. The man with the briefcase jumps out. 'Well, so long, give me a ring some time.'

'What's your extension?' shouts the other man after him. The man with the briefcase is already out of earshot.

Desk Job

We sat in a row across the stern of the boat sweating in the late afternoon sun. It was quiet out there tied up at the landing in front of the yacht club between a mahogany cruiser and a tubby white yawl. The traffic on the Fourteenth Street Bridge was a distant hum. Only occasionally, when the sleek brown harbor water was stirred by a long ripple moving in from the channel that set the boats faintly seesawing for a moment, did some piece of tackle rattle or a pulley creak. On the opposite bank the trees along the parkway made a string of closeset bundles of dense juicy green between the bright lead color flaked with blue of the river and the lavender sky. A couple of slim tilted white triangles of sails moved smoothly against them. In catspaws from the long gleaming reach of river down towards Alexandria came now and then a puff of cool air that chilled the wet skin where your shirt clung to the small of your back and brought a little country sweetness into the old Potomac smell that rose from wormeaten piling and tiedup boats and weedy debris floating in the sluggish backwater. As we sat talking, every now and then our voices were drowned by the roar of the four motors of a graygreen bomber that swerved low across the basin and, slowly gaining altitude, headed eastward down river.

The curlyhaired man in the pale blue seersucker suit had been talking for a long time. He had been telling about a curious experience he had had that morning. He'd gotten up from the breakfast table to answer the phone and found a faintly familiar voice asking for him at the other end of the line. The voice was that of a man who'd worked in the government department from which the man who was telling the story had found himself suddenly and un-expectedly removed a few months before. Bright and early one morning he had gotten down to his desk and found a memoran-dum on it acquainting him with the fact that the office he held had been abolished. 'I was responsible for your removal. You probably suspected it, but I wanted you to know,' was what the voice at the other end of the phone said to him. 'I was the one who gave certain people the idea that you were talking too much up on the Hill and to newspaper men. The motive was jealousy and I'm damned sorry I did it.'

While the man in the pale blue seersucker was telling the story in a tone of interested surprise as if he were telling of finding some odd kind of bird in his backyard, a sunburned young man in bath-ingtrunks had hopped aboard from the stubby white yawl in the next berth and stood hanging onto the shrouds scratching the calf of one leg with the big toe of the other foot as he listened. 'I swear,' he suddenly interrupted, 'that's the sort of thing that makes me wonder whether I'm awake or dreaming half the time in this town.'

'You mean the guy's making a clean breast of it?'

'No, I mean that for every man that's trying to do a job, there seem to be two men after him to stop him.'

He was urged to sit down, a glass of bourbon and water was pressed into his hand. He crouched on his heels on the edge of the deck and began to talk. 'Some people fly into this town, some people come in by train and bus but I came in by the old Potomac River. It just happens that I've spent a great deal of my life floundering around on rivers . . . in everything from a pirogue to a sternwheeler . . . I've done some designing of shal-low draft boats, barges, motor tow boats, stuff like that. That took me to South America and South America brought me to Washington. Well, not so long after Pearl Harbor an old friend of mine got a job in this town and first thing I knew the wires were hot with this guy trying to get me up here. I must drop everything and fly . . . to hell with family problems . . . your country calls and all that . . .'

A bomber drowned out his voice as it passed low over oui heads, swerving across the basin, and soared off eastward.

'Gosh, I wonder where he's going. Those boys bring it all close, don't they?' somebody said in a low voice.

The skipper was pointing the whiskey bottle at the young man in bathingtrunks like a gun.

'Thanks . . . just a small one . . . Well, I've been here a year and a half. The first six months I sat up nights getting ready some plans I had for a fleet of shallow draft riverboats. I thought I would be back down there any day to start building the damn things. I even had a fellow down there hiring hands. The cream of the notion was we were going to build 'em down there out of native materials with native workmen. Nothing needed but the engines from here at first. Later I even thought we could build the engines down there. No drain on any materials needed for war. Down there good neighbor business . . . foment native industry. I thought the plan was a honey. I'm not saying my ideas were good just because I thought they were . . . maybe they were lousy, but the big boys who hired me seemed to think they were all right. All the swells on these committees for coordinating this and that seemed to think I was the albino wonder. They led me around this town like a prizewinning poodle. That was the honeymoon period. A government corporation was set up. Orders went out to give me the green light on priorities all down the line. They gave me a nice airconditioned office and a better salary than I'd ever had in my life. And I'd come up here to make a sacrifice. Jeez, I thought I was going to town . . .'

He paused, drank off his whiskey and wiped his mouth with the brown back of his hand.

'But then one day I discovered I had a boss, a queer fish from way down east. He'd run a fleet of excursion steamers or something like that. The only reason I could imagine they'd picked him was that he was probably the only Democrat in those northern solitudes . . . But gosh, I'm dragging this story out too long . . .'

'Go on,' shouted the man in the seersucker suit. 'This is very, very interesting. This fits in with other things.'

'Now, I may be crazy. It may be my own fault. I may be going nuts. I don't sleep at night. I say mean things to my wife. I yell at the kids. I can't get a damn thing across of what I want to do and I find I spend all my time keeping this goddam boss of mine from doing what he wants to do.'

'Well, isn't that what bureaucracy's for?' somebody muttered into his whiskey glass.

'What he wants to do is build nothing, spend all the money buying up old scows. He waited till I was away on a field trip to put the deal through. One of the damned old scows went to pieces in the rapids and drowned six men. "What's six natives," he says, "when there's a war on?" But hell, I knew the guys and their fat wives and their little yellow brats . . . they signed up with this business because they knew me and knew I was on the up and up, see . . . I can't get over the notion that that bastard was put into our corporation by somebody who wants to stop anything getting done. And you liberals complain there isn't any after the war planning . . . By God, there's more of that kind of planning in this town than you can shake a stick at . . . planning in re- verse . . .'

'But can't you take it up over this guy's head?'

'Sure, I've taken it up from hell to breakfast. I been up to see the chairman of the committee of committees, the cleanlimbed young scion of great wealth who's actuated by motives of pure patriotism, and he is, goddam it! He says sure he thinks my ideas are hotsy totsy but that this excursion boat king was very highly recommended. All these swells, they've got a little feller, some- thing between a family lawyer and a valet sitting around telling 'em what's what. I know who recommended my boss and why. But where can I go tell my sad story? I wish somebody would tell me whether they want boats on those rivers or whether they just want to keep their office chairs warmed. Ought I to hold on, on the chance that somebody higher up may change his mind and let me get to work or ought I to go fly a kite? I seem to be acting like a louse whichever way I play it . . . God, I bet the psychiatric wards around this town are filling up. Well, now I've talked too much.'

The roar of another bomber overhead drowned out somebody's soothing answer. The young man let himself drop onto a cushion in the cockpit. When we could hear ourselves speak again we waited for him to start talking but he went on sitting there with his mouth pursed up tight.

Unloading the Detail

We sat on iron chairs on the steaming brick paving of a small backyard. There was no breeze. On every side we were closed in by walls of old brick houses. The late afternoon sun lay heavily on the spongy trees like a red hand squeezing out heat. Before we could half drink them, the ice had melted in our collinses.

I was asking my host to explain one more thing. What was the actual procedure when his agency took over an industry in the course of a labor dispute?

'That's easy . . . first we call a meeting of department heads . . .'

'But aren't they all busy up to the hilt right now?'

'Nobody's ever so busy he can't take on something more, if he knows how to unload the detail.' There was a trace of impatience in his voice. 'Well, to continue . . . at that meeting we set up the blueprint of an organization.'

'But what happens right in the plant . . . where they produce the product?'

'Oh, in the field? . . . Well, we swear in the presidents of the companies as enforcement officers. They are instructed to haul the flag up over the plants and to exhibit the posters we send out explaining the situation to employees and management alike — last time we beat all records with the posters . . . we got them out over the weekend.'

'But what about production?'

He was already looking at his watch. 'You must excuse me. I have a dinner engagement.'

'But is anything done to make production more efficient?' He didn't seem to hear. Already we were on our feet, shaking hands.

'Thank you very much.'

'Goodbye.'

The Public Interest

'It's a feeling of frustration,' said this man, summing up his flood
of description of his eighteen months in Washington. 'In my
office we've all had the same experience. We came down here full
of beans, most of us giving up better paid jobs in private industry,
because we felt we could help. Now look at us.'

We were sitting on a terrace high above the street under the
awning on the roof of a hotel. He was tall and sandyhaired. A
big normally cheerful-looking man from the Middle West. No,
he wouldn't take a scotch. He was drinking lemonade. He had
to give up drinking, he'd said when we sat down; found he was
hitting it too hard. No, thanks, cocacola kept him awake. Maybe
his wife would take a spot. We were all sweating as we sat there,
in spite of the trickle of water across the awning over our heads.
The big man had a wilted look that came from more than the heat.

There was an oddly illassorted air about the men and women
seated round the little tables to right and left of us. It wasn't an
Atlanta crowd. It wasn't a Philadelphia crowd. It wasn't a
Detroit crowd. It was the kind of random assortment of medium
business men and their wives you would have found on a New
York to San Francisco boat before the war. Perhaps half the
men were in uniform. There was little of the shrill chatter of cocktail hour. People looked tired and sat talking sluggishly or else
slumped in the wicker armchairs watching the bright trickle of
water off the scallops of the wet awning. There was a feeling of
sitting on the porch of a particularly dreary summer hotel.

Why is it like that? you're asking.

'Well, I'm trying to explain. The industry I represent . . .' he
flushed and stammered a little. 'I don't mean I represent the
industry. I'm trying my damnedest to represent the public,
honestly, I am — or was until I began to just sit on my tail and
let things drift . . . is divided into two groups. One group is progressive, wellorganized, easy to get in touch with . . . The other
is made up of maneating sharks. Not one of that gang who's
come to Washington but isn't ready to cut the other fellow's

throat. They won't get together. They won't work in the public
interest or even in the industry's interest or any other but their
own interest. Tell 'em there's a war on and they turn a glazed eye
on you. My job is to pummel some idea of the public interest
into these guys' heads. That wouldn't be a great job if a man
could feel there was some organization behind him, some definite
plan. You never know whether what you do is going to be backed
up or not. You work in a vacuum. Higher up everything seems
cloudy and drifting. The clouds form and scatter and reform.
It drives you crazy. What a man does doesn't seem to gear into
anything. Take an example. For the last eight months I've been
working out arrangements for increased production of x commodity, a damned necessary commodity. I've sweated for hours
at the phone, I've gone around to see everybody concerned, I've
bullied and cajoled and begged them to establish a certain line of
production, working out raw material problems, labor problems,
shipping problems, the question of profits, standards, what have
you? All down the line I've gotten a lot of selfwilled men to make
concessions, to agree to cooperate for getting out this commodity
that the war economy needs like hell. I was so worked up at one
point I didn't sleep for a week. At last it seems as if everything
is smoothed out and everybody is going to be happy. Then at the
last moment somewhere in the higher brackets it's no go, a bottle-
neck, other considerations. It's like trying to work a telephone
keyboard with half the wires cut and you never know which ones
are cut.'

He paused and swallowed some lemonade with the desperate
gulp of a man trying to drown himself in whiskey. 'Now while
I'm trying to get a new directive, one that will stick, I'll tell you
what's going to happen. The juice will all ebb out of the proposition. The guys I've sold on it will start looking out for number
one. How can you blame 'em, goddam it! Selfseeking is so
simple.' He paused for another gulp of lemonade.

'This feeling of living in a fog affects even the secretaries and
the stenographers, even the people who sweep out the offices. I
can see the greatest difference in them between now and a year

ago. At first everybody came to work on the dot. They stayed on till six or seven in the evening. Nobody minded coming back after supper. They were in a fever to get the work done. They'd come here to work for their country like the rest of us. And now look at 'em . . . By half past four they are so restless the office is a madhouse. At five o'clock it's a panic. You'd think the building was on fire the way they stampede for the elevators.

'Gosh, I envy the guys down here with expense accounts trying to wangle advantages for the big concerns. They have no problems. They know their organization'll back them up. All they've got to do is get places at the feeding trough. They only have themselves to look after. The public interest is so damned complicated. It's no wonder our men one by one join the four eagle club.'

'What's the four eagle club?'

'You don't know what the four eagle club is?' He laughed creakily and lit a cigarette from the butt he held between shaky stained fingers. 'Well, we have the two eagle club. That's for the men who get lunch and dinner out of the representatives of business interests. There are no lobbyists any more, no, no, only representatives of this and that. The three eagles get cocktails, too. The four eagles get a room at the Mayflower or the Carleton. Board and lodging all complete. Four eagles is tops.'

Arrivals of Representatives

The hotel lobby is full of people. Army and Navy and Marine Corps uniforms, Wacs and Waves, civilians in Palm Beach suits and summer dresses are thronging towards the glass doors of the cocktail lounge in the corner from which comes the low jiving hum of a band and an inviting smell of gin and lemon peel and bitters. Opposite the desk stands a row of new suitcases. Across the starspangled carpet arrivals are hurrying through the crowd to take the room clerk by storm. The room clerk is a bilious young man, very dark under the eyes who looks as if he suffered from stomach ulcers, obviously 4F. A large man, broad and

smooth as an egg, has grabbed the room clerk's hand and is shak·
ing it impulsively as if he had just heard of his election to office.
Before the first man has dropped his hand a tall fellow in light
tweeds has leaned across the counter and started to coo his first
name in his ear. Behind them a large imposing man stands with
his arms folded, glaring silently through smoked glasses. He's the
man who really knows he has a reservation. He's waiting for the
room clerk to remember his name. All eyes are fixed on the room
clerk's face as he studies his book with his lips in a thin pout. All
eyes follow his glance as he looks up at the keyboards and then at
something invisible posted inside the cashier's cage. There's a
hush in the line of men as he reaches for a key. He taps with it on
the glass counter. A pimply schoolboy face appears above a
frogged uniform. 'Take Mr. Selz up to 416,' pipes the room clerk
in a peevish voice. Several jaws drop. Mr. Selz is a small silvery
man who's been standing towards the end of the line, dreamily
looking up at the ceiling as he polishes his nose glasses with a
handkerchief with a blue monogram in the corner.

The Perfect Bureaucrat

'No, there's no corruption in Washington,' said the tall man with
crinkly gray hair pushed back from narrow temples.
    'No, of course not,' I echoed his words.
    'Of course there's no corruption, not in that sense of the word,' a
sallow sharpfaced man who had just slid into the seat beside us
chimed in. He let his breath out in a whisper. 'Unless you mean
the corruption of power.'
    We were jammed into a corner of an airconditioned bar. It
was cool, but there was something clammy about the air of the
place that kept you feeling swampy in your damp clothes after
the honest sweat in the searing sun of the streets. There was
something morose about the tone of the voices around us. The
only sound of cheerful drinking came from a table in the center
of the room where three young aviators had just been joined by a
fourth. He'd come a long way. They hadn't seen him for a long

time. They thought he was a great guy. There was no hinder thought back of the cheery whoops they greeted him with. There was a breeze in their voices. They were on leave. They had money in their pockets. They had the evening before them. The world was fun.

My own voice sounded flat and cagey in my ears. 'Don't you think we protest too much about no corruption?'

'Yes,' whispered the tall man . . . 'There's no money being handed around in satchels. From that point of view there has never been a war administration with such clean hands. But there are other ways. Maybe it would be more accurate to say that there are no more cash transactions in this town.'

'Put it this way,' said the thinfaced man. 'In the old days money was power. The dollar was almighty. If you wanted to get something out of a government official you slipped him a damp wad of bills in a dark corner of a saloon. Now it's the other way around. If you've got the power the money comes to you of its own accord. A man who's been in government, even who's made a flop in government, comes out so magnetized with power that the greenbacks fly right to him . . . you know how if you rub an amber cigarette holder you can pick up little pieces of paper with it.'

'That's only the exceptional story . . .' said the tall man slowly stirring his drink as he slowly began to talk. 'The great majority of people who have come to work in this town are caught in the web like me . . . I can hardly remember how I felt when I first came here a year ago. My gosh, the sophomoric hopes! . . . I've worked with cooperatives all my life. I think that's the way we can get the individual back on his feet in this country. I'd been hopeful there would be things in the war effort could be done that way . . . I thought the government might really be forced to gear the latent democratic forces of the American people into the war effort . . . But we didn't have to. Our productive potential was so great we found we could do without the people. Everything's done with the higherups. War belongs to the higherups just like peace . . . When I discovered that I thought I'd pull out. Then

I decided I'd take just one more crack at it first ... Now I'm
thinking that maybe the way things are is the way things ought to
be. That's the final stage of the perfect bureaucrat.'

A Generation of Young Men

A sallow sharpfeatured young man was talking.

'This is a town of people who spend their time sitting at desks,
writing little things on little pieces of paper, dictating letters into
machines, talking on the telephone to people they never see.
It's a town of people who never see the results of their work.'

Under the informal almost collegiate manner there was something sharp. Behind the brooding thoughtful look in his eyes
there was the glint of a coiled steel spring. He was slightly built
and seemed very light on his feet when he slipped out from behind
his desk, piled high with papers and folders, to come around and
lean against the front of it.

It was a big darkpanelled office in one of the great satrapies of
administrative departments. Out the window across a broad
street shimmering with sun you could see the even ranks of windows of other long low white government buildings.

'In a tankfactory, say, you can see the product rolling off the
assembly lines, but here we never see our end product. That's
one reason why it's so hard for us to keep our feet on the ground.
We live an airconditioned life ... It's hard to get a window open
on the country ... But it's work that's got to be done. Now a
whole lot of us came to this town full of lofty ideas of what we
could do here. There's never been a generation of young men
before in this country so anxious to devote their lives to the public
interest. The normal thing in Washington in the past has been for
people to come here to serve some particular interest. That's the
way our political life has been run, a thousand tugs of war of various interests all passing through Washington. But we thought we
could devote ourselves to the public interest straight. A whole lot
of people have put in a lot of the best years of their lives at this
job. They've invested everything they had in it. We don't want

to forget that in the final reckoning. Now, I don't know. The Administration sometimes seems as full of rifts and fissures as ice on a pond breaking up in the spring. Maybe all we can do is hold on and see what comes. I for one think it's important to hold on. We are here and we've got to stay here. I happen to work in a department that's solid from the top on down. We've got a great organization and a solid man for a boss and we don't have that feeling that people have in some other departments that the minute they step out to do something somebody's going to stab them in the back.' He smiled faintly. 'Here you can hold on with a quiet conscience. A man feels his career is secure.'

As I got up to go I couldn't help referring back to what he'd been saying about the end product and asking what he thought the end product of Washington was; taxes maybe? He didn't smile. 'People in this country won't get it through their heads that government is a necessity,' he said a little peevishly. 'There's such a thing as national sovereignty.'

Sour Grapes

'Well, how do people strike you round this town?' asked a newspaper man of my acquaintance whom I met in the before luncheon whirlpool of people in a hotel lobby.

'Don't they seem to you kinda frustrated?' I asked him back.

He was a small yellow man with a sharp nose. 'So you're falling for that line,' he said in a tone of voice infinitely wise. 'A lot of these people who complain that their good intentions are always being frustrated in this town are frustrated because they ought to be frustrated. They weren't any good in the first place. They're not frustrated over in the Pentagon or down at the Navy Department . . . That line reminds me . . .' Suddenly his face became round with smiling wisdom. He'd said this before. It amused him. People had laughed. 'That line reminds me,' he picked up his story again — 'of the sad tale the local prostitute told the college boy. She was a good girl but a travelling man deceived her.'

Already a large tweed suit that had a look of coming from Detroit was bearing down on my acquaintance. It was his luncheon
engagement. We parted laughing.

The New Deal Fades

After sitting some time on a lightcolored leather couch in the
waitingroom admiring the pretty receptionist's handsome hairdo
I was ushered into a large corner office. The man I had come to
see was sitting behind a bare desk set cattycornered between the
windows. He was roundheaded and blueeyed and looked dapper
in his meticulously cut light gray suit. His hair was curly with a
touch of silver at the temples. There was a touch of silver in his
richly modulated courtroom voice. This was a man who'd kissed
the blarneystone early. A glister of success played over his large
eyes and his crisp hair and his neat white teeth and his handsome
bare desk. Sitting there in the afternoon light pouring in through
the windows he was a very persuasive individual indeed.

I led off by saying that as he was one of the oldest inhabitants of
New Deal Washington, I wanted to ask him how he thought the
New Deal was getting on. Having a private practice these last
few years must have given him a good chance to see from the
outside what he had seen so much of from the inside. He ought
to have a pretty objective view. How was the battle going for
his old colleagues who were still sweating and bleeding in government?

He smiled and pointed his chin in the air for a moment and then
said in a dreamy tone that before we got to that question we'd
have to remember back to how it was in Washington ten years ago
when this Administration moved in. The big business wiseacres
had thrown down their cards. The politicians were on the ropes.
The country was waiting to be saved before going down for the
third time. A lot of young men fresh from college and lawschool
were handed a fresh pack and told to deal fresh cards and to make
up fresh rules as the game went on. His voice grew eloquent as he
talked about the magnificent period when everything was hopeful

and new. In those days the government was still within human proportions. A couple of men working as a team could still keep an outline of what was going on in Washington in their heads. The city itself had a kind of horsecar look. He spoke in nostalgic tones of how Connecticut Avenue hadn't been widened yet and was still outlined by the old trees and had only a sprinkling of storefronts: rugmerchants, antique dealers, oldfashioned caterers, jewelry stores. His voice became silver mellow when he spoke of the beauty of the jewelry stores glistening under the trees in the evening on Connecticut Avenue. 'It was a great time and some of the things we accomplished stuck.' His voice rose.

'Why hasn't it gone on?'

'People get tired. They get distracted . . . In those days we really had a team. There was teamwork all through the New Deal. We had a pretty good idea of what we wanted to do and we knew how to get it done. When we needed to be backed up by the White House we got backed up . . . Now that's all gone.'

'Why did the team break up just when you would think teamwork was most necessary?'

'Maybe the Boss didn't think it was needed.'

'What's going to happen now?'

'Nothing's going to happen now so far as the New Dealers are concerned. They are all washed up. There's no fight left in them . . . One thing has often occurred to me about these bright young men — you know they used to call them the hot dogs — who came up fresh out of lawschool into government jobs. They'd had no experience outside. None of them ever really had to walk the streets to find himself a niche in a lawoffice or to put up his shingle over a drugstore in a smalltown. They suddenly found themselves rich, at least for boys just out of lawschool, and powerful and protected. They never had to take any course in the university of hard knocks. They never had any experience with going out and making themselves a living in the market place. Now, I tell you, they are scared to death. They've married and settled down here. If they were thrown out now they wouldn't know what to do for a living. Naturally they hold on to their jobs instead of to their principles.'

'Do you suppose anything like it could ever be done again?'

'Some group of men has got to start working together in the public interest in this town. Maybe people will be able to get together on a pure national basis. The New Deal for the underprivileged is all washed out. The Boss is through with it.'

'Don't you think maybe we'll all end up underprivileged?'

He shook his head and smiled dreamily. He was looking up out of the window at a corner of sky. 'It would have to be new men, new ideas, a brandnew team.'

It was getting late. He was beginning to fidget a little behind his polished desk. The telephone rang. 'Yessir, that was all fixed up this morning. You needn't worry about that situation. It was all fixed up,' he was saying into the receiver. As he put the phone down I got to my feet. 'The boys came to this town with high ideals,' he said. 'Now what's left of them are just holding jobs. The fire has gone out of them.' His voice sank to a bull-fiddle whisper.

He escorted me to the door. As he turned away the bright understanding smile faded off his face. His mind had snapped back to business. With a preoccupied frown he strode back through a side door into another office.

'Well, the man I've just been talking to says the New Deal's all washed up,' I said to a friend I met in the lobby of a hotel a few minutes later.

'Tell me something new,' he said drily. 'Waiting for you I've been having a wonderful time watching the arriving lobbyists storming the room clerk. This business of hotel rooms has gotten to be one of the great rackets.' I was following him through the lobby into the bar. Through a hedge of waiting summer uniforms we could see that every table was taken. It was the same thing in the lounge. At last we managed to get ourselves a place to sit down to a drink in the diningroom.

'After all, speaking seriously,' my friend said, 'we mustn't go around writing off the New Deal. Like all reform movements it failed partly because it succeeded. Something has been accomplished. A certain measure of citizenship has been restored to the workingman. An idea of public interest separate from all other interests has been established in the country. Farming to a certain extent has been put back on its feet. A beginning has been made towards restoring the family size farm. Where would the war effort be without the great public empires like T.V.A.? People accept the successes and forget them. Only the failures stand out. There have been plenty of those, too. But we mustn't write off the New Deal until we have something to put in its place.'

'What are we going to put in its place?'

'"The evil that men do,"' he answered, '"lives after them, the good is oft interred with their bones" ... Did I get it right?'

'That's not what you said a minute ago.'

He didn't answer. He sat silent staring at the olive at the bottom of his martini.

The Punishment

It was an immensely hot still night full of chirping and shrilling of insects. My friends and I had come to call on a man we all admired very much. On the way over we had been talking about his career. He was a man who had had a successful business of his own in a Southern state. During the first years of the New Deal he had found that he was losing interest in just piling up money for himself and his family. All around him the nation seemed to be going to pieces. In Washington, under Franklin Roosevelt in his first administration, there had appeared a bunch of men who seemed to him to have a plan to rebuild a real commonwealth where every man would have a fair show. The more he thought and read about what was going on in Washington the more he lost interest in the humdrum of his own business. He wrote to the then Secretary of Agriculture telling him that he wanted to go to work for him. The Secretary answered that he sounded just like the kind of man he liked to work with and that he himself had come to Washington for the same reason, and offered him a job. He wound up his business, packed up his family and settled in Washington. Now he'd been there ten years, on the whole successful years. In the course of them he had invented one of the most effective administrative methods in the entire setup that had kept the machine of production going and people comparatively well fed and well clothed during the period when the country was climbing out of the Great Depression. He was a man who didn't think in the terms of ward politics or in the classroom cant of economists or social reformers. Everything he said and did showed that his mind dealt with people as living people, with farms as real farms. This man, we agreed, had one of the best minds any of us had ever come in contact with.

When we walked into the rather bare whitepanelled sitting-room, he was hunched, his shortsleeved white shirt open at the throat, beside a reading lamp. His hands hung limp off the arms of his chair. His hands and face were floury white. His cheeks had deep hollows in them and the skin round his eyes had the bruised look of sleeplessness. When he saw us at the door he pulled himself with some difficulty to his feet. His wife who had been sitting by the fireplace came forward to greet us with her customary quiet hospitality, but as she came forward her eyes were still on him. She had the expression of a woman caught sitting up at the bedside of a very sick child. It took a moment for her to switch her mind from her intent determination to pull her invalid through, to the business of pleasantly meeting friends. As he pulled himself up to shake hands I hardly recognized the sturdy reserved man of slow decisive speech I had last seen a few months before. He let himself drop back heavily in his chair.

We sat down in a halfcircle facing him and talked haltingly about this and that for a while. The wife poured out some ice-water for us from a glass pitcher beaded with moisture. As we talked the unspoken knowledge of the bereavement this man and woman had suffered in the loss of their son clutched harshly at each one of us. Under the lamp stood a photograph in a silver frame of an alive largeeyed young man in flying uniform. My friends fell to talking about the tough time another couple they knew was having whose newborn baby was sick and likely to die. 'My,' this man said, 'the suffering there is in the world.'

When we came in a breeze blew through the room. It dropped again and we sat there sipping the icewater with the slow sweat trickling down our backs. No sound came in from the road. It was very quiet in the close room, in the isolated suburban house under the breathless trees.

He had been sitting there with the expression of a man who was groping in his mind for something to take hold of. After a while he roused himself from the slumping position of complete weariness and his hands tightened on the arms of the chair. He spoke with a flicker of the old smile. 'Too bad it's too dark to show you my Victory garden. I'm right proud of it. It's the first time in my life I've ever really done any physical work. I'd never imagined a man could take such pleasure in growing a few rows of corn and beans.'

'He'd have lost his mind if he hadn't had it,' his wife said eagerly, filling in the silence. 'He's out there first thing every morning hoeing and grubbing.'

Her cheerful tone of voice brought a little blood back into his face. Shaking his head as if to shake loose some painful tangle of thoughts he said that the main trouble was he couldn't seem to get to sleep any more; he was only getting two hours' sleep a night and that, combined with being hammered by the congressional committee all day, was wearing him down. If he took sleeping medicines it made him feel dopey so that he couldn't use his head and God knows he needed it.

'I've just been figuring up . . . while I've been doing this job each month interdepartmental rows have taken up more of my time. In the last few months I figure that ninety percent of my time is taken up in trying to get cooperation from other agencies and only ten percent in helping win the war. Since I've been up before the committee it's been all my time. If I were to tell you how many men I have detailed to liaison work — that means mainly to knockdown and drag out fights with other agencies — you would be mighty surprised. That means we are putting in too much time fighting off administrative encroachments from other agencies to keep our minds on our work. Things can't go on this way. There's got to be a showdown.'

We all sat silent. The breeze had come up again. An occasional puff of barely perceptible coolness was seeping into the room from the open door in one corner. Moths thudded against the screen.

His voice was stronger when he continued. 'Our side has been too decent. We've kept our mouths shut when they flayed us publicly and impugned our motives and called us every name under heaven. They've been allowed to have plenty of scapegoats from our side. It's time we made a few scapegoats. We've got plenty of ammunition, even if the full record can't be pub· lished till after the war. It's about time we used it. It's time we made a scapegoat.'

He paused. Nobody said anything. In everybody's thoughts the question: Will the Boss back you up? was as clear as if it were written on the white paint over the fireplace.

'There ought to be some way a man who's going to take an important administrative job in this town could have it all out before he starts work. He ought to be able to appear before both houses of Congress and tell them exactly what he intends to do and how and then put it up to them to let him work or tell him to go home. It's this infernal sniping that gets you down. Never knowing exactly where the enemy is, a shot from here and a shot from there. No man can take the punishment I've been taking for the last few weeks and not fight back. We have got to fight back.'

Again the silence hung heavy in the room.

'My particular boss will back me up.' He ripped the words out of his chest with rending sincerity like the tearing of a sheet. 'He's the best boss any man ever worked for.'

Driving home in the station-wagon we were all pretty thoughtful. 'It looks like the Alamo,' somebody said.

'But in the Alamo they were all massacred. The enemy took it by storm.'

'That's what I meant.'

Chevy Chase, Maryland, June, 1943

IT WAS EARLY on a steamy summer morning. The sunlight down Connecticut Avenue, almost empty of traffic, still had a rosy hue. The bus was jouncing along full of young women in frilly summer dresses and of older men with straw hats, in freshly laundered wash suits. The trees, receding in ranks into the haze down long empty avenues or standing hugely in groups in the open spaces between apartment houses, were swollen with greenness. In the middle distances they seemed gummed together with blue mist like trees in a painting by Correggio. The bus was slow. When I looked at my watch about halfway into town I found I was late for my appointment. I scrambled out of the bus and hailed a cab.

I told the driver I was in a hurry. 'Hurry,' he echoed scornfully. He was an elderly man with white hair and a banker's carefully trimmed white mustache. 'Nobody ever used to be in a hurry in Washington,' he said, looking back at me as if it were my fault.

Crossing the Connecticut Avenue Bridge we began talking about the old days in the District. How Rock Creek Park had changed. 'I used to hunt through there before it ever was a park . . . Greatest place in the world for squirrel . . . The squirrel I used to shoot . . . I've never had better birdin' either than up

[161]

Rock Creek an' out through Paul's Addition . . . quail mostly
. . . a few doves . . . All built up now with apartment houses . . .
and rabbits! My Lord, there was rabbit!'

To keep my end up I said my father used to shoot reedbirds
in the marshes at the mouth of Anacostia Creek.

'I know the place,' he crowed cordially. 'We used to go duckin'
there too . . . there was a small brownish black duck. We used
to call them peewees. They used to come in flocks in the fall of
the year. So thick you couldn't miss. Made great black streaks
in the air. My, they was good eatin' . . . But there ain't no game
in this world I'd change for squirrel . . . squirrel stew or squirrel
pie. I kin remember like it was yesterday goin' out one Sunday
mornin' when I was a boy. There was an old widder lady lived
acrost from our house. Her little girl was sick, an' the old widder
lady, she wanted to make her some broth, so my mother, since
it was a case of sickness, she let me go gunnin' on Sunday. We
didn't worry about no game laws in those days. It was in the
fall of the year after a frost. I remember the persimmons were
ripe. I shot three red squirrels on a beech tree right about where
the Connecticut Avenue Bridge now is an' brought 'em home
an' the old lady stewed 'em an' we sent the broth over to the
little girl who was sick. I can remember how those squirrels
tasted to this day. The taste of squirrel, that's my house.'

CHAPTER 9

Washington Is the Loneliest City

IT WAS A BIG APARTMENT HOUSE with a marbleflagged lobby. The first people who moved in must have felt they were doing the fashionable thing. Now instead of a doorman there was a spinsterish woman at a desk. The not so young visitor asked if the young lady were in. The spinsterish woman gave him a look and plugged in the number and cooed into the telephone: 'Dearie, here's your dinner date. Shall I tell him to wait in the lobby?' The not so young visitor turned red. Unfortunately that wasn't the situation at all. But it was no use trying to explain. 'She says please go up,' crooned the spinster, goggling her eyes.

The apartment had been at one time a large comfortable family place but it had been very much subdivided. The visitor had the feeling of having strayed into a college sorority house. The place was packed with girls rustling and giggling and scampering behind thin partitions. The girl he had come to see met him smiling in the hall. Yes, she had finished the typing she was doing for him after office hours. A couple of other girls poked their heads out and were introduced. He had a feeling of being the only male in the building. He felt like a highschool boy making his first call. He wished he had time to take them all out somewhere. All he had time for was the business about the typing. Coming down in the elevator two girls, very much dressedup, were talking about the Virginia Association dance. 'I'm not really a Virginian,' one girl was explaining, 'but I have a cousin who is. She's going to take me.'

'You're in luck,' the other girl said. 'I haven't been to a dance in six months. Washington's the loneliest city.'

The Old Washingtonian

It was a hot June afternoon. I was sitting on a bench in the backyard of one of the houses built on the edge of the low house-crowded ridge that cuts across the northwest section of Washington to form the rim of the shallow bowl in which the downtown city stews. The grass in the sloping yard was very green. The sky over the rooftops in front of us was very blue. A few big tattered white clouds shaded at the base stood motionless in the midst of it.

For the first time in my life I was finding Washington beautiful. When I was a very small child I used to hear my elders talk about the beauty of Washington and never could figure it out. There had been, to my childish mind, a certain cosy dilapidation about Georgetown, vinegrown brick walling in little lives of elderly female relatives sitting in parlors behind drawn shades; there'd been the stately degradation of Alexandria, 'the deserted city,' the colored people used to call it; there'd been Rock Creek and the false feeling of being in the mountains it gave you; and green swampy meadows and the haze over the mudcolored Potomac. My parents used to talk about the beauty of Washington. To me it seemed stifling and hideous. Now I was discovering that I was old enough to find Washington beautiful. Maybe it was the city that had gotten old enough.

The old Washingtonian who was sitting beside me on the bench was working as a checker on the streetcars. He'd never done a job of that kind before, but he was enjoying the work. He liked the idea that he was being useful in the war effort. As we looked out at the grassy yard and the ailanthus trees and the nondescript bushes along the fences and the backs of brick buildings, he told me with cheery enthusiasm about his days standing on street corners or in the full weight of the sun on traffic islands, noting the times the cars passed and the number of people on them. Sizing up the number of people in a car at a glance was a trick it took him some time to learn. The work made him feel busy, useful, and in an odd way, free.

He was enjoying the life of the streets, the varieties of people he saw; the change in personnel as the day wore on; the early workers less welldressed, the oldfashioned American mechanics who worked at the Navy Yard or the Bureau of Printing; the floodtide of office workers between eight and nine; the housewives going shopping; the school kids; the random specimens in the afternoon, fashion plates from embassies, tourists, soldiers and sailors on leave, young women going to the movies in pairs; the great flood of tired heatwilted clerks struggling to get home between five and six; the evening life of the town; people in fresh clothes on the loose, citysized crowds in search of a place to eat, a movie house you could find a seat in, a cocktail bar you could get a table in, a dump to drink beer, aimlessly hopelessly roaming about in what was still a vastly overgrown small Southern town in that stagnant hollow between the Potomac River and Anacostia Creek.

When he came home at night often very late my friend said he'd sit a while on this bench smelling the rankness of wilted leaves the damp brought out from the heattrampled vegetation, listening to neighing voices out of darkened windows, girls' voices making fake dates with men, young men's voices yodeling that they'd be right over. Wartime Washington was essentially a town of lonely people.

We decided to go downtown to eat supper at Hall's to renew a torn fragment of recollection that lingered in my mind of the shadow of foliage against gaslit brick and curlycued gilt mirrors and towboat captains in embroidered suspenders drinking beer in their shirtsleeves against a black walnut bar, and the powdered necks of blowsy women, and of a greataunt of mine, a lame old lady in her seventies who wore a black silk dress with a lace yoke, and who used to like to shock her daughters by saying that her idea of heaven was sitting in Hall's beergarden eating devilled crabs and drinking beer on a Sunday afternoon.

We walked out through the lodginghouse, a big old place that had been a family mansion not so long ago, now partitioned off into small cubicles where lived a pack of young men and women clerks in government offices. The house was clean, but it had the feeling of too many people breathing the same air, of strangers stirring behind flimsy walls, of unseen bedsprings creaking and unseen feet shuffling in cramped space.

Going out the front door it occurred to us that it might be in Washington that the Greenwich Village of this war would come into being. Around the period of the last war it had been in the slums of downtown New York that young Americans, fresh from the uneventful comfort of onefamily homes in small towns, had holed up like greenhorn immigrants in sleazy lodgings to get their first taste of a metropolis. In this war it might be in Washington. Maybe Washington was the new metropolis in the making.

Walking down the densely shaded street I remembered that when an uncle of mine had moved out to a house on this avenue, we had all thought it pretty fine, almost like taking a house in the country. My friend, the old Washingtonian, murmured that it would be all right now if it weren't so near the colored district. There was quite an overflow, especially at night. It was a dark street, he went on, laughing, in more ways than one. At night young negro girls and boys filled up every unlit corner and alarmed the lodginghouse keepers with their obstreperous necking under the trees and on the stoops. Shouted physiological terms flopped in through the open windows to offend the ears of the more respectable lodgers. It was almost as if they did it on purpose.

That started us talking about how people with different colored skins were getting on together in this crowded town.

For a while my friend said it had looked as if a bloody race riot were brewing. On the streetcars, in the continual shoving for seats or for a place to stand there was every opportunity for trouble. Some colored people had bad manners. Some white people had bad manners. Everybody was in the habit of giving the colored people the worst end of everything. Remember the moment of painful tension when a car or bus crosses the line into Virginia and the colored people have to move into the back seats. Some of the younger negroes had gotten very uppish. Whites resented it. There were days when he could feel in the background among the crowds on the street a teasing whisper that there was going to be a riot, that there had got to be a riot to teach the niggers a lesson.

Wasn't the streetcar company more or less of a storm centre? Yes, the latest organized negro protest had been against the streetcar company because they wouldn't hire negro conductors and motormen. The company had canvassed its employees and found that if they did, most of them would look for other jobs. He himself, certainly not a man to throw an extra stone at an outcast, had said he would leave if there were colored men hired in his department. Nobody minded having colored men in jobs that could be all colored. It was the mixture the white men resented. They felt that in some jobs there'd be too much rubbing elbows in shelters, at the carbarns in close quarters. It wouldn't be practical.

After all most of the employees were Virginians or old Washingtonians, and old Washingtonians of all Southerners were most set in their ways. My friend said he'd gotten to know them and liked them immensely, found them very nice to work with. They felt they were doing a good job, they were certainly doing their best in a very trying setup. They resented this effort to force them to accept situations they didn't want to accept. As it was, the company was having a hard time getting new motormen. Youngsters who didn't know the routes kept getting their cars on the wrong tracks and snarling things up. Driving a streetcar was a job a man had to learn.

Anyway, the tension seemed to be easing off now. Things had been pretty much touch and go at the time of the mass-meeting in Garfield Park. The town had been full of that sullen sense of a storm brewing. There had been the rumors, the little groups with their heads together, the hysterical individuals suddenly starting to whoop it up for a fight. Luckily, the demonstration had turned out to be more of a circus. The parade to the park had been fun. Colored people couldn't help enjoying things like that. The music and the bands had cleared the air. The cops had been ready to quell an insurrection, but they had done nothing to keep one from starting. Somehow the good sense of the majority of people colored and white had staved the riot off. Since then my friend said that hardly a day passed without a colored man's coming up to him at one of his streetcorners and trying to explain to him that the negroes in Washington wanted no trouble with the whites.

While we talked we had been walking eastward. At a corner on U Street we climbed on a streetcar. Sitting in the car my friend started talking about the Civil War. He had been reading Freeman's life of Robert E. Lee. We fell to speculating on the treacherous morass Washington had been during the Civil War, wondering whether there had been less regard for the public interest by officeholders then than now. Looking back on it, it was a miracle that this strange nation of ours had ever held together, the same kind of a miracle the nation was performing right now.

As the car ran east a change was coming over the street. It was losing the vague look of an uptown thoroughfare and becoming a main stem. The color of the population was changing. At every stop white people got off the car and colored people got on. They were as welldressed as the whites and their way of speaking and their manners were about the same. The street was becoming garish with signs, storefronts were taking on the tinselly look of a central city neighborhood. Pavements were crowded. We were riding through the main street of a negro city.

Meanwhile my friend was talking about Winfield Scott. It surprised me that it was to 'Old Fuss and Feathers' that he attributed the North's grand strategy that eventually destroyed the Confederacy, the giant pincers movement, the military economic strategy on which the German conception of warfare has been based since that time. We found ourselves arguing about that.

When we changed cars to go on down Seventh Street we were still arguing about it. A popeyed young negro had been standing beside us. When he started to work his way past us to get off the jampacked car he nodded in our direction and said in a ceremonious tone, 'Gentlemen, I've enjoyed listening to your conversation. I'm sorry I have to get off the car.' My friend threw a couple of remarks at him as he left on the subject of the war to see if he had anything special to say, but the car had already jolted to a stop so there was no time. 'Doesn't sound like hard feeling, does it?' whispered my friend. 'I think that was a rather nice little incident.'

We got off the car at the edge of the Mall. We looked up at the Capitol recumbent on its hill of darkfoliaged trees, every column and pediment standing out in high relief in the brilliant strawcolored light that poured out from the west. The sky behind the dome was deep opaque blue. Against the brightness when we looked the other way along the Mall rose the slender shape of George Washington's obelisk and the red pinnacles and gable ends of the Smithsonian. To head for the river we turned our backs on the long white cliffs of the government buildings along Constitution Avenue that were streaked vertically with alternate column and shadow where the hard glancing light harshly brought out every detail. As we walked across the Mall our heads were turned again to look up at the Capitol.

We were wondering if it would have looked better with its original low shallow dome. It had been during the Civil War that the present dome had been built. Lincoln had insisted that the work go on.

At the foot of the hill the glasshouse for tropical plants, with its whitewashed bays and domes of glass that used to remind me of a scary story in Hans Andersen, was still standing. Seeing it made my mind swoop back through the years. Walking down Seventh Street we found ourselves right away back in the leafy redbrick Washington of years ago. Suddenly the wartime tension was gone. People rambling limply along the street were in no hurry to get anywhere. Customers in the dim corner stores seemed in no hurry to be waited on. Young men in their shirtsleeves stood in groups at the corners not talking about anything in particular. In every face there was that look of shiftless poor white relaxation that I remembered had driven me halfcrazy when I lived here as a child.

We walked, sweating prodigiously, clear on down to the river There we found a heatwilted crowd of men in shirtsleeves and girls in light dresses filing up the gangplank of a rusty old excursion steamer. We walked out to the edge of the wharf to look at her. There was a faint freshness off the water but no breeze. Out on the greenishbrown stream the sails of some little racing boats hung limp. The trees across the water were oozing intense green as the day drowned in hot pearly haze.

We both had recollections of Potomac wharves. We stood a while on the edge of the piling beside the excursion boat talking about the time when people in Washington used to buy oysters right off the schooners at two dollars a barrel. A policeman who had been preventing three grimy little boys with their shirttails out from buying tickets for the boatride came up to us and suggested civilly enough that we must either go on the boat or get out of the way. To say something I asked him if this was one of the old steamboats of the long defunct Potomac and Chesapeake line. 'The skipper can tell you.' He pointed out a roundfaced man who was standing bareheaded beside the ticket office watching the government clerks, the stenographers, the secretaries, the highschool kids and the soldiers and sailors and their wives or girlfriends shuffling past to buy three hours of evening breeze on the river.

I sidled over and asked him what had happened to the old

Three Rivers, the river boat that used to make the Virginia and
Southern Maryland landings round to Baltimore, and that I had
travelled on so often at one time in my life. I almost hoped that
this might be the old *Three Rivers* rebuilt and altered. No, this
was an old Albany dayboat. Before I knew it we were thirtyfive
years back in the days of the river boats. He said the *Three
Rivers* had burned years ago on a newsboys' excursion out of
Baltimore, and not a few of the newsboys with her. There had
been a big story about it in the papers.

'You remember the old inside cabins?' he asked.

'Sure.'

'You know they opened on an air space between them and the
outside cabins. Well, they didn't know about that and they got
to throwing matches out of the windows and the partitions caught
and the boat burned down to the water's edge.'

The *Three Rivers* launched us into a rambling conversation
about Captain this and Captain that and the old *Northumberland*
and the time she stayed aground so long halfway up Saint Mary's
River. We were still at it when the whistle blew for departure.

As I walked away I was remembering what it was the brackish
backwater smell of the wharves had been reminding me of. It
was the smell of an inside cabin on the old *Three Rivers*, the smell
of old paint and musty old settees upholstered in red velvet and
of crabshells and oysterbarrels and fertilizer, and steam and
grease from the huge slow engines; and with it came the memory
of how the river freshness came in the window after you left
Alexandria and the silence after the slapping waves of the broad
river when the boat turned into the glassy smoothness of one of
the creeks at night, and the engineroom bells and the thump of
the hawser on the loose planks of a wharf; and the rattle of the
small ironbound trucks on the gangplank as the ragged negro
roustabouts, singing, chattering, whooping, loaded and unloaded
freight at country wharves all night long, and the smell of farm-
lands and pinewoods and clover crowding aboard as the old
steamboat blundered through narrow channels with splash and
surge of paddlewheels; and the seethe of the broad wake astern

and the cries of startled terns circling about the sandspits at the bends in the river.

Talking about the river life, remembering the cranky wharves and the ragged negroes who sold steamed crabs and the shaggy fishermen from Tangier Island with tobacco in their cheeks and all the Mark Twain world I used to scurry through with my heart in my mouth as a child because it was so rough and rank and noisy, and how the old dilapidated coal wharves and oyster wharves had gone and with them the bugeyes and the white Chesapeake schooners and the old colored men sculling skiffs and the stench of rotting fish and crabshells and flies, we walked up the street to Hall's.

Hall's was as I'd remembered it, the bar was there, and the garden fenced off from the street by a wooden paling, and the gaslit look of green trees against redbrick. We walked past the great painting of a very undressed-looking Adam and Eve being told to get out of the park, it's closing time, by a rosy and ineffectual angel, and settled down in the yard to eat devilled crabs and drink beer. Across the green wooden framing for the awning over our heads yellow cats scampered back and forth and snarled and caterwauled. As we sat there smiling across our mugs we felt, just for the moment of the first tingling cold gulp, that thirty years had rolled off our shoulders.

2

Washington Is a Bivouac

'I was born in Moscow, Russia; maybe you've heard of the country,' says the taximan in tones of sudden scorn as he starts around Dupont Circle. 'That's why I have a right to say people don't know what war is in this country ... I've been in this country thirtytwo years. Sure, I'm American citizen, ain't you? Americans don't know what hardship is ... My mother was born in Smolensk. My grandfather he fought Napoleon with wagons ... Look at this city. You call it the national capital and the people don't know there's a war on ... You eat too good . . . You go on strike when you like . . . You ain't got no respeck . . . In Russia we know about war and hardship . . . You can take the man out of the country but you can't take the country out of the man.'

1 didn't have time to argue with him because I was late to lunch. I jumped out of the cab opposite the embassy of our transatlantic cousins. How the world has changed, I couldn't help thinking as I looked up and down the table in the cafeteria in the basement at the soberlooking young people, each dressed for his own comfort, who ate there. They looked more like students at a coeducational college than like the stiffcollared underlings of the pompous hierarchy of the Foreign Office I remembered from times past. It may have been their informal clothes that gave them such an alert free and easy air, but I couldn't help feeling that the grim restraints of wartime had freed them from some of the ancient restraints of the protocol, collar and tie and calling card. They had a businesslike look of determination about them. What's in their minds? I kept thinking. What are they planning?

The young man I'd gone to see was delighted when I asked him what he thought of Washington. After lunch we sat on the concrete wall in the shade of a horsechestnut tree behind the office building. In spite of the gypsy look his gleaming black hair and olive skin gave him he was very much the don. His speech was a rapid Oxford flutter: 'But of course it's wonderful and horrible but it's not a city,' he said, 'not as you conceive of the great European capitals of the recent past as cities. It's more like a vast temporary headquarters during a campaign . . . you know the city of Santa Fé that housed the Catholic kings during the siege of Granada, or something Genghis Khan might have put up . . . Washington is a bivouac.'

Later that day, coming into the Pentagon Building, I thought of what he'd said. There's a look of impermanence about the place in spite of its immense weight and size. The concourse, with its low ceiling held up by two rows of vermilion columns and its brightly lit chromium-trimmed drugstore and cafeteria

and barbershop behind plate glass round the sides, gives you the
feeling of arriving at a temporary station specially built to serve
a world's fair. The people you see swirling round the stairways
that lead to the busses and taxis on the lower level look like New
Yorkers. Some of these clerks and office workers are in uniform,
some are in civilian clothes, there is a large proportion of negroes.
There's the feeling of a giant institution suddenly set up but not
much sense of its being military in the oldfashioned armory
sense. No smell of horses. Not a sentry or a bayonet in sight.
No tramping and clanking of squads changing the guard. To get
to see someone in the fastnesses above you go to a girl at a desk,
as in any other office building, and wait on a leather sofa in a
panelled alcove until a messenger comes to escort you up. Ramps
and escalators lead upstairs. On the upper floors the long gray
halls make you think of the passages on an immense ocean liner.

I was chatting about what kind of a bivouac Washington
seemed to the military with two captains I had come to see while
we sat squeezed together among the crowded yellow desks of
one of the public-relations sections, when a sudden windfall appeared in the shape of a onestar air general only two weeks back
from the Pacific theatre. Asked if he'd talk for publication he
said with a resigned air, sure, he would. He was a slowspoken
sandyhaired man with blue eyes. This was stuff that had to be
gone through and you could see he'd made up his mind to grin
and bear it. Underneath he was full of the elation of being home.
He looked barely forty. He pondered the questions carefully.
Obviously he was a man who liked to talk accurately.

'I guess how I felt getting back home after two years,' he
said, 'was confused, just plain confused. In San Francisco I tried
to get a room in the hotel where I usually go and they laughed
at me. Finally, the manager put us up in his room. Here in
Washington, my home is here, I'd been planning to get out the
old car and spend my leave driving around seeing some friends.
I thought I could take my family for a little vacation. I went
down to the ration board but no, siree, they won't give you
gasoline for any such purpose. We took the train and, my, what

a business that was! And now I've got my income tax to make out . . . My homecoming certainly didn't turn out the way I'd planned it out there. I needed a pair of shoes. I lost all my stuff in a plane accident. Of course, I got down to the store and had the shoes all picked out and then discovered I'd forgotten my ration book. The first thing I'd been planning when I got home was to have a nice steak and a bottle of whiskey and to drive around in my car and see my old friends. I did get hold of some whiskey. My friends got wind of it and came around and drank it all up, but I haven't seen the beef-steak yet.'

After the general had been swallowed up in a conference, my friends took me to see some recently returned men in their new bare offices.

'I find Washington life delightful,' said a young colonel who had just come back from Sicily. The way he stressed the word delightful was positively contagious. 'I'd heard such tall stories of life in Washington I honestly felt bad when I was ordered home for headquarters duty. I expected to sit at a desk and suffer. But I find the work very interesting. I managed to get myself an apartment, after I'd been here three days, from a woman whose husband was a naval officer and had just been ordered out to the Pacific Coast — just looked it up in the advertisements in the evening paper and walked across town and took it. Everybody abuses Washington nightlife, but I don't think it's bad . . . I even find people quite cordial. The other night at a place I was in, a whole bunch of people put their tables together and started talking though none of them had ever met before. Everybody was so friendly and nice, we had a wonderful time. Even the food in the restaurants seems fine after what we were getting out in the theatres. I find it delightful.'

There was another tall young colonel, hawknosed and black-eyed, at a desk in the other corner of the room. 'Don't forget the rent gouging,' he broke in. 'Don't forget to put that down. They get out of the ceilings because there's no ceiling on furnished places. So they just drag in some five-and-ten-cent store furniture and charge anything they like. Once we're stationed in Washington they've got us just where they want us.'

'Don't listen to him,' said the young man we'd first talked to, grinning over his desk. 'I find it delightful.'

The Daily Humiliation

The office was small and cramped, but the chairs and the desk and the dictaphone were the best money could buy. The lawyer had a gray skin and a broad face and high cheekbones. There was a touch of New England in his way of talking, though he assured me he was a Washingtonian born and bred. He had in-troduced me to his father, who was senior partner of the firm, an elegant dark old man with cottonwhite hair, in starched shirt-sleeves, who greeted me with oldfashioned ceremony.

'Every problem of the negro in this city,' this lawyer was telling me, 'centres about segregation. We admit that the posi-tion of the negro has improved economically. For the first time in many cases we are getting equal wages for equal work. But suppose we want to invest our money, suppose we want to buy a home. We have to pay a fourth more than the white man who buys a similar home, and the trouble we have to find a place to live . . . Every way we try to branch out they wall us in. En-tertainment now . . . The theatres for negroes — there's only one chain of them — are inadequate to the population. We never see a first run feature. They've got us walled in. Down here it's the hardest thing getting lunch. It's a daily humiliation. Either my father and I have to munch a sandwich at our desks or on a park bench or we have to go ten blocks to a lunchroom. It's the daily humiliation. As we are a little better off economi-cally than we were, we feel it more than we did. Can you blame us for wanting to break through the daily humiliation?'

The Protocol

My hostess had said to come 'around fiveish.' Green light poured up into the room through a tall narrow window reflected from the brilliantly sunlit grass and dense shrubbery of the garden in back. It was a high narrow dark room with a moulded gesso ceiling in an old brick house that smelt cosily of books and waxed parquet. My hostess sat on a couch in the shadow against the wall behind a beaded pitcher of iced orangeade, listening with a small indulgent smile to a question I kept presenting to her in various soggy shapes. How much did she suppose social life really counted in Washington? Was it a major factor in shaping people's careers, in influencing them to behave like honest men or like scoundrels in their jobs?

The Judge came in and stood listening for a moment. 'Are you entering into competition with Lucius Beebe?' he asked sarcastically and went out of the room to fetch some whiskey.

When he came back with a pint of rye, I tried to explain that since it happened that society, like golf, was a sport I knew very little about, I had to go around asking questions about it. If you didn't play the game yourself you had to get information from people who did. The difficulty was to find anybody sufficiently detached to admit they played it at all.

'Of course we don't have any choice,' whispered my hostess thoughtfully. There was some dismay in her tone.

'The ladies really understand that subject because they never take it seriously.' The Judge turned towards the couch. 'Speak up as an entity in your own right,' he said.

'Sometimes . . .' she began. But the Judge was already talking again: 'For one thing the protocol is stricter than in any other capital in the world. Even people who knew St. Petersburg and Vienna under the old regime say the same thing. It's often struck people as odd.'

'I suppose you know,' my hostess said with her small smile, 'that there are still great unsolved problems. There are people the Chief Justice can never eat dinner with because the problem of precedence has never been worked out.'

'Problems that await the solution of some Beebe yet unborn,' cried out the Judge.

He spoke of Jefferson's effort to introduce what he called the rule of *pêle-mêle*. When dinner was announced every gentleman should take the lady nearest him into table and seating should be accidental or arranged as in an ordinary Virginia gentleman's house. This procedure at the White House had horrified a certain Mr. Merry, who was then British ambassador and a great stickler for the etiquette of the Court of St. James's, and he had written copious memoranda complaining about it to the Foreign Office. In the long run it had been the British ambassador's idea that had prevailed, not Jefferson's.

'At least people still pursue good food,' my hostess said. 'I've never seen people pursue food and drink so frankly as they do in this town. It's not a dressy town, as you know. People don't care what they wear. The money goes into catering. You have to have good things to eat if you want to have a crowd at your afternoons at home. You know there are certain officials whose wives have to have afternoons at home whether they want to or not. Even the day of the week is set for them. It's one of the laws of the Medes and Persians.'

Did a man's social rating affect his career in government? I asked.

Well, there were the wealthy young men who gave big parties. There was the embassy crowd. There were the hostesses of great wealth who liked to have the latest celebrities. There were certain embassies whose invitations had a political intent. But on the whole social life was mechanical.

Wasn't one reason why so many people cracked up there that there was so little social relaxation? Didn't the town lack any real society?

We talked a little about what was meant by society. We decided it might mean, in the good sense, a sort of republic of equals. Once you were admitted into such a group competition and social climbing ceased. The nourishment and relaxation of such a society came from the fact that people inside it could freely exchange ideas, gossip, jokes — could feel at ease among equals. Jefferson's dinners had aimed at a republic of entertaining conversation where good breeding was taken for granted. Perhaps

people would use their heads better in their jobs if they had that kind of refreshment in the evenings. There was the moral check on a man that came from feeling that he belonged to a group whose judgments he had respect for. Ethics depended in some degree on your respect for the judgment of your peers.

We fell to talking about various mutual acquaintances who had come to Washington. Some had struggled hard to go out to dinner with the right people and not to be seen with the wrong people. Some had drifted innocently. None of them had gotten much nourishment out of it. In the long run it made very little difference one way or the other, not so much as it would in London, say. It was a man's position on the political or bureaucratic pyramid that determined his value as a dinner guest rather than the other way around. The halo of celebrity hovered fitfully about this or that man's head for a while, then it vanished and left no trace.

But hadn't the new population that had come in during the last ten years changed things? Some of the best brains in the country had poured through Washington. Hardly. Washington wasn't a city where people had much curiosity about why they behaved as they did. New Deal or old deal the Judge suggested, the same dignitaries still kept on inviting their opposite numbers to dinner. Maybe the protocol was an accommodation. With the protocol you didn't need to think. It was the unexamined life, he said with a smile, that Socrates had not thought worth living.

'We haven't any Socrates'; my hostess made a little face, 'and now the war has put a stop to formal entertaining anyway. And to tell the truth,' she added cheerfully, 'it's been quite a relief.'

Street Scene

A man is walking along the street with a bundle of soiled clothes under his arm. He's been to three laundries already. He's been told there is another in this block. He's in a hurry because he has an engagement downtown in fifteen minutes. He darts in under the pale blue sign and stands against the counter in the dense smell of damp linen under the flatiron. The girls working in the back of the room won't look at him at all. At last his pleading attracts the attention of a swarthy young man with short legs who is arranging packages of clean clothes on a shelf. 'We don't take no new customers,' he says sharply. The man starts to explain that he's in a hurry, that he's away from home. Maybe if he paid extra. The swarthy man turns his head away. 'You heard me the first time,' he snarls out of the corner of his mouth.

The man with the bundle of soiled clothes stalks out in a rage. Outside he meets a cop. He asks the cop where, in God's name, he can get his laundry done. The cop says there's a Chinaman three blocks across on the other side of the street. Sweating profusely, the man with the bundle of soiled clothes hurries across the broad sunbeaten street. When he gets to the Chinaman's he finds the glass door locked. The Chinaman, his yellow face wrinkled like a hand that has worked too long in hot water, is inside going over a pile of painted slips of paper. The man raps on the door. The Chinaman doesn't even look up. When he's tired of rapping, the man notices a piece of cardboard with some words scrawled in blue pencil: 'No More Cloes until Friday.'

While he's trying to decide what to do he goes into a corner drugstore to have a cocacola. The curlyhaired girl from the deep South at the fountain, pretty as a picture but no more interested, looks at him blankly. 'Well, if you haven't got coke give me buttermilk.' 'We got sweet milk,' she drawls. The man clutches the bundle to his ribs. It's beginning to come undone. 'I'm in a hurry. Give me something. Just give me something wet in a glass,' he says in a gasping voice.

Beside him stands a dapper young man with a suitcase in his hand who has asked for a cup of coffee. All of a sudden he is filled with hope. The young man knows a laundry. He must be just taking his clothes to be washed in that suitcase. He asks him. The young man smiles and shakes his head wisely. 'If I were you,' he says, 'I'd wrap that up in brown paper and take it to the nearest postoffice and mail it home.'

'I guess you're right. No use trying to get anything done in this town,' the man says, mopping his brow.

'Now maybe you can tell me where I'm going to sleep tonight,' says the young man seriously. 'I've been in this town four days and I haven't found a room yet.'

3

The Battle of Washington

The Reporter was a small precisely dressed man with deepset eyes and a preacher's forehead. I sat down at his table to have a glass of beer with him while he finished his supper.

'Well, how's it stacking up?' he asked me.

'There are the people who tell you sob stories and there are the people who think it's wonderful here ... After all, a whole lot of them have better jobs than they ever had in their lives.'

'Goddam termites! They are eating out the structure of the government like termites in an old house. My people are farmers. I get an idea from their letters of how things look from the outside, from the Nebraska side. There's the darnedest rift widening between Washington and the country.'

'Here when they talk about the rest of the country they talk about "out in the field."'

'Sure. The farmers, storekeepers, small businessmen of this country are just natives ... I can tell you one thing. They don't like it.'

He wiped his mouth decisively with his napkin. 'Now I'm through. Want to walk around the town some?'

We walked out southeast through the sweltering treeshaded streets towards the Navy Yard. This was again the Washington I remembered as a child: the stifling streets choked with trees where all the life seemed to be going into the vegetation, the families sitting out on their front stoops and in their tiny dooryards; men in undershirts, dank little halfnaked children sitting

out in swings, women fanning themselves on settees and rockers
in their tiny front yards, the streetlights muffled by lowhanging
branches, light filtered through leaves, the shadows of branches
thrown on brick walls. The young men and girls and boys lined
up limply at the dingy sodafountains. The feeling of slack life
stagnant in a jungle.

We walked for blocks and blocks through wilted white neigh-
borhoods of narrow brick houses with elongated windows, through
colored blocks littered with squirming black children all over the
pavement, where girls in slacks with black hair slicked smooth
against their heads sauntered beside young bucks in opennecked
shortsleeved shirts and trousers cut tight to their narrow hips.
Four and a Half Street was one of the streets I wanted to find.
In those days it had been full of poolparlors and bars and honkytonks, the main stem of waterfront characters, fishermen and
Chesapeake Bay boatmen. 'As I was walkin' up Four and a
Half Street' was how the towboat captains and brackish water
sailors used to start their more scabrous tales of night life ashore.
I was disappointed. So far as I could make out it has been
swallowed up in Fourth Street.

It was surprising to find the Navy Yard so immensely enlarged.
The old building with the 1830 look of the pediment over its
arched entrance was lost in the midst of a great industrial plant,
great concrete sheds full of greenishviolet light. By the time
we were abreast of the shabby old entrance we were all in from
walking so far through the steamy night in heat so dense that it
was like pushing your way through a swamp. We turned into
various bars but they were all out of beer. At last we stumbled,
dripping from every pore, into a small beerparlor and lunchroom.

We were asking each other just exactly how Washington officeholders had changed in the years since we had known the town.
As a small child, I tried to explain, I dimly remembered a board-
inghouse where my mother's father and mother lived, a place
that smelt of camphor and chicken dinners, full of very old
people whose youth dated from before the Civil War. They were
all 'in office.' I used to wonder what the words meant. There

was Colonel this and Major that and General so and so, relics
of both war bureaucracies, old fellows with white goatees and
bushy mustaches who went to work ceremoniously at ten and
vegetated in their offices until four. It was hard to explain the
peculiar lack of verve or ambition with which they performed the
routine that furnished them with room, board, tobacco, and an
occasional suck out of a whiskey bottle when their wives weren't
looking. In those days nobody ever imagined those duties meant
anything to the world or the nation or were other than a tedious
method of obtaining a small addition to an old soldier's pension.

'I guess it was Wilson brought righteousness into Washington,' the Reporter said. 'Roosevelt's ardor for social reform
means righteousness multiplied by itself. We get the righteousness and we don't get the reform.'

Two Marine Corps sergeants sat drinking beer in the next
booth. We asked them to have a glass of beer with us. One of
them got to his feet with his glass and his bottle in his hand.
The grayfaced Greek with sagging eyes who ran the place rushed
over all of a fluster. 'No move drink.'

'No can move,' said the sergeant, dropping down in his seat
again. 'District regulations,' said his friend.

'That's the sort of thing,' said the Reporter. 'The last war
gave us prohibition. You just wait and see what this one will
give us ... How do you like Washington?' He turned to the
sergeants and hurled a question at them in his prosecuting at-
torney manner.

The sergeants snorted. 'Lousy,' said one. The other nodded
vigorously.

'What's the matter with it?'

'Lousy.'

'Don't people here treat you right?'

'They don't know there's a war on. This guy and me we enlisted eighteen months ago to go to the war and here we are,
bored to death ... This here battle of Washington ...' he spat
the words out.

'It's not that we don't do all right,' the other sergeant said in a judicial tone . . . 'Those two treated us all right, didn't they, Bill? Just now? . . . No, they weren't hookers either. We don't have to go to hookers. We can get it any time we like . . . But it's the atmosphere . . .'

'Lousy,' echoed the other man. Then they both jumped to their feet as if they were afraid they'd been spilling military secrets; shouted back, 'Goodnight, gents. Thanks for the beer,' from the door and strode out of the joint.

When he brought us two more steins the Greek hovered over our table dabbing at it with the wet rag he carried in his hand. 'Hot,' he said.

'How's it you have beer when the places down the line don't?' the Reporter asked him severely.

He smiled a sallow smile. 'I store plenty kegs upstairs. I got two places.'

'Business good?' asked the Reporter.

'Sure.' The Greek sat down beside him. 'Make big money. Rent this place only thirtyfive dollars. I come from Houston, Texas.'

'Before that, where did you come from?'

'Athens.'

I murmured soothingly that I'd been to Athens years ago and that it was a beautiful city.

'My wife there, three little children. For more than a year I get no letter. Maybe starved. We try send food, everybody in Greece starved. Here I make good business. Last week I buy four thousand dollars in Liberty Bonds.'

'I know a fellow,' said the Reporter. 'He's a countryman of yours. He has a liquor store. He's had it only two years. It's on a good block, I guess.'

'In Washington,' said the Greek, 'all blocks good blocks, only some pay expensive rent, some pay cheap rent. You pay cheap rent, you make money.'

'Well, this fellow took me into his back room and opened up his safe . . . I'd been kidding about how he wasn't doing anything for the war effort. He opened up his safe and showed me eighty thousand dollars in war bonds. He had to take them out in different names.'

We all sat in silence, thinking about eighty thousand dollars.

The Greek shrugged one shoulder and tapped his long putty nose with one finger and, smiling his sallow smile, sidled away from the table.

'Hell, let's move on,' said the Reporter.

We went on slogging up the street. In the old brick residential blocks every house looked as if it had been turned inside out. Men, women, and children were draped in drowsy huddles on brick steps. Elderly people were sitting at open doors in dimlit hallways. Stout women were leaning out of windows.

It was a long walk. We had come out into the open spaces of trees and grass and shrubbery in front of the Library of Congress before we noticed that there was a moon. The Reporter was telling me that the Capitol grounds were the place where service men went to pick up girls, like a smalltown cemetery these days, full of couples rolling in the shadows. Walking across the gardens, the white uniforms of sailors stood out bright in the moonlight. There were girls' voices giggling. A soldier was asleep on the grass. The Capitol looked immensely quiet. The dome slept solid as a mountain in the moonlight.

The Reporter hailed the sentry who was walking back and forth halfway up the steps on the House side. 'Howdy, soldier?' The sentry brought his gun up to attention. 'At ease, soldier. I'm just a newspaper man.'

The soldier looked at us suspiciously from under his bulbous tin hat. 'I'm not rightly supposed to talk,' he said.

'I won't let anything happen to you,' said the Reporter in a napoleonic tone.

'I got a furlough comin' up. I want to git home to see my wife.'

'I'll see you get your furlough. What do you think of that?'

The sentry had walked down the steps towards us and stood with his gun at rest looking at us. He kept running his tongue over his lips. He was a quiet thoughtful looking man.

'So you are married?' asked the Reporter.

He nodded. 'I married me a little girl down South.'

'When you went for training?'

The soldier nodded.

'How long have you been in?'

'Two years. They let me out once and I got married. Then they hauled me back in again. I been all over this country. I trained down South. Then I was out in Oregon guarding forests . . . I like that . . . out in the woods three months at a time.'

'They say there's a lot of monkey business goes on at night around the Capitol.'

'I wouldn't know that. I only been here a week.'

'Where are you quartered?'

'I don't rightly know the street yet. We march down here in formation.' The soldier had a leisurely quiet voice.

'What do you think about the antistrike bill?'

'I guess it's all right. I don't know much about it.'

'How do you like Washington?'

'When you're in the army, you take what comes.'

'Do you think Congress is doing a good job?'

The soldier ran his tongue over his lips. 'Mister,' he answered after a pause, 'when a feller's in the army he don't think much about what's going on outside.'

'Well, I'll bet you a bottle of beer I can get you a furlough.' The Reporter took down his name and address and we walked on. 'Nice fellow,' he said.

'Say,' I asked him, 'did you suddenly have the feeling that there was no date to that conversation? It might be during the Civil War.'

'Don't tell me that. My business is getting news.'

Suddenly we remembered there was a concert in Meridian Park. At the corner of the Senate Office Building we found a cab. We tumbled into it and sat back and waited for the breeze the car made to chill through our wet shirts.

'Have you been reading about Hopkins Institute? The high class call house up on Connecticut Avenue that's been running as a massage parlor all these years. No article on Washington will be complete without that,' the Reporter was saying.

The husky blond young man who was driving the car let his breath out through his teeth with a whistle.

'If they asked me,' he said, 'I could write a book. Washington's a wide open town. The cops don't know they're alive. Just the last few days I've seen about fifty of those girls. They've all taken jobs as waitresses until this blows over. When they start investigatin' these things they won't never ask nobody whc knows about it. They never ask the cabdrivers.'

'Do you think they ought to stop things like that?' asked the Reporter.

'How can they? Ain't everybody has the luck to be happily married. If they shut up the professionals, the amateurs take over. Look at all these nice girls from small towns with no place to go in the evenings. Look at all these boys away from their families. I call this the city of lonely hearts.'

Out on Sixteenth Street it was cooler. Meridian Park turned out to be opposite Mrs. Henderson's castle, a building that had since childhood given the locality a faintly comic flavor for me. We said goodnight to our cabdriver and walked up the steps towards the music. Beyond the trees pale shapes of tall apartment houses glimmered in moonlight. The small park was crowded with white people and colored people sitting in chairs or standing in rows behind the chairs round three sides of an oblong pool. At the far end in the white orchestra shell a violinist was playing. You could hear perfectly. The sound of the violin came sweetly across the water. The crowd was quiet. Floodlights lit the black figures of the violinist and his accompanist at the grand piano. The reflections from the rippling water lit up very faintly white faces and dark faces, motionless, listening. When the piece was over immense applause came out of the darkness packed with people under the trees.

'Have you ever thought,' the Reporter asked me, 'that if Washington was Rio everybody would say what a hell of a picturesque place?'

4

The Merest Courtesy

The grand ballroom was full of dressedup people. At one end was a long table with silverware and piles of giltedged plates and bowls of caviar in ice and lobster salad and cold salmon stretched out on plates in a sea of ornamental mayonnaise. The man of great wealth who was giving the party for the bride of an official was a great believer in the simple virtues of champagne and caviar. It had never occurred to him that there was any other way of giving a party than to spend plenty of money on champagne and caviar. The band played. Couples danced. The air was rich with food and drink and perfume and cigarettesmoke. Women shook out the ruffles of their long dresses. Men puffed chests out under pleated shirtfronts. It was all lavish. It was all free.

A man of some position and his wife had just danced together and were innocently headed with watering mouths towards the suppertable when they met a friend, another man in what is known as a position of trust.

'Hello.'

'Hello.'

The two men eyed each other.

'I didn't expect to meet you here.'

'Well, I didn't expect to meet you.' There was a pause; the man who had spoken first was looking uneasily around the room.

'Maybe neither of us ought to be here.'

As they looked at each other, the saliva dried in their mouths.

'How could we help it? Simple courtesy,' murmured the wife soothingly.

'But it's war time. The press might get the wrong angle. I've seen faces . . .'

'Who?'

A name is mentioned. They haven't advanced any nearer to the magnificent suppertable. Instead, they are headed for the cloakroom. Every familiar greeting is torture. 'We don't have to be in such a hurry, the house isn't on fire,' the wife says drily. She was just beginning to have a good time. She hates to leave all that caviar.

'After all,' the men say to each other, as they wait for their hats, 'we had to look in for a moment . . . the merest courtesy.'

Washington, D.C., July, 1943

'*IT'S ALL A PLAN*,' the elderly New Englander was saying as he gazed thoughtfully across Lafayette Square so buoyantly green in the sunlight. Beyond the statue of Jackson saluting the crowd from his bronze merrygoround horse we could see the pediment and columns of the White House between the trees. On the benches under magnolias colored people sprawled munching their noonday sandwiches. Some white girls from offices in white green pink dresses were eating lunches out of paper bags. An old man was feeding the pigeons. Two sailors were holding out peanuts to a squirrel. A major, stout and grayhaired, with a briefcase under his arm, came picking his way carefully through the pigeons that rose and fluttered about him. Young starlings in their shining tweeds hopped about the bright grass. A racket of dryflies came from the trees. 'It's all a plan,' the elderly New Englander was saying, raising his voice to draw back my lagging attention. 'There are no two ways about it. It's been a plan from the first to change the system of things in this country and to substitute for our welltried ways socialism and dictatorship.'

CHAPTER 10

The Two Ends of Pennsylvania Avenue

1

Several men and a woman are sitting at breakfast along a yellow refectory table. Through the screened French doors, from the small garden laid out in the open spaces between dense trees, comes the smell of lilies trodden under the heavy sunlight, and the reedy note of a redbird from the linden.

One man is explaining: 'The first man he ought to see, if he wants to get an idea of what makes this town tick, is Joe.'

'Isn't Joe a pretty hard man to see?' asks a second man.

'Frank can fix that up. Frank had me on the phone for over half an hour before I was out of bed this morning telling me about his talk with Joe yesterday afternoon.'

'When I had lunch with him last week,' a third man says, 'Martin told me Joe was going bigger than ever.'

'Eddy don't think so,' says the second man in a dogmatic tone.

'Well, why can't he talk to Eddy?'

'No use talking to Eddy,' the first man says emphatically. 'Eddy gets everything from Harold and it's six months since Harold knew anything he didn't read in the papers.'

'I thought Eddy and Harold were on the outs,' mutters the second man. The first man begins to laugh   Outside in the hall the phone is ringing. 'If you ask me,' the second man insists, 'Martin's the man for him to see if he wants straight talking. Martin's the brains of Harold's little combination, anyway.'

'Well, talking to Martin's just like talking to Don.' The third man insistently raises his voice to be heard above the phone that rings and rings.

'Where do you think Don gets his ideas? He sees Joe every night before he goes to bed.' The first man calls back over his shoulder as he sidles off to answer the telephone call.

'Now that that's settled, won't somebody have another cup of coffee?' soothingly suggests the smiling woman at the head of the table.

In the linden above the lilies the redbird keeps on singing.

2

The Power of the Word

This taxidriver thought I was an Englishman. He spoke with a strong east of Europe accent himself. He'd hardly started the motor before he began to take me to task. 'Those sentimental prelates you have over in England are raising Cain about our knocking down the old churches. They ought to button up their mouths. That's sentimentality, if it ain't worse than that. We oughta bomb them Germans out of existence, wipe out everything they've got and then let 'em starve in their own ruins, men, women, and children, let 'em all starve.'

I found myself taking up the cudgels for the English prelate; for a moment I felt I was the English prelate trying to explain that if we were going truly to defeat Naziism and that sort of thing oughtn't we to behave as little like them as possible?

'That's appeasement talk,' he shouted back out of the corner of his mouth. 'They'd oughta shut up those imperialist appeasers. We'd oughta do to them like they'd do to us if they got a chance. Wipe 'em out.'

'What use would it be to lick them if we turned out just like them?'

'Anybody who says Americans are like Nazis is a goddam liar.'
'You're talking like a Nazi yourself.'

By the time he unloaded me in front of the House Office
Building we were about ready to have it out on the pavement.
It was only the stately nature of the surroundings, the rhododen-
drons, the Capitol dome like an inflating balloon rearing its
august architraves among circling pigeons behind the trees, the
tall receding colonnades of the office buildings ranked in the sunlight, that kept us from slugging each other. I was so sore I
hurried up the steps without giving him a tip.

The Congressional Mind

Inside the House Office Building the cool staleness of the air
under the high ceilings, and the courtesy of the whitehaired
guard of whom I asked my way, restored my feeling of dignity
as a fullfledged citizen of this republic that the taxidriver's
yammering had ruffled. Thickness of marble walls shut out
the heat and discord of the city. Walking down the tall corridor, I read the modestly lettered names of the representatives on the narrow darkstained doors of their offices, placed far
apart along the soupgreen walls. At least in the physical setup
of the buildings around the Capitol there was something left
of republican simplicity. I found the door I was looking for, and
was told by the pleasantvoiced young woman in the outer offices
to go right on in; I was expected.

The freshman representative I'd come up to see was a lively-
looking young man. His face didn't have that look of being
trampled by crowds you see in seasoned politicians. He was a
man who had done other things in his life than chew cigars in
hotelroom conferences and breathe out platitudes on public
platforms. He told me that he'd made the decision to run for
Congress only because he honestly believed that, as he couldn't
serve in the army, he ought to serve his country in some way at
a time like this. He talked so plain about it that I believed
him.

Well, here he was in Congress; how was he planning to go to work?

Before he answered that question, he said with a wry smile, he had to make some explanations: the first thing you came in contact with when you sat down in your office as a new arrival was the rigidity of the House organization. What went on on the floor was mere byplay that had very little to do with the real business of legislation. That went on in committees. The committees were in the hands of the Old Guard of both parties. A new man could be made effective or helpless by the men who nominated the committees. If he rubbed them the wrong way they could sponge his name off the slate. The House was an oligarchy of oldtimers who had arrived at their posts by seniority.

Many of these old men were honest old men who really wanted to do right, others were living up to political commitments they'd made years ago, some of them were . . . well, we'd better not go into that . . . but whoever they were, their real contacts with real people and things had been made fifteen or twenty years ago. We mustn't forget the time lag. Since then all they'd seen or known was Washington and their political machines back home. The routine business of their work, doing favors and necessary jobs for constituents, answering letters, committee meetings, the hours spent on the floor, took up so much of their lives they didn't have leisure to read or study even if they wanted to. About all they could do was read the papers.

Most of them were lawyers. Lawschool or training in some county lawyer's office had already given their minds a verbal bent that made it hard for real events to get through. Life on the Hill fostered a feeling of selfimportance that hardened the shell on even the most receptive mind. And there weren't very many receptive minds in this typical enough collection of middle-aged middling-income Americans. We were living in a time when changes came so fast it was hard on even the liveliest understanding. Only the most resilient and best-trained minds could keep up. Sometimes he doubted if any of us could. Why should we expect congressmen to think quicker than their constituents?

He hadn't been there long but, gosh, he'd come to the conclusion that under the circumstances it was surprising that the House did as well as it did.

Suppose you had something definite you really wanted to get accomplished, how would you go about it?

The first problem was to get yourself on the right committee, or to get some senior member to take up your bill . . . Suddenly he paused and gave a startled look around the office as if he expected to see somebody hiding behind the calfskin bindings in his bookcase. Now if he talked freely I must please not quote him by name or identify him in any way. His voice dropped to a whisper. Talking out of turn by a newcomer was the best way to get in wrong. If he got in wrong right at the start he might . just as well have stayed home and made himself a pot of money at his business. Had I ever noticed how few men of prominence in other walks of life had ever made effective congressmen? The problem was to use what brains you had without letting your colleagues know you had any. I wasn't to think that the freshmen of this congress weren't putting their heads together trying to dope out some way of making themselves felt. They were. Their problem cut right across party lines. Most of the new Democrats and new Republicans were not professional politicians, but men like himself who'd let themselves be sent to Washington because they thought they might use their brains or their experience to some good purpose there. And they were all up against the same stone wall: seniority.

Did they have any definite plan?

There'd been agreement on some details. One thing they'd decided was that congressional committees needed more expert advice, congressmen needed expert secretaries who would really be able to give accurate information about questions that came up.

Did he mean a brain trust?

Sure; set a brain trust to catch a brain trust. He laughed. He went on to explain that he meant there ought to be more information work of the sort some of the Senate committees were doing. Congress so far this session had been a bull in a china shop. It had done a pretty good job tearing down the New Deal wing of the Administration. The question was: could it be gotten back to constructive work?

What kind of constructive work? What kind of thing had he hoped to accomplish when he packed his grip to come to Washington?

'My . . . my . . . That sure is the sixtyfour dollar question,' he said, pursing up his lips. 'There are so many things it's hard to put into words.'

A bell like a schoolbell rang through the building. It was twelve o'clock, time for the House to convene. We get to our feet. 'Whew, that lets me out,' he said laughing. 'I've got to get on the floor.' He held out his hand. 'Well, this has been very interesting.' He shook my hand vigorously. 'I'm glad I don't have to answer that one.' We were both laughing.

The House in Session

Dawdling a little so as to let the congressman get ahead of me I followed him down the corridor and out of the building into a stream of men in twos and threes and fours who were walking slowly so as not to get too hot in the blaze of noonday heat as they crossed the street and rounded the edge of the curved pavement towards the House wing of the Capitol. It was so hot that sparrows hopping around in the grass had their bills open as if they were gasping. In the shade of the stone arches under the steps it was cool again. Under the vault dimly lit by dim electric light bulbs there was a press of people that gave a little of the feeling of a theatre lobby just after the curtain has gone up. Down a corridor I found a small lunchroom and sat up on a stool and ordered a glass of buttermilk and a sandwich.

Beside me sat two tall men in stetson hats, undoubtedly Texans. 'Now, look here,' one of them was drawling in the other's ear. 'I'm agoin' to get Dick to come out and visit with us in the lobby and I want you to talk to him good. He's goin'

out on that floor and make a speech against meat prices this
afternoon, and I want him to feel he's got some stockmen behind him. You tell him the truth about the price of feed. Half
these politicians round here don't know the hind end of a steer
from a taxicab.' They slipped off their stools and moved off
with toothpicks in the corners of their mouths.

Swallowing the last of my buttermilk, I climbed the broad
stairway. As I went I craned my neck to look up at the painting
named 'Westward the Course of Empire' that used to send a
chill down my spine when I saw it as a child. The stairway was
full of soldiers and sailors on leave rambling around taking in
the sights of the Capitol. On the upper landing a guide had
marshalled quite a flock of them along with a few schoolteachers
on vacation and some young girls and small children, and was
about to lead them into the gallery for a glimpse of the proceedings. While they filed past the guard I walked over to look out
of a window that opened on gray architecture and blue sky and
the leafy gardens of the Hill and the avenues crowded with cars
at its foot. A wedgeshaped formation of planes made up of three
threes was passing so far away as to be tiny specks in front of the
streaked white clouds that hung over the irregular rim of buildings across the horizon. I went back to let myself be frisked for
weapons by the elderly and genial guard before being let into a
seat in the gallery to see for myself what the House was up to.

The appearance of the hall had changed since I'd last seen it
years ago. The desks and the red carpet had gone and instead
there were semicircular benches with high backs freshly upholstered in blueish gray. The steel girders painted olivegreen
that were put in to hold up the glass ceiling when it was con-
demned as unsafe gave the whole place a temporary and transi-
tional look. The representatives themselves had a more citified
air than I remembered. They moved about more than they used
to. The noise of the desks was gone, but there was a great
babble of conversation. In spite of the public address system and
the portable mike that some of the members hung round their
necks when they spoke it was hard to follow what was said from
the gallery.

I found myself sitting in the front row between a strange character with a long not too clean face tanned by the open and long slatecolored hair loose over his collar, who looked like a medicine show Indian or a professional hermit, and a young corporal with blond hair cut in a brush and a turned-up nose who kept asking me who this man was and that man was. We were right opposite the bare bulbous head of the Speaker who sat looking straight in front of him with an expressionless face as solemn as a hound dog's.

A gentleman from Montana was addressing the House in opposition to a federal scheme to build a dam to store water for the Columbia River hydroelectric project which he said would ruin one of the grandest and most beautiful and productive valleys in the whole state and that just for the benefit of another state. A gentleman from Maine rose to congratulate the House on the reporting out of committee of a resolution stating that the House was in favor of having a foreign policy. He got a round of applause when he said that this resolution did not in his opinion mean a conspiracy of the starryeyed to elevate the wages of the tin miners of Bolivia or the living standards of the banana growers of Nicaragua. A gentleman from New York spoke in defense of the Administration's rationing plans and in favor of subsidies for food producers. A gentleman with a rich South Carolina accent came out in favor of price control all down the line and of the elimination of unnecessary middlemen between producer and consumer.

From the gallery it was hard to trace any continuity in the arguments. Speech stood up after speech like peaks out of a mountain range drowned in mist. It took considerable effort to imagine what kind of ridges joined them together. Nothing seemed to gear into anything else. The speeches were good, wellphrased and welldelivered; during this particular segment of an afternoon they seemed the sincere opinions of sincere men, but the end result of the orderly and goodtempered proceedings was a sense of stagnation. It was hard to connect the voices with the faces or backs of the speakers. Voices tended to lose

themselves in a vague babble. Irresistible drowsiness was steal-
ing over me. I came to from a catnap with a start for fear the
guard had seen me nodding and would come down to throw me
out. Sleeping, reading, writing, and demonstrative behavior
are forbidden in the galleries of Congress. After that I sat up
straight and practiced deep breathing and tried to look as if I'd
been awake all along.

The corporal and the hermit had gone and their places had
been taken by two countryclubby looking men in light tweeds.
Down in the House a slender cool looking lady, with a finely cut
profile and her hair in a pompadour, was talking. She was pointing out that for many years this nation had had no foreign
policy, that we still had no foreign policy in spite of having been
at war for eighteen months. She suggested that the basis for a
foreign policy should be a military alliance with the British
Commonwealth of Nations.

The House listened with a good deal of attention. It was a
good speech, delivered in a crisp rather superior tone of voice.
Whether you agreed with it or not it contained concise and
definite statements that could be used as the basis of an argument. The galleries listened with rapt attention. The gallery
sitters seemed to have the feeling that this speech was an oc-
casion. Their sense of importance was heightened by being present in person at an event that would be headlines in the newspapers. This cool looking lady was a celebrity. Down on the
benches the younger Republicans seemed pleased. But looking
down on the grizzled heads and tweed shoulders of the oldtimers
seated below me I imagined I could see the hackles rise on many
a congressman's neck.

The speech ended in a general discussion of the Administration's foreign policy. A gentleman from Texas began the re-
buttal by laying a smoke screen of official doubletalk over the
argument. He made an effort to turn the whole thing into the
good clean fun of a mock battle between Democrats and Republicans. There were tart references to the clever gentlewoman's newness in these surroundings and to her beautiful and

devastating phrasing. The gentlewoman received a dignified spanking for bothering her pretty little head about such abstruse matters, but nobody answered the pert question she put to the distinguished member of the Committee on Foreign Affairs when she asked him to describe clearly and simply in what was left to him of a fiveminute period the foreign policy of the President of the United States.

When the argument suddenly merged into a discussion of the affairs of the unhappy island of Porto Rico, I felt all at once I'd been sitting there long enough and threaded my way up over the seats through what was only a scattered handful of listeners out of the gallery. At the door I noticed that the elderly doorkeeper was arguing with a creamyfaced page boy. I stopped beside them for a moment to listen.

The page thought the speech was wonderful. He thought the gentlewoman was wonderful. 'She said things a guy could understand,' he kept saying. 'Now why can't we go over there to say to the British how about it? just like she said.'

The doorkeeper shook his head sourly. 'She'll never get away with that sort of thing, not in this House,' he was saying. 'When you been around here as long as I have you'll know more about this sort of thing. You watch, they'll nip her right in the bud. You can't come out and say things like that.'

'But that's what's so wonderful. Nobody ever does.' The page's voice broke.

'Things don't work that way.'

'But they ought to,' whined the page, almost tearful.

'Well,' said the doorkeeper in a sententious drawl, 'she had the pleasure of hearing herself talk. If you ask me, that's all she's going to get out of it.'

3

Investigating Committee

This is a small committee room in the Senate Office Building divided into an inner and outer office by a row of bookcases

masked by green silk curtains. There's a large desk in the back
and two small ones facing each other in the outer part. There's
nothing else in the room but chairs. The electric light is overhead and mixes wanly with the daylight coming in through the
tall windows. I've been sitting there a long time beside the reception girl, across from a keenlooking young man with a long
nose working at the opposite desk waiting for the Secretary to
come back from a hearing. The stale airconditioning gives me a
feeling of being cut off from the world like the feeling I used to
have as a child kept in after school. The girl is carrying on a
whispered telephone conversation about going out in the country
with a girlfriend on Saturday. When I begin to stir uneasily in
my chair the young man at the desk gets to his feet and suggests
that as the Secretary is late maybe he'd better pitch in. He
begins to tell me about the committee's work.

One thing that has been kept in mind, he says, is the experience
of the Committee on the Conduct of the War during the Civil
War. These congressmen drove the commanders in the field
almost crazy, they had their fingers in every pie and balled
things up generally. 'Strategy and tactics we keep away from.
The aim of the committee has been to keep Congress informed
on the efficiency of war production. Our business is to be a
spotlight, not to recommend legislation. Our reports are for
information. Our real weapon is publicity.'

I had begun to bring up the point that maybe through such
committees Congress was developing new and valuable tentacles
with which it could deal with real happenings and real people.

Before the young man could answer the Secretary himself, a
husky tall lightskinned man with short sandy hair and a downright manner, hurried in and took me over.

'We started to work more than six months before Pearl Harbor to try to find out what was being done about national defence. We started by calling in the heads of departments to
testify and then we worked through procurement officers and
businessmen right back into the factories where the stuff is produced. We've plugged along the same line ever since. We want

to know what's being done, how well it's being done, and whether it's being done efficiently. If money and time are being wasted, why are they being wasted? To save money and time ourselves we take a subcommittee to the scene of the investigation instead of the old method of bringing the witnesses to Washington. Everything we've accomplished has been by publicity. If we say out loud that the building of army camps and cantonments was wretchedly planned at first and that more than two hundred and fifty million dollars were wasted right off the bat, then that makes the War Department more careful next time. We've done more by the mistakes we've averted than by what we've actually accomplished in uncovering fraud and incompetence.'

I brought up my theory about the new organs Congress needed to keep its end up in the face of the giant proliferation of the executive branch. He said maybe this was one of them. At any rate this committee had developed an effective method for getting at facts. Facts in this town were pretty goddam scarce. A fact had a hard time staying alive in a political atmosphere.

Once you had the facts, how could you put them to work?

Well, some things had happened in that direction. Long ago the committee had uncovered the fact that seventy percent of war production was in the hands of great corporations and that the procurement officers just naturally felt safer dealing with them than dealing with the small fellows. The tendency of all the regulations was to make things hard for the small independent manufacturer and easy for the great corporation. Recommendations of the committee had had, he thought, a good deal of influence in getting the facilities of the smaller plants used.

Wasn't small business cooked, anyway? Wouldn't that brave new world after the war the advertisers tell us about, be entirely in the hands of great cartels?

There certainly had been a very definite trend that way, he admitted. But he didn't think that small business need give up hope yet. The committee was trying to foster the idea that after the war there could be room for all kinds of interests, big, little, and middling, if businessmen would only keep the national interest separate from their own interests in their minds and learn to put it first.

'Honestly,' I asked him, 'do you yourself think there's any hope for small business after the war?'

He gave me a sharp steely questioning look and his face went blank. 'A good doctor never gives up hope till the undertaker comes ... A good deal of it depends on who our Doctor Schacht is in this country.'

'Well, who is our Doctor Schacht?'

He gave a short harsh laugh. 'Well, you'll just have to find out for yourself, Mister. You just stick around Capitol Hill.' I studied my notebook for a while. He started rattling with his pencil on the edge of his desk.

'National interest means the needs of the individuals who make up the three great segments of the population — labor, farming and business — doesn't it?'

'That's one way of putting it,' he said, yawning dreamily. I began to feel I'd been taking up too much of his time.

Cassandra Speaks

Down the hall I went to call on a Senator I knew. I told him I'd been talking about cartels. 'Cartels,' he shouted, staring in front of him as if at some invisible and ghastly scene of carnage across the room. 'They are sweeping everything before them. Our society is headed towards monopoly, restraint of competition, enforced scarcity on a vast scale ... And will the Administration take any measures to stop it? I have most regretfully come to the conclusion that the answer is, No, it will not.'

He looked at his wristwatch and suggested that I come down in the elevator with him. The Senate was convening at eleven. This was going to be a busy day. 'One more stage in the reaction,' he said mysteriously. 'The passing of the antistrike bill over the veto is on the cards for today.'

The elevator, run by a man in a wellpressed light gray suit, who had a carnation in his buttonhole, took us down to the basement.

When we stepped out, my friend pressed a pushbutton in the wall opposite, marked in large letters 'Senators Only,' and we walked around through a curving plaster tunnel to the little monorail car, with its superannuated toyshop air of something thought up by Jules Verne and exhibited as the hope of the future at the St. Louis World's Fair, which trundles the Senators through a short tunnel to the Senate elevator. 'I gather, Senator, that you're pessimistic about cartels?' I mumbled, as I settled down in the little car beside him. 'Yes, sir, I am pessimistic. It is a very terrible thing to see everything we have fought for all these years going to ruin and destruction. Let me tell you that there are still some men who have not given up the battle. I have been defending the cause of the people against the cause of monopoly year after year. I intend to go on defending it. The fight's not over yet.'

The car came smoothly to a stop. We nodded to the ancient mechanic in a blue uniform and made for the elevator. The elevator was packed with Senators. There were greetings and introductions. When we got out at the floor level the Senator cornered a small pageboy. 'Son,' he said to him with a flourish, 'this gentleman is a very particular friend of mine. I want you to take him up in the gallery and to place him in a seat away from any of these pillars or obstructions, a seat from which he can have a full view of everything that takes place.'

The Hill Becomes Volcanic

Though the girders supporting the ceiling give the Senate Chamber the same look of transition the House has, the old desks are still there, and it has less the air of having been in the hands of an interior decorator. The Senate Chamber seems lighter and the figures of the Senators loom larger than do the crowded congressmen in the House. This particular morning the Senators have an easy and wellslept look in their light clothes. They look like men who have enjoyed good solid leisurely break-fasts. The clerk is calling the roll. Senators are coming in, in twos and threes, stopping in the aisles to exchange a few words or stooping to lean over the back of a seated colleague; they form small knots in the rear and to the sides of the presiding officer's rostrum, nod heads over papers and scatter again. There's a good deal of stretching and slow moving around. They move rather ponderously as if they had difficulty in lifting their feet off the carpet. You are reminded of groups of bears on a fine morning in the bearpit at a zoo.

The proceedings gather momentum as the morning dribbles away. Communications are recorded or laid on the table. The Senator from Virginia announces ceremonies to commemorate the Jefferson Bicentennial in Charlottesville the coming fourth of July. The address he has prepared is included in the record, but, thank God, not read. Gradually a full dress debate is getting started on the perennial subject of subsidies to food producers. There's great opposition to the Administration. The clerk reads an amendment cutting subsidies out from the pending bill. An amendment is offered to the amendment and an amendment to that amendment. It becomes obvious that strong feelings are stirring behind these gentlemen's ponderous courtesies.

A letter from the Secretary of Commerce defending the Administration's subsidy program is introduced into the record. Suddenly the Senator from Missouri is on his feet. He has a paper in his hand. He is complaining that one of these letters was placed on his desk while he had stepped out of the Chamber for a moment. 'It was not even folded.' There was a quiver of irritation in his voice. 'Mr. President, I say that that is an exhibition of indecent lobbying by the Secretary of Commerce . . . I say that the Secretary of Commerce sat out there in the lobby yesterday afternoon, conferring with Senators as they passed by to try to raise some doubt in the mind of someone, any doubt in the mind of anyone, as to the wisdom of the course the Senate was about to pursue . . . Mr. President, I say that I think this is an indecent practice. I think it is a practice forbidden by law. In all truth and candor I think this is a practice for which the Secretary could fairly be impeached by the House of Representatives, and if he were impeached I should vote to convict him . . .'

The Senator from Texas shakes his white ducktails and lifts up his voice in defence of the Secretary of Commerce. The Senator from Alabama agrees with him. The Senator from Colorado announces that it was he who asked to have the offending letter sent purely for information and who introduced it into the record. The Senator from Missouri says he never asked for such a letter. He takes the still unfolded paper off his desk and shakes it. He goes on that everybody must have seen the Secretary of Commerce sitting there on a couch all yesterday afternoon. There had been no secret about it. The Secretary is a large man. 'Anybody can see him with the naked eye. It is not necessary to put on glasses to see him as you pass by. So as I saw him out there buttonholing Senators, whispering in their ears, I knew exactly what he was doing . . .'

The Senator from Alabama tries to spread oil and balm. He is delighted, he says, that the Senator from Missouri says the Secretary is a large man. He himself considers the Secretary a large man in many ways. He hoped that is what the Senator has in mind when he uses the adjective 'large.' He adds that there had been a luncheon yesterday in an office up here in the Capitol and that the Secretary had been invited, but that little of the conversation had been on the subject of subsidies. Another Senator injects a little ruefully the remark that he hadn't gotten in on the lunch, but says he considers that the Secretary's behavior has been perfectly proper.

The Senator from Alabama returns to the defence of the Secretary of Commerce. At a time when there has been so much complaint against the bureaus and agencies at the other end of the Avenue, that they didn't cooperate with Congress, he thought the Secretary of Commerce was much to be commended for his attitude towards Congress.

The debate got back into the groove of the amendments. Senators were drifting away from their seats. It was lunch time.

While I waited for a Senator who had asked me to lunch, I sat in the dark lobby on the lower floor under the crawling design of ornate red and gilt arabesques on the vault, against which the faces of presentday American politicians, lobbyists, newspaper men, visitors, and our clothes and our manners, looked strangely incongruous.

Did the man I'd been talking to that morning mean that Jesse Jones was the Doctor Schacht of the regime? I was asking myself. He'd dug the New Deal's grave all right, was he doing the same job for small business? And wasn't it democracy's grave they were all digging? Was there any use in finding the criminal, dragging out the scapegoat? The Greco-Roman stage setting of the Capitol was filling my mind, as it was intended to by its designers, with notions out of ancient history. Cicero thought he had saved selfgovernment in Rome when he got rid of Catiline; all he did was to prepare the way for Caesar.

The Senator who had asked me to lunch was already standing in the arched entrance waiting for me. He looked much younger than his age, with his round glasses and his shortcut hair and his student's manner. We walked down the stairs to the diningroom in the basement.

The Senate diningroom, with its white starched napkins and tablecloths and its elderly colored waiters in white coats, still has that oldfashioned New World air that is so pleasant around the Capitol. There's something plain and dignified and self-respecting in the manners of the guards and of the elevator men and of the rambling citizens roaming around the building, looking at the pictures and statues and eating in the public sections of the lunchrooms, something that goes with the sense of civic dignity and spaciousness scaled to the human figure, that the architects tried to impart to the dome and the colonnades and the crude painfully worked and earnestly stiff carving on the old part of the building. It's pleasant to sit in the Senate dining-room. It makes you feel like an American of two generations ago, when all the institutions and hopes that seem so precarious now, were still among the unchangeable verities. The food is plain and good, oldtime American dishes. It reminds you of the food you used to get in station restaurants as a child in the early years of the century when there still was such a thing as distinctive American cookery.

As we ate we talked about the drifting eddy of cross purposes Washington became when the New Deal collapsed. It hardly seemed possible, we were saying, that our immense production for war could be directed from here. And yet somewhere in the welter of frustration, recrimination, interdepartmental politics, useful decisions were being made and carried out. Some way or other the stuff was being produced and taken where it was needed. To accomplish that miracle, the nation's energy was draining off into war. There just wasn't the energy left for anything else.

The trouble was that you couldn't divide the war from the nation. Successful waging of the war depended on health at home. This was the afternoon when the mine strike situation would come to a head. The President was going to return the antistrike bill with a veto. Congress probably would pass it over the veto. What would that do to national unity? None of this, the Senator said, need have happened if the Administration had retained the momentum of the old New Deal days. Whichever way the vote went, the Senator said, all he could see ahead was rifts and more rifts.

After lunch I sat in another arabesque lobby at the other end of the building, talking with another Senator, a Southerner this time. I was asking him if he didn't feel that the Administration, while conducting the war, so most people admitted, very well, was losing touch with the folks back home. This was a mighty confusing time, he said. Some days he felt dismayed, and some days he didn't feel so bad. This coal strike business was mighty bad. Ought never to have been allowed to happen. Never would have happened if the President had been properly advised about it. He didn't feel they knew at the White House how intense the feeling through the country was against labor. Keeping in touch with your constituents was the most important thing in the world. He himself, he said, made it a point to spend a few days every month down in his home state. A feller had to trim his fences. They would have the hide off him down there

in no time if he didn't. Why, he even prepared recorded addresses to be broadcast once a week from a local radio station.
This was no time to take any chances.

I had still another Senator to look up, and was waiting for him
in the little niche right off the entrance to the Senate floor when
he blundered out through the door. At first he didn't recognize
me when I spoke to him. He shook his head as if to bring his
eyes into focus. I must forgive him, he said. He was extremely
agitated. His head was spinning. He was very confused. He'd
have to put off our conversation because the President's veto
message had just come and he must return to the floor immediately.

He bolted back into the Chamber and I ran up the stairs to
the visitors' gallery. There was considerable briskness in the
usually lackadaisical air of the corridors. The old man who
opened my coat to look for weapons had a pleased inscrutable
look like the look of the boxoffice girl on opening night when the
show begins to look like a hit. The gallery was crowded. By
great good luck I managed to get into a corner seat that was not
behind a post. Young men, old men, welldressed women, girl
secretaries, heavyfeatured lobbyists were sitting on the edges
of their seats. The press gallery was full. An unusually large
number of Senators were sitting in stiff attitudes of attention at
their desks on the floor below.

The Senator from Texas stood well back in the middle of the
Chamber, his white head tilted on his shoulders so that the long
wisps of hair were ground into his collar. His jaw was thrust out,
his mouth tight closed so that the curved lines that joined the
flanges of his nose to the turned down corners of his mouth were
deeply accentuated. He was asking the presiding officer that
the President's message might be laid before the Senate. The
Senator from Alabama asked the Senator from Texas to yield,
so that he might suggest the absence of a quorum.

While the roll was being called, the tension mounted. Men
answered to their names sharply and with an air of decision.
They sat stiffly in their seats. Their voices were tense. It was

like the roll call in a company of soldiers about to move up to the front. They were in for it now. They'd made the decisions that would end or make many a man's political career. Labor and antilabor were both forces that had long organized memories. The vote that many a man was going to cast would mean re-election or defeat.

A quorum was announced. The Chair laid before the Senate the message from the President vetoing the antistrike bill. When the veto message had been read, the presiding officer put the question:

'Shall the bill pass, the objections of the President of the United States to the contrary notwithstanding?'

It was the big moment for the Senator from Texas.

'Mr. President,' his voice had a low bellow to it like a bull heard in the distance. 'I am sorely disappointed. The Senate is sorely disappointed. The House, I am sure, is sorely disappointed. The people of the United States are sorely disappointed. Every sailor and soldier on the seas and on the land and in the air is sorely disappointed ... The President has a right under the Constitution to veto a bill, and the Senate has a right to pass a bill over the President's veto. I hope the Senate will exercise its high constitutional privilege.' There was applause. Voices broke out. In the gallery there was an occasional handclap and stirring and scuffling of feet.

The Senator from New Mexico was joining his voice to that of the Senator from Texas. The Senator from Wisconsin made a point of order that the Senate was not in order.

The gavel rapped. There was no need for motions, the question came up automatically under the Constitution. The roll was called. Fiftysix voted yea, twentyfive voted nay, fifteen abstained from voting, and there were a number of absences.

By this time the Vice President was in the chair. In an expressionless resonant voice he announced: 'On this question, more than twothirds of the Senate having voted in the affirmative, the bill on reconsideration is passed, the objections of the President of the United States to the contrary notwithstanding.'

Something snapped like a rubber band stretched too tight. The galleries were as full of stir of people leaving as the bleachers in the last inning of a dull baseball game. On the floor Senators were slumping back in their seats like rowers at the end of a race. In the crowd of civilians and men in uniform pouring down the stairway from the gallery there was a feeling of exultation. They'd seen the home team score against the visiting team from the other end of Pennsylvania Avenue. Most of them seemed to feel it was their home team that had won.

4

The Land of Plenty

In the hotel palmgarden music shrills above a din of tongues like the racket of an aviary in the zoo. The air smells of rolls and sizzling butter and cocktails and cigarette smoke. Packed in beside a little wicker table between other tables, all crowded with rattling groups of dressedup men and women, my friend and I have to talk loud to hear each other above the racket.

'Who is the man whose historic function, as the Marxists call it, corresponds to Doctor Schacht's in Germany?' I am asking.

'You're always asking about personalities,' he complains. 'Personality is only important when it's relevant to the machinery.'

'But in the long run how the job is done depends on what the man is like.'

'How about saying that the job makes the man? The job of supply for the army is getting done all right. The army at least has men in this town who know how to get it done. Their job is seeing that we get places fastest with the mostest men and equipment, and they are doing it.'

'But on the way the job is done depends the shape our society will have after it's over?'

'You mean that as they do the job they ought to remember it takes wealth to create the money they are spending?'

'And that if the history of the United States has proved anything it has proved that liberty creates wealth ... I mean,' I said, shouting above the din, 'the turnover to war is reshaping the nation.'

'They don't know about things like that in the army. They've got to get things done. What we have is some extremely efficient organizers on a short term basis. They know how to get the most money out of Congress and they know where to spend it.'

'That means they can't help building up big business.'

'Sure ... They are no more worried about where the money comes from or the future liberties of the average citizen than the hunters on the great plains were worried about where the buffalo came from ... They were brought up to think of this as the land of plenty.'

Plans

This flyer couldn't have been more than twentyfour years old. He was a thin, seriousfaced young man. He'd just gotten over a bout of fever he'd picked up on a Pacific island. Yes, he said, he found trying to get settled in a place like this was pretty complicated. Maybe it was because he was going to get married soon, but all the details of life did seem more complicated to him than they used to when he used to wish he was home out there in the theatres ... Out there they all wanted to find things at home just like they'd left them. They liked the country the way it was. That was one reason they were so sore at labor, they felt laborleaders were trying to change things. Did that make any sense? ... One thing really had surprised him since he'd been home. That was how little people talked or thought about what was going to happen after the war. In New Guinea there'd been all kinds of discussion groups. There'd been great enthusiasm for this sort of discussion. They had let in the enlisted men because they showed so much interest in what the plans were for after the war. Their attitude was they didn't want any changes made till they got home. They all wanted to have a hand in

things. But here in Washington nobody seemed to feel that way.
It was natural that around the office where the work was so
pressing and interesting, most of the talk would be shop but it
was really surprising to many of the fellows coming back from
the theatres, or at least to some of those he knew — one man's
experience was pretty limited you know — to find so little excitement at home about plans for after the war.

Practical Man

In the anteroom an elderly man with a hammer under his arm
was standing in front of the receptionist's desk holding out a
large framed photograph, taken from the air, of the dark land of
Kiska between shining sea and mist, and of transports and destroyers in formation headed towards the island. The receptionist was telling him he couldn't hang it now, there was someone in
there. If he'd lend her his hammer, she would hang it herself
later. 'I'd never get it back,' he said, shaking his head. 'I'll
come back later.' He leaned over and stood the big photograph
carefully up against the wall.

When whoever was in there left, I was ushered into a large
bright office, where the man I had come to see sat with his back
to a broad window open on the Potomac and the white buildings
among green trees across the river and the broad morning sky
above. He had a round light head and a large pale rather irregular face. When I said something about his being pretty
busy, he smiled and said, 'Well, not so busy as last year. Then,
we were in a jam getting all this started. Now, the team is in
the field. For better or for worse, the training program is
launched. Then, we didn't have anything. We had to make
everything up as we went along.'

'What kind of a country are we going to have after the war?'
I asked him.

The question didn't seem to faze him.

'A great country,' he answered smiling. 'Two things have surprised me in the course of this work. One has been discovering

the deep traditional selfless patriotism of the old line army men
... I always knew it was there but I never knew how deep it
went before . . And the other was the discovery that we have
military brains in this country. We hadn't shown any particular
sign of them since the Civil War. I suppose we didn't have any
use for them . . . That's why I don't feel too discouraged when
people go around hanging crepe about how we'll never solve the
postwar problems. Well, we found the brains for the army when
we needed them. Maybe when it becomes absolutely necessary
we'll find the brains for the postwar problems too.'

5

The Architecture of the White House

I met my friend at the corner of Lafayette Square. We drove
out in his car to his place across the Potomac. He wanted to
do some work on his garden. While we hoed the hard red dirt
between the rows of corn and beans, I got to asking him what it
was like in the White House these days. At first, he didn't say
anything. I was afraid he wasn't going to talk. Washington
officials don't much like to talk to outsiders whether they are
friends or not. When he reached the end of his row, he leaned
on his hoe and said:

'Well, you know, there's always that feeling of dignified calm.
It comes from the architecture, light pouring in through tall
windows off green lawns shaded by big trees; it always seems
quiet and serene there as if nothing outside mattered.'

'That's Jefferson again, the influence of Monticello.'

We got off our subject talking about the stately setting for
the young republic that Jefferson had imagined more completely
than any other man. You felt it in the Capitol, you felt it in the
Treasury, you felt a last distortion of it even in the pompous
burlesque of a Greco-Roman style of the Hoover period buildings
along Constitution Avenue. But most of all you felt it at the
White House. His design for the building was rejected, but
Jefferson did more than any other man to launch the style in

which the building was finally built, a style that expressed an aristocratic kind of pride in republican simplicity.

As we talked and hoed every now and then a plane passing low overhead drowned out our words. The hot blue air over the Potomac valley was full of planes. As they banked in the distance they glinted like minnows in a brook.

'I wonder how much that feeling influences the occupants?'

'It does,' my friend said. 'I believe it does.'

Then I brought out the question that had been in the back of my head all morning:

'Does that help to keep the President out of touch with the country?'

'Is he? I wonder. It isn't like it was before his old private secretary got sick. She was an extraordinary woman. She had a knack of keeping the human side of things uppermost ... something about the way she arranged the papers to go on his desk ... she was pretty conscious that he needed to have the channels kept open for him so that he should be in touch with what real people did and thought and felt. It's not like that now.'

Hoeing made us run water like fountains. Gradually we stripped off our clothes as we worked, until we were working in bathingtrunks. The sun was so hot it made your ears hum and red spots swim before your eyes. The clay was red and hard, but out of it corn, beans, broccoli, lettuce, peas grew strong in astonishingly rich and varied greens.

'Do you have a feeling that the whole place is under a bell-glass? I mean the White House.'

My friend didn't answer. We set the hose so that it would sprinkle the lawn and went into the house for showers. While we were dressing slowly in front of a fan so as not to start sweating again, I asked him whether the quality — intellectual, moral, put it any way — well, whether the human quality of the people who went in and out of the White House hadn't deteriorated in the last few years. Outside of the army and navy, outside of purely war matters he thought perhaps it had. We mustn't forget how much of the country's best energy had gone into the war.

A certain restraint was growing up between us. I rephrased my question, but he wouldn't rise to it any more.

We decided we'd better go out to have a glass of beer and a sandwich. Along the main road, by this time pretty well sprinkled with cars, there were a number of white and glass fancy-roofed luncheon places. Every one of them was packed to the doors with citizens sweating in clean Sunday shirtsleeves, and their families, and service men in light uniforms, and girls in pale colored dresses. At last we came to one that advertised curb service. We stood in the shade of its awning facing a little teasing breeze until we could waylay a little girl hurrying a tray of beer-bottles and glasses out to an old sedan packed with the squirming and screeching and wisecracks of a bunch of sailors and their girls. We induced her to treat us as if we were a car and to bring us out a tray. As we stood there munching and drinking, the great graygreen bombers kept passing overhead. It was like being under a bridge on a main road full of traffic. Across the back lots we could see the civilian transports circling to land at the airfield. My friend made a vague gesture with his hand. 'That's where the big swells land. They come in by bomber from . . . from everywhere . . . and hurry right to the White House.'

Close to the President

It was late afternoon. The man I had come to call on in his comfortable apartment overlooking the Avenue greeted me in his bathrobe, apologizing for it with the explanation that he couldn't keep his clothes on, it was so damn hot. Coppery clouds were building up over Georgetown, giving a reddish glow, as if it were heated from within, to the asphalt of the street. He handed me a dripping glass of beer. 'I had to bring this in on my back. You can't get anything delivered,' he said, and we started chatting about the District. Did I know that the old gentleman who ran the brewery was still alive? He was over a hundred. A living advertisement for his product and for the healthiness of the city. Maybe people complained about the Washington weather too much. If people lived to be a hundred it couldn't be too bad.

Did this man, who was what is known in the press as 'close to the White House,' feel, I asked, that the war had cut the President off from the country? 'Every time he takes a trip,' he answered, a little aggressively, 'he comes back very much refreshed. Maybe he's a little like the Greek mythical giant who lost his strength as soon as he ceased to touch the earth . . . I think he's quite conscious of the importance of keeping that touch.'

'Can he do it? Can he get away from official channels enough to do it?'

'Well, he still sees his old friends . . . all sorts of people turn up who have no connection with politics or business of any kind — family friends, legal friends from New York, casual acquaintances. He can't give them quite as much time as he used to. But he certainly sees them. Some people feel that he gives them too much time . . .'

'It must be hard for the man in the White House to keep in touch, though. It's so much easier for people to tell him what he wants to hear. I should think the longer he stayed there, the harder it would be for anybody to tell him any bad news.'

'That would be true of an ordinary man. A man has naturally to be a genius at that kind of thing. I think this man is . . . How about another glass? A bird can't fly on one wing, you know.'

Press Conference

About the only change war has brought to the procedure when you go to the President's press conference is that the secret service men have to find your name on a list at the gate before they let you walk across the drive to the entrance in the West Wing. If you are not a regular attendant, you are ushered into the long panelled room filled up by the great mahogany table

Aguinaldo gave. You sit there remembering the bronze general on his rearing horse taking off his hat to all of us whom you walked past as you came and the sailors talking to girls on the benches of Lafayette Square, and the pigeons drinking at the drinking fountains, lifting their pink bills and puffing out their rainbowcolored breasts and stretching their necks to let the cool water run down their gullets; remembering the stately simplicity of the main porch of the White House, the spacing of the trees, the box bushes in tubs you got a glimpse of as you passed, the Augustan afterglow in the style of ornament of the portal you came in by. It's still the sort of thing Jefferson meant. In this long room you are sitting in, the panelling has a certain dignity; there's a hellenic reminder in the dentated cornicing. The minutes pass. You sit on a red couch, one of a row of men you don't know. From the hallway outside comes a faint babble from the regular newspapermen in the hall. You go over your notes. You jot down appointments, you try to remember your expenses, that taxicab, the check at dinner. The minutes drag on.

All at once the newspapermen are pouring down the hall. A suave tall gentleman in a cutaway has his arm across the door. As the crowd thins, he lets it drop. We come in at the tail end of the procession into the oval bluegray office. The brownish velvet curtains are new. The pictures of boats are the same, the flag and the eagle. Across the shoulders, past the ears of the newspapermen who got there ahead of you, you look down on the President of the United States seated at his desk.

On either side behind his chair stand secret service men. One of them is a burly middleaged man with a red beefy face, the other is a squarejawed expressionless young man who might be a floorwalker in a department store. Beyond you can see the green lawn sloping down the hill to the great enclosing trees. Lustrous in the crosslights behind the President's head, stands a large globe of the world. It is against the blue Pacific Ocean that you see his head uptilted.

As always he's handsomer when you see him face to face, than he appears in his photographs. He hasn't changed so much since I saw him seven years ago in the early days of greensickness and accomplishment of the New Deal. His hair is grayer. He still has the fine nose and forehead, the gray eyes blandly unabashed under the movable eyebrows. Looking down from this angle you don't notice the broad stump speaker's mouth, the heavy jowl.

Today he looks well rested. He's in high good humor. At breakfast they brought him the news of the capture of an island. The reporters shoot questions up over each other's shoulders. So long as it's on the foreign wars it's fun. His manner is boyishly gay. He shoots the answers back with zest, blowing out his cheeks the way he does when searching for a word, lifting his eyebrows to make the questioner feel he has all his attention, man to man, for a moment; cosily scratching an ear or the back of his head as he formulates one of his sparkling improvisations. The boys are being made to feel at home in the headmaster's study.

It's only when rationing, the coal strike, price control, come up that a frown appears on his forehead. He begins to talk about deep water. His manner becomes abrupt. A querulous note of vexation comes into his voice. He won't talk about these things. Congress will have to decide them, he says. His face takes on an air of fatigue, there's a sagging look under the eyes of having been up late at his desk, of sleepless nights.

'Thank you, Mr. President,' a voice says. The President's gray face is hidden by the younger fresher unworried faces of the reporters turning to make for the door.

Only a Handful of Men

When you have an appointment with someone in the East Wing of the White House you have to go first to a little glass sentry box set up in the middle of the short barred off street that divides the White House grounds from the Treasury Building. The secret service men check your name with their list. When you have been identified, you walk past the barricade and up the low steps to the porch. In an airy corridor a few men in khaki are lounging on a rushbottomed colonial bench. A sergeant ushers you into a little office where a blueeyed girl with a pompadour tells you that the man you have come to see has been detained, and won't you please wait a minute, and hands you the morning's *New York Times*.

It's quiet and cool there in the small modestly furnished office. You read through the news columns that interest you, and then you read the book reviews, and then you read the financial page, and at last you turn back to the editorials. You've read all the letters and are starting in on the sports when the young lady, who from time to time has encouraged you with accounts of how things are progressing in the inner office, at length tells you with a smile that you can go in now.

The man you have come to see is sitting at a desk in another small office with a window behind him. He is a tall stooping man with a high forehead and nose glasses. For a flitting instant there's a recollection of Woodrow Wilson's long pale stubborn face. You can see that he has been ill. There's a waxy almost transparent look about his skin. At first he has a little difficulty finding his words as he talks. He stammers a little. There's no side about him. He doesn't talk like a man who's holding back half his mind. You feel that he trusts your respect for the seriousness and selflessness of his purpose, that he feels that if it is his purpose it must be a good one.

The place has an air of seclusion like a den in a large house in the country. It's quiet in the office. Perhaps you only imagine the faint hum of energy like a generating plant. Is it real or imagined, the feeling like terror that comes from being close to a source of power over the destinies of many men? As he talks, he keeps looking away from you across the green sheltered lawn towards the pedimented main building of the White House.

You have to start him off with questions. They are the old clumsy questions. Is there a rift appearing between the White House and the country? Is it possible for the commander in chief in a global war, the man a Southern Senator has said his dearest wish was to nominate for President of the United States of the World, to keep in touch with the picayune unglobal needs and aspirations and reactions of the people of the fortyeight states of the Union on this segment of a continent? The questions aren't very well put. You don't have much confidence in questions anyway. Nobody ever learned anything by asking questions.

The man you have come to see is patient about the questions. He doesn't evade them or bristle at them. You feel that he doesn't hear them. Some time ago he made up his mind and closed its windows on the world. He starts talking about how the running of the war is necessarily in the hands of a few men. Only they know the facts. The President knows things nobody else knows. A great deal of his time, a great deal of his thinking, has to be on the level of the four leaders of the United Nations — Roosevelt, Churchill, Stalin, the Generalissimo. There are decisions that only these four men can make. Below that is the level of general staffs, of coordination of campaigns, the worldwide allocation of munitions, Lend Lease. The facts upon which these decisions were based are known only to a handful of men.

Several times he used the phrase 'only a handful of men.'

I mentioned Congress and strikes and food production. He frowned. A lot of that was politics. The press was always puffing up the importance of domestic problems. Problems made a great splash at first and gradually they were solved and people forgot them. In the White House they were bored with this way of looking at things. If the war were brought to a successful issue, all these troublesome things would fall into line. Did I realize how much work had to go into every separate decision as to what munitions were to go to what front, for an example, how much time had to be taken up on the level of the four leaders? Only a handful of men had the information on which to base an opinion. It was boring to come back to the petty misunderstandings of domestic problems. They should wait until victory. With the victory all these things would fall into line.

'How?' the small question was in my mind but I didn't ask it. It was time to go. He had talked pleasantly and patiently and he was a very busy man. I said goodbye.

As I walked out, past the limp guards, enjoying the civilian-in-uniform look these young men still had in spite of years of military training, and past the broadfaced secret service men in the little glass shelter and out onto the hurrying noontime crowds and cars and taxicabs of the street that the flailing sunshine lashed like rain, I pictured the man I had been talking to walking back with long unsteady strides across the secluded lawn to the central part of the White House where life went on on the level of the four leaders.

6

Departure

It's dark under the great soapcolored Roman vaults of the Union Station. Not much daylight gets in through the grimed windows. The electric bulbs have the redeyed look of having been up all night. So many people have absorbed all the light. The floor, the benches, the entrances are dark with shifting masses of people. About half of them are young men in uniform. Negro families are spread around the benches. Cues fan out in shifting tentacles from every ticketwindow, from the information booths, from the newsstands, from the telegraph offices. In the telephone room men sitting on upended suitcases wait glumly for a chance at the booths. In the dim blurred light of the glass trainshed sailors in whites with their heavy canvas seabags on their shoulders are being mustered into ranks. A stream of men, women, and children is flowing sluggishly down the platform towards the New York train. No seats in the coaches. Everything booked in the Pullmans. Just as I'm sliding into a place at a table in the diner, I see a man I know.

'Hello,' he says, as he shakes hands. 'You ought to have called me up sooner. I bet you've seen nothing but liberals.' He grins. He has protruding brown eyes and a brown round face with a big jaw in it. We sit down side by side. 'I used to think I was a liberal once. But they've turned out no good.' He made a downward gesture with his hand. 'I don't mean they don't mean well. But they've proved themselves unable to put their ideas across.

They don't stick together. They're not coherent. They aren't tough enough to survive in the battle of Washington, they're too yellow to slug it out man to man, they're not efficient. My quarrel with a lot of these New Deal agencies is they don't deliver. I been in all of them. I'm working for the army now, thank God . . .' He suddenly rubbed his hand across his forehead. 'Here I am spilling my guts and I haven't even had a drink yet. Hey, waiter!'

We ordered some drinks and lunch. 'Well, go on!' he shouted above the thumping of the train. 'What have they told you? You spill something now.'

'For sheer human suffering the foxholes of Bataan have nothing on the foxholes of Washington.'

'"Don't cheer, men, the poor fellows are dying."' He threw back his head and laughed uproariously.

'In all the conversations I've heard for and against this man and that man, nobody has ever mentioned whether he was doing a good job. Efficiency never seems to come up in Congress or in any of the powwows I've listened in on at all. It's all — Is he right politically? Has he the right ideas?'

'Hell, that's natural. This town's a vast clearing house. There's no real work done here.'

'But there must be some people doing an efficient job of paper work.'

'The country does the job. Washington is no place for bright-eyed idealists, even if their ideal is efficient work.'

'Why not?'

'The stakes are too high . . . Has there ever been a time since Cleopatra's barge when the stakes were so high? . . . Ever read about the Roman Empire? Since the days of Caesar and Crassus and Pompey there's never been a time when so much direct power was within the grasp of a few men's hands.'

'All the more need to work in the public interest.'

'Interests in the plural is the thing in this town. Lately, I've had a good deal to do with the British. The difference between our boys and the Britishers is that the Britishers always put England first and the old firm second. With our boys, it's the other way around.'

'Do you honestly think so?'

He nodded vigorously over his plate. 'Look at your idealist. Look what happens to him. He comes down here in the public interest. That's what he thinks, anyway. If he has any brains he's probably had theories and spouted them around at some time in his life. The Dies committee gets on his trail. Right away he's a red. Maybe he's been a tulip fancier or gone in swimming without any clothes on. He's a crackpot. He's a nudist. The Kerr committee makes him miserable digging up his past. He either runs to cover and stops trying to do anything or else his boss puts him in cold storage. He's not a party man. Say he's just out to save the American people some money. The first time anybody needs to be fed to the wolves, out he goes on his fanny. What comeback has he? A letter to the *Nation*. If he's a real conspiratorial Communist the party protects him. He sits pretty. If he's a crook he's got partners in crime. An unattached individual citizen has no more chance than a man trying to fight a tank with a croquet mallet. We live in a world of machines. Some machines are made of steel; others are made up of men.'

'Isn't a good deal of the government machinery antiquated? I don't mean that selfgovernment is antiquated. It hasn't really begun yet.'

'Antiquated! They've got an engine built for a side-wheeler, one of those old excursion boats, and they're trying to fly an airplane with it. What do you expect?'

From the train whenever the line passed through a town or near a group of houses we could see Victory gardens, carefully tilled plots rich in curling ranks of corn, stately poles of beans, fat cabbages, lacy patches of potatoes in flower.

'Look how well we cultivate gardens,' I said. 'I bet half the people growing vegetables this year never had a hoe in their hands. They are doing a hell of a good job.'

'Sure, but don't forget that the knowhow exists. Any fool can read a book and plant a garden. The science of government ain't.'

'What about the Constitution?'

He suddenly looked tired. 'This is over my head ... I'm a realist,' he said in a shaky voice. 'All I meant, I guess, was that the present gang has shot its bolt. We got to have a new outfit, new leadership, new ideas.'

Beyond Baltimore when we came out into the sunlight after the tunnel, the train passed between vast low factory buildings prettily camouflaged with clouds and hills and pictures of trees and houses.

'Now that's a good job,' he cried. 'My work's part of that, that makes me feel good.'

Across immense runways new fighting planes stretched in ranks as far as you could see. 'I don't care whether it's just for war or not. It's wonderful ... I was born in the old country and I know it's freedom we are fighting for. You can't separate any of it from freedom here and in England ... If freedom could find a way of running its own affairs ... that would be democracy.'

Washington, D.C., Summer, 1943

THE TRAIN was a local. At this particular dingy brick station it waited a long time. Through the smudged windows of the daycoach you could see a string of coal cars, the black tipple of a mine standing up in the fold of a hill beyond the bleak storefronts of the main street of the little town and behind the tipple the plumcolored hills streaked with blue coal smoke. On the worn brick pavement of the platform under the window, a group of people was gathered round a redfaced young soldier. He'd been home on leave and they had come to say goodbye. There was a grayfaced stocky man in a dusty black hat with coal dust in his brows and lashes, who was evidently the father. There was the mother, a dumpy pansyfaced woman with little wrinkles radiating from the corners of her eyes and mouth, looking quite crushed under a Sundaybest coalscuttle hat of black velours. There was a lanky careworn man in his shirtsleeves with two front teeth missing, who might be the older brother. There were some embarrassed small boys and an overdressed yellowhaired baby girl led by a noisy busty woman in a picture hat, who was probably the sister-in-law. And standing a little apart there was a skinny largeeyed thincheeked girl with skimpy blond hair who didn't seem to know what to do with a large new white handbag with spangly embroidery on it. The children looked forlorn except for the small boy who was carrying the helmet, but the older people were all aggressively cheerful. The soldier was a wellbuilt young man who had the air of being the smartest and the best nourished and the best educated member of the family. He waved his arms and jumped about and kept up a continuous rattle of talk. Every sentence seemed to end with, 'And didn't we have a time?' He told stories. He teased the kids. He grabbed his sister-in-law and started to show her how to do a new dance step. He ribbed his old man. He slapped his mother on the back. All the while he and the girl with the white handbag never dared look at one another.

When the brakeman shouted 'All aboard,' and the engine bell started to clang, he grabbed his pack off the ground, took the tin hat off his little brother's head, and boarded the train with one leap. As he came down the aisle of the crowded coach the old man with drooping white mustaches and a kind of a Civil War veteran look in the seat in front of mine made room for him by letting him slip past into the place by the open window. When he leaned out as the train began to move his broad khaki shoulders filled the window. He kept on laughing and shouting and even started telling a rambling story about an Irish sergeant who lost his boots. He never got it finished. The train was rattling fast past the shacks and shanties on the edge of town before he pulled his head back into the car. He straightened his cap and sat there staring ahead of him, his face set and stiff and colorless.

The old man had been watching him. 'Son,' he said in a low conversational voice as if they'd been talking together for a long time. 'It reminds me of a story I used to hear when I was younger, about a famous clown ... I don't rightly remember his name ... a famous clown in the circus, who went through the whole show one night with a telegram in his pocket, and nobody in that immense audience noticed a thing. Indeed, some folks thought he was funnier than usual that night, and all the time he had a telegram in his pocket telling him that his little girl, his only child, was dead.'

CHAPTER II

The Men Who Dig the Coal

T HE MAN who was driving brought the car to a sudden stop opposite the tipple when the track hidden in deep grass seemed about to plunge into a gulch full of crumbling slate and refuse dumped from the miners' shacks. It was one of those September days when the sky is moulded out of bright concrete, cobalt blue shading to violet. A few great cottony clouds stained with a little ochre and indigo stood motionless overhead as if trapped inside the shining dome. We had driven out from the smoking industrial city, with its bridges over leaden rivers, its endless ranks of stacks, its black rows of houses scattered helterskelter over steep short hills, and come out of a tunnel into an intensely green gorge that had widened into hilly pastures and cornfields. After we had turned into a side road up over the flank of a hill, the trees had begun to look stringy and brown, and the fields to take on a starved eroded look. At the top of the hill there had been a filling-station, some stores and beersaloons, and then the mournful ranks of twofamily frame houses. We had wound through them and past a row of shakylooking onestory cabins along the edge of the gulch, and stopped in front of the last unpainted shack.

Old Style Patch

We piled out of the car to see if the road went any farther. A yellowhaired young man was sitting slumped in a chair on the porch with his feet on the cracked old two by four nailed across it for a rail. I went up to him to ask if you could drive a car over the ruts that I could now see curving round the bottom of the slatedump up towards a brick building by the railroad track that seemed to be the office at the head of the shaft. While he was answering in a slow West Virginia drawl, I noticed that his feet inside of tattered slippers were in plaster casts. I asked him what the trouble was.

Arthritis, he said, he'd just come out of the hospital. He'd be three months before he could work, the doctor had told him. 'They was all twisted up. He straightened 'em out.' He looked up at me with a bright smile. 'Hit's something we miners git,' he said.

Wasn't it horribly painful? He nodded unconcernedly. How would he make out? Oh, he reckoned he'd get some kind of compensation. How about his rent? It was twelve-fifty a month. Company house? He nodded. He'd work it out when he got well. And his groceries? They let him charge at the company store. He'd work it all out some time. Had he a family? He had a wife and four little children, he explained with a certain pride.

At the same moment both of us smelled the good smell of fresh bread baking that came from inside the shack. I noticed a scuttling of ragged little figures in the darkness inside the door. He smiled again, sniffing the baking bread. 'We make out,' he said, and let his head drop back on his shoulders.

What he thought about the strike? He'd been too sick to worry about it, he answered in a tone of relief.

Had the union improved things for him since it had come?

'What could I do,' he drawled, 'settin' here like a log of wood, without the union?' But a strike in a time like this? 'If you can't strike when you have to, it ain't no union.' He smiled and added, 'I ain't worryin',' as if to say, if I'm not worried about it, why the hell are you?

The sun was hot. The grass smelt pleasantly underfoot. The clank of coalcars and the chugchug of a switching engine came distantly through the drowsy zizzing of dryflies. He responded politely but without enthusiasm to the hope I expressed that he'd get well in less than three months.

As I turned back to the car remembered objects in the landscape fitted into a picture, and I suddenly recollected I'd been in this same patch eleven years before. That was when the Communists were trying to launch a miners' union of their own, and people writing in the liberal weeklies spoke of these regions as the class war front. It had been in the late fall, a day of driving sleet, that I had driven out from the industrial city with a man who worked for the labor press. He had the addresses of two organizers he wanted to talk to, but was afraid the detectives would arrest us if we drove up onto company property, so we had left the car at the foot of the hill, and after considerable stealthy reconnoitering had found a big grayfaced negro and talked to him outdoors in the shelter of a storebuilding. While we talked, we had had to keep stamping our feet to keep them warm. He had told us that none of his people had seen any money for a year, they were all in debt to the company store; many days they didn't even make enough to pay for their explosives. The manager was barely letting them draw out enough food to live on. Their children were hungry. If it weren't for Red Cross relief they would be starving. If they knew you were union, no more relief. Their clothes were worn out. Sure, they'd make a revolution. Couldn't come soon enough. The Communists had told them all workingmen, black and white, were comrades, and they would take over the mines and the mills and run them for their own profit, and there would be no rich and no poor any more. Sure, it was better to get killed that way than to die starving by inches. Surely the Lord hadn't brought human creatures into the world to live like he and his people were living. When we had left the big man had shaken our hands ardently. We must tell the comrades that his people were ready whenever they said the word.

We had picked up the other organizer, a white man from the South, at a little Italian store near the railroad station down in the valley. Driving back into the city, he had talked of secret meetings, and organizers beaten up and left for dead by the company gunthugs, and marches of miners across the hills, in a black huddle behind the flag they always carried at the head, on their way to strike new mines, and broken heads under the clubs of the coal and iron police, and the savage jailsentences read out to strikers arrested and herded into court. Whenever he spoke of the operators or the old line labor leaders his voice had hissed with hatred. He took for granted with a kind of savage exultation that everybody who was not for him was against him. He had enlisted in the class war for the duration, was the last thing he had said before he left us and ducked into a doorway with his head sunk in his coatcollar.

As we turned back into the main road the lawyer in the backseat suddenly blew up. He hadn't said much while we were walking through the patch. 'It's awful,' he cried. 'People oughtn't to be allowed to live in places like that. I believe in housing. The only answer to that problem is firstrate government housing. There are limits of decency below which people ought not to be allowed to drop.' He was a smiling quietspoken man. His vehemence took us by surprise. 'I've seen it work,' he went on. 'Get people out of slum housing and all their standards rise.'

'Well, that was a bad one,' soothingly said the man who was driving.

'I was just thinking,' I said, 'that it wasn't so bad as I'd remembered it eleven years ago.'

A Carload of Bureaucracy

The man who drove the car had been in the florist business in one of the suburbs full of steelmills of the great industrial city. He told us that his wife was running the store by herself since he'd gone to work for this federal agency. Yes, there was a lot of money going around. Not much to spend it on. There was profit in flowers and knickknacks. Those hunkies were spending heavily for weddings and funerals. Why, a small downtown store had been found selling twentyfour-dollar wedding dresses for eighty dollars to poor people who were too shy to go to the big depart·

ment stores where they might get a square deal. The young man who sat beside him on the front seat, and who had, he somewhat bashfully admitted, been an actor, piped up that there was plenty of chiseling going on. During the drive against pleasure driving all sorts of odd things had cropped up. A girl belonging to a wealthy family who was driving home a car belonging to the secretary of the local Communist Party had been picked up with a lot of loose T coupons in her ration book. He pronounced the words Communist Party as if belonging to it were a mark of respectability. How things had changed in eleven years, I kept thinking.

There was a story about a priest who said he was on his way to collaborate with another priest on a sermon, whose car had been found parked at a race track . . . 'The boys didn't like that business much,' broke in the lawyer. 'They didn't like the attitude the public took towards them.'

He went on to say that he would be leaving the agency soon himself. He had a commission in the army waiting for him. He was going to do organization and government work in captured cities. The other two men cried out at once that they hated to have him go. Where would they get another boss like him? You could tell they meant what they said. 'Well,' he said smiling shyly, 'let's get back to the miners.'

Where the Coal Miners Live

As we drove along the highway that wound through the steep hills so green under the blue sky, we talked about miners' wages and the price of living. They'd found that the setup varied a good deal in different places. At the lower end of the scale was a company-owned patch a little like the place we'd just left. Population about five hundred. No church, only a community hall where services were occasionally performed. Two stores, one independent, one company. All the men worked in the mines or in a machineshop. In the machineshop they made from forty to fifty dollars a week. Mixed population of Italian, Russian,

Polish, Slavic, Negro and American origin. The machineshop men hadn't gone out on strike though they were all union members. They paid from $10.30 to $12.60 for company houses.

At the maximum end of the scale, said the lawyer, who was looking up the figures in a mimeographed report, was a big modernized mine where the houses were brick or tile and rented for $18 a month. There loaders took home an average of $350 for a two weeks' pay period. Drillers made slightly more and cutters slightly less. Even common laborers averaged $168 ... The place you could consider typical for this section was a rural mining community of fifteen hundred, half American, half Italian, Slavic, and Polish. It had one Protestant and one Greek Catholic church, a company store and two independent stores. The houses were built on top of a steep hill. The company owned fiftyfive houses that rented at from ten to eighteen dollars a month. Forty houses privately owned, most of them by miners, paid an average yearly tax of thirtyfive dollars. The mine's four hundred employees averaged seven dollars a day. They'd gone out on strike and stayed out five days. The president of the local was an unusually intelligent fellow, who was also the town barber. There, too, the complaint had been that particularly the miners with small families didn't get enough meat and potatoes to keep their strength up for their work. Their rubber boots cost $6.20 a pair and wore out in two or three weeks, instead of lasting nine months as they used to. They seemed more worried about scarcity than about prices ... In the general area, these government agents told me they had discovered that violations of ceiling prices amounted to only 16 percent of cases investigated. The company stores, many of them large modern chainstores, seemed to comply better than the small independents. A lot of the small storekeepers just didn't understand the regulations. The commonest complaint was about the scarcity of meat and potatoes, and the high price of rubber boots. The miners kept saying that a man couldn't do the work if he only had lettuce sandwiches in his lunchpail.

What the Cutter Had to Say

We had driven through a pleasant college town of redbrick Victorian houses and green lawns and treeshaded streets, and climbed a hill and stopped beside a string of miners' houses along a road. These were frame houses, but painted and kept up, with grassplots and dahlias in their dooryards. We stopped to talk across the picket fence to a whitehaired broadshouldered old man in his shirtsleeves who was standing in a doorway under a sign, 'Justice of the Peace.' We were asking him whether the mines were working today. Some locals had voted to work and others not to work on Labor Day. He was pointing out that the mine at the top of the hill was working some. Some coal was being cut, but it wasn't being brought up to the surface.

'That means we'll have a big day tomorrow,' said a young man with light curly hair who walked out from the next doorway.

'Why didn't they want to go to work?'

'Some of 'em are tired . . . We've been putting in some mighty long weeks.' He stood looking at us across the fence with his arms crossed. He had firm blue eyes. His face had a Slavic look with high cheekbones and a turned up nose, but his English was very good. The big square nails on the hands that clasped his bulky upper arms were clean and carefully trimmed.

'How much do you make?'

'I'm a cutter. What I make depends on how much the loaders can load up and haul away.'

'How many cars does a man load a day?'

'I've known a good man to load twenty cars and go home before twelve o'clock. But you can't do that every day, not with the food we are getting now. The mine is shorthanded, too. Six hundred where we ought to have a thousand . . . A man can't work on sliced tomatoes. Unless you've got a large family of small children there's no way of taking any meat down in your lunchpail.'

'What did they think of the strike around here?'

'Nobody likes to strike. But they don't like to work without

a contract, either.' A darkhaired Russianlooking man with no
shirt on, who had come strolling down the road swinging his bare
arms, joined us.

'Men work hard. They got to have a holiday,' he said. 'Men
get tired on six-day week.'

'Why are you so shorthanded?' we asked them. They replied
that the population of the coal country had been going down for
years due to slack times in the mines. Then there was the two
year law passed by the state by which, unless he had worked
there for two years, a man couldn't get a job in a mine without a sponsor who was responsible for him. That meant that
only sons and relations of miners went into the mines. A lot of
the younger men had gone into the army or the war industries
where they made much more money for much easier work. Now
those that hadn't moved out were stuck for keeps.

We asked if they could see any way the present production
could be stepped up. Not on the money and the food they were
getting now, they both said emphatically. Or with the present
equipment. Lots of mines needed new equipment. We asked
them how much they made. The cutter said he doubted if he
averaged over seven-fifty a day. The other man who was an
outside man paid regular wages said he made seven. We drove
on.

Old Welsh Superintendent

At a mine with an immense burning slatedump that almost filled
the narrow valley with its long black ridge smudged with smoke,
we had a long talk with an old Welsh superintendent. He had
silky white hair and finely chiseled fastidious features. It was a
pity, he said, the men didn't take more interest in their union.
The meetings sometimes got so rough that most of the intelligent
steady men didn't attend. The whole thing was run by twenty
or thirty radicals who didn't want to work and were out to get
the company in any way they could. Some of the radicals believed they were doing right, he had to admit that, but the other

men didn't dare talk back to them. That was the pity of it. They followed like a lot of sheep. He'd talked to a lot of them about it. What they said was if the President of the United States couldn't control the president of the United Mine Workers, why should they try? 'If you can say two words "fight" and "strike" you can always be a leader among the miners.'

On the subject of going to work Labor Day, a lot of young fellows had sprung a meeting without notifying anybody and had voted not to work. That meant losing two days at time and a half that week, because you had to work your six days to get time and a half Saturday. Well, then, the miners had gotten together and had another meeting and voted to work, and they were working right now.

'But that sounds as if the majority sometimes had its innings,' somebody suggested.

'Not often,' said the superintendent. 'Twenty men control six hundred. Since I was a boy miners have lost the habit of continuous work. Too many slack times. There's not the incentive to save. They figure the government will keep them when they get old. Of course, in all fairness I must say that these big records per man can't be kept up. A man can do it one day. Then he's tired and falls down the next . . . If it wasn't for these troublemakers we'd do all right. I've had a man tell me he made more money staying away from work than he did working. Now, what did he mean by that?'

'Were they striking against the union? I mean the men who stayed out after the rest went back?'

He smiled mysteriously. 'They got the idea the union wanted them to stay out . . . What they say is they can't go back to work until they get the telegram from the national office in Washington. They say they didn't get the telegram.'

He Worked His Way Up

At another mine the shaft went horizontally into the hillside in the gorge of a noble green winding river. The office in a modern

brick building was very spick and span. The superintendent
was a brisk young man built like a halfback. He sat at his desk
talking with his helmet pushed back on his head. He wore very
highly polished glasses and turned from time to time as he talked,
with evident pleasure, to the big blueprint of the mine hung along
the wall beside him.

He said he had worked thirtyfour years in coalmining, so he
must have looked younger than he really was. No, they had not
had much trouble there, he said. If they could only get rid of a
few professionals of union politics he didn't think they'd ever
have any trouble. It was a professional union official's business
to make trouble, just as it was his business as superintendent
to get out coal. We mustn't forget that the miner was an independent kind of cuss, he said. To do a good job getting out coal
you had to know the miners. He thought one reason a lot of them
stuck to mining, when they could be making better money else-
where, was that a man was his own boss once he went into the
mine. He could plan out his work as he pleased. He could
knock off for lunch when he felt like it. For a while the company
he worked for had tried to train superintendents in technical
schools. They'd put in youngsters who knew the theory but
who hadn't been down a mine before. It hadn't worked. They
couldn't get anything out of the miner. They didn't know
anything about operations. Now most of the superintendents
like himself were men who had worked their way up from the
bottom. He could hire people to do the accounting and office-
work, to write a letter in grammatical English. What he couldn't
hire was knowledge of the miner. Without that you couldn't
succeed in operations.

An older man, also in stained blue workclothes, had come into
the office. 'Don't forget to tell 'em,' he said, 'that the feller
who's really badly off is the salaried man. Our salaries are
frozen. Our expenses go up all the time. Sometimes I don't
know how we're going to make both ends meet. No kidding.
The miner's doing all right, but the salaried man, he's in the soup
proper.'

'At a time when everybody else is making really big money,' the superintendent said as we got up to go, 'I can't see why the miners shouldn't get it too. I'd raise their wages if they would let me. Sure, I would.'

How They Spend Their Money

On the way back to the industrial city, we went through the suburb where our friend who drove the car had his florist shop. His wife was busy mopping up the floor of the shop. No help. She'd had a niece working for her, she explained, but the niece was leaving at the end of the week to go into a mill. Still, she'd done seventyfive dollars worth of business already today. Pretty good for a holiday. 'Business is good, we can't deny that,' our friend said, rubbing his hands.

He explained he was going to put in a line of wedding dresses. Already he was conducting wedding ceremonies for people, furnishing the ornaments, the flowers, and arranging the party. He rented out a section of his store to a jeweller who was doing a great business in engagement and wedding rings. 'The foreign people we have here,' he said, 'they love to spend money on a wedding.'

Our friend was the perfect host. He poured us out drinks and showed us every detail of the store, from the glass refrigerator in which the actual flowers were confined, to the lines of vases and jardinieres along the walls, and the window full of a strange blooming of knickknacks and parlor ornaments: gilt shiny gazelles and firebirds, silver goats and turkeys, immense Disney piggy-wiggies and quackleducks of bisque, nameless objects pressed out of plastic, tarantella dancers, and brown hula girls, and koochie figurines in terracotta, and streamlined Holy Virgins in pale blue with kewpie Infants.

'I just finished doing the window . . . what a job!' said the wife, still panting from her mopping.

'It looks . . . it looks like a Christmas tree!' somebody stammered.

'I've got a whole new line stored in back,' our friend was explaining enthusiastically, 'but I won't touch a piece of it until this is all cleaned out. You ought to see how fast it goes. These people make big money and they haven't got much to spend it on. You wouldn't think you could do six thousand dollars worth of business in a month in a little hole in the wall like this.'

Aftermath of Trouble

This aging lawyer had been counsel for some of the miners convicted under the Smith-Connally Act. When I asked him how they felt about this business, he leaned back in his chair at his desk and spoke slowly and thoughtfully: one thing they'd told him, and he had half a mind to believe them, was that they couldn't get it into their heads that the United States Government really had taken over the mines. All they could see was the proclamation posted up. Otherwise, everything had gone on as before . . . same bosses, same superintendents, same deductions from their paychecks for debts at the company store . . . They'd felt that this business about the government taking over the mines was just a cheap trick to keep them from striking. Their attitude was they would show the world they wouldn't fall for it . . . We mustn't forget how out of the way many mining towns were, lost up eroded valleys, rows of shacks on stilts with their outhouses perched crankily on the edges of old slatedumps where the clay washed out in runnels between the houses: no relaxation but the store and the beer saloon . . . Of course now some of them did have radios and cars and read the metropolitan papers. But they were still cut off from the community. For years all they had they felt was their own was the union. The leaders had hammered it into their heads that they shouldn't work without a contract. They hadn't wanted to strike, but they hadn't wanted to work much either, so when some went out many others went out just so as not to scab on their neighbors. If one shaft went out the shafts in the same valley thought they ought to go out, too. The fellers over the hill didn't feel obligated.

'Why do you suppose they stick to mining coal?' I asked him. 'I've often wondered,' he said. 'I've doped it out this way. Being brought up in those isolated patches in the hills makes men a little shy and timid. They are afraid of the competition if they move into the great brawling industrial cities. It sounds funny to talk about miners as timid people, but I think they are, perhaps . . . Then there are the union seniority rules. If a man moves away he loses his seniority. When he wants to go back he has to start in at the bottom of the heap again. That holds them as much as anything. I suppose the men who have stuck this long are there for keeps. The young move away as much as they can. At least they did before the government froze them.'

A Small Town in the Coal Country

It was a pleasant redbrick town set in a valley among tightly folded green hills. The main street ran along the bottom of the valley. The office of the Mineworkers' Union was in a large stone bank building. I went up in the elevator. The secretary had a mean heavyset pokerfaced look. No, he couldn't tell me anything. Any information had to come from Washington. The miners were sore at the way they were being treated, that's all he knew. A large coal company had its office in the same building. There it was the same story. Any information had to come through public relations at the main office.

The independent operators were more hospitable. A gray-haired man with a pleasant round red face, who had his office in a brick Queen Anne style building next the courthouse that looked as if it ought to be full of lawyers, talked about the difficulties of carrying on his coke business. He said they would like to increase production, but that if they bought new machinery it would have to be run as a capital increase on their books, and he thought they would get stuck when production dropped after the war. If he could charge it off taxes it would be another story.

Oh, yes, his men had gone out. He didn't think ninetyfive percent of them wanted to strike; they were in pretty good shape now, their take-home was about fifty dollars a week after all deductions. Five men had driven up in a car and cleared out the coke yard. They left the ovens burning untended and ruined a whole twentyfour hours' production.

What he'd like to see was some scheme for assuring selfgovernment to the union local. If they had a secret ballot on these issues and the men felt they would be protected he didn't think there'd be half the trouble there was now. Absenteeism? Yes. Frankly, it was bad. As high as thirtytwo percent after payday. He'd never seen so many blue Mondays.

In the back office of another coal company two brothers, noisy middleaged men, sat with piles of papers in front of them at either end of a long table. 'We don't know anything,' shouted the older of them cheerfully. 'We just live with coal eighteen hours a day. We're too busy making out forms to send to Washington to know anything. We don't know whether we own our own mines. All they did when they took over was to ask for the managing director's name and to send us some posters. Half the miners thought we were spoofing 'em. They didn't know what they wanted. All they knew was what they heard over the radio. We found that highly confusing ourselves, so I don't blame the miners for getting balled up . . . A few boys went around in a truck and pulled 'em all out. It sure gave 'em a turn when they were all standing around talking big about how they was goin' to strike, government or no government, to a bunch in workclothes they thought had come from a mine over the hill and these birds pulled back their lapels and turned out to be dicks from the F.B.I. You oughta seen those organizers run.' They rolled back in their chairs and laughed.

'Things have changed in the coal country,' said the other brother slowly. 'More miners own their own homes, for one thing.'

'Sure, a whole lot of these concerns unloaded their houses on the miners and then moved out of the mines,' shouted the older brother.

'Do you think production can be increased?'

'Can you go above one hundred percent? Answer me that . . . In another ten years there'll hardly be a coal mine in the county. All the available coal will have been taken out. All we hope to do is not to go broke in the process. We'd like to get out with enough to get us a ranch somewhere and raise some whitefaced cattle.'

At the Chamber of Commerce the secretary was busy with a naval officer getting up an exhibit of captured war materials for the War Bond drive.

'Compared to the last war,' he said, when the naval officer had gone, 'there is not quite the boom situation in this town that there was, no such inflation of wages and prices, but it's my opinion that prosperity is sounder and more general. Seventy percent of the people own their own homes. Many miners who work in mines around about, own their homes in town. We have a firstrate school system. A number of small industries, a shirt-waist factory, a radiator plant. Three banks in excellent financial condition . . . We are the headquarters of the district for the miners' union . . .' 'How times have changed,' I whispered. He went on hurriedly: 'There was a time when people felt differently, perhaps, about the union, but it has become a solid and stable organization now. They cooperate in local welfare work. They are possessed of considerable capital. They have their committees, their officials, their nationwide organization.' He went on talking and talking in the same slick-paper tone of voice.

Village the Mines Deserted

The bus from the highway ground up the steep hill in low and lurched to a stop in front of a small dilapidated firestation. Opposite in a fragmentary business block there were a couple of beersaloons closed because the day was Sunday, a grocery and two softdrink parlors, with a few men and boys standing in the sun in front of each. The wooden and brick houses of the village, most of them freshly painted in white or cream, strung out along the roads that climbed to the big yellowbrick highschool at the top of the hill. They were set irregularly among trees. Back of them were sloping gardens of cabbages and turnips, broccoli and corn, potato patches in flower. There were a lot of petunias everywhere and big dahlias hung over the picket fences. There was a white Catholic church on the flank of the hill, and a Greek Orthodox church with a tin onion dome painted bluegray in the hollow behind the firestation. In the sultry late-summer afternoon the little scattered houses perched pleasantly on the hill between green valleys where the slatedumps of abandoned mines looked like burrows left by gigantic woodchucks. In places, the sappy vegetation had healed over the scars entirely. In others, toppling moraines of slate and coal choked the brooks in the bottoms and towered black and forbidding over small pastures where cows grazed. The smell of burning coal was gone and instead the place smelt of hay and chickenyards and cowbarns. Flocks of white pigeons fluttered overhead. It was the familiar Appalachian country, but something about the grape arbors over the back doors, the way the vegetables were planted in the steep gardens, the flowers along the picket fences gave the place an East of Europe look.

The roads were full of cars. Every car seemed full of pretty girls in lightcolored dresses, girls with fluffy hair of light sandy and light red colors, with the slightly prominent cheekbones and chins you associate with South Slavic people.

The man I had come to visit was up at the Social Hall, they said. I followed a red clay road round the edge of the hill through gray shivering cottonwoods until I came to a rambling gray frame building that looked as if it might at some time have been a gristmill. Cars were strung all along the road in front of it and parked in every level space on the hillside. From inside the hall came a muffled clatter of tongues in a foreign language. A man stuck his head out of one of the doors, and I asked him if my friend were through with his meeting yet. He disappeared, and I sat for a while on the steps watching a storm make up over the intensely green valley at our feet, patched with welltended farms and vegetable gardens. On a tree across the road was

tacked the picture of a man in the baseball outfit of the Brooklyns
who was running for sheriff on the Republican ticket.

They Don't Read Careful

When I was asked to come upstairs I found at the end of a clean-
swept meeting hall a group of elderly men in their Sunday
clothes sitting on the stage round a table that had ledgers and
accountbooks piled on it. In the centre was a pile of bills and
small change from the dues they had been collecting. The
windows behind them shone with cleanliness. The table looked
scrubbed. The floor looked scrubbed. The men looked scrubbed.
My friend was secretary of the organization.

Wouldn't I sit down until it was time for them to go to another
meeting? So I wanted to know what the miners thought, did I?
asked an old man with a handsome head of silvery hair who had
lost two middle fingers of one hand. 'Around here they don't
do good. Cost of living too high. Transportation . . .Some men
have to go twentyeight miles to work. Too many expenses —
tools, powder, caps. They don't make money.' The men
around the table shook their heads. 'Eighty-three cents a ton
for machine coal and $1.03 for pick coal don't make the miner
money . . . Many mines old. We spend all day moving posts and
track. No money that way. Too many accidents.'

A longnosed young man with a shock of black hair who wore
a very white shirt open to the waist had been listening to what
the older men were saying, standing with his legs spread wide
and looking up at us from the floor of the hall. 'I don't give a
damn what anybody says,' he broke in. 'They ain't giving us a
square deal. Sure, I'll go into the army. A hell of a lot easier
an' a hell of a lot less dangerous work than minin' under the
conditions we've got today. Let 'em put us in the army and put
the soldiers down the mines. I'd like to see how much coal they'd
get out. And that War Labor Board — how many cars of coal
would they load? If the people in this country understood what
we was up against, they wouldn't treat us like this.'

'The trouble with the American pipples is,' began one of the old men at the table, 'they ain't informed. They don't read enough. They read headlines. They read funnies. They don't read careful ...'

The Opinions of the Slovenes

It was time for another lodge meeting to begin. A big blond man, very Germanlooking with his hair clipped short, who said he was a mine carpenter, took me down to the bar on the ground floor to have a glass of beer. The bar was a cheerful noisy white-painted room where the jukebox continually roared. The walls were ornamented with calendars and advertising posters and the faces of local political candidates in the fall elections. It was filled with miners drinking beer out of bottles as a chaser to little glasses of whiskey. When the carpenter and I were each on our second bottle of beer, he turned to me confidentially and said: 'Now look at me, I'm a pretty good carpenter, maintenance man, repairman for engines, I can do blacksmithing, anything that's needed in a mine. I've got two boys in the army, one in the navy, and a girl who's working in a munitions plant. She and her husband both work there. She makes twice what her fader make. That makes a man feel cheap. Nothing left at home but me and the old woman. I'm a pretty good worker, but I'm telling you I can't make a go of it if I can't save anything. We don't eat good no more ... Now I'm telling you a lie; I save the ten percent they take out for war bonds. I'd go in the army tomorrow if they take me at fiftytwo years old. I make sixsixty and if I'd had the sense to move out before the jobs were frozen I'd make twenty a day.'

A young man with a broad cherub face and curly yellow hair spoke up. 'In the old country they treat the miners better than they do here now,' he said. 'They get pensions when they retire. The work's not so hard. Safety precautions are better regarded.'

'No, no,' said the carpenter. 'I'm American citizen. I never go back ... here good school for the children, spirit of freedom, big great American country.'

'How about being frozen to your job?' asked the young man bitterly.

An old man standing at the bar beside us whose cleanly cut regular features jibed strangely with his big mutilated hands, accepted a small glass of whiskey. 'Beer bad for my stomach,' he said. He tossed off the whiskey and stood looking down at the glass in his gray hand that had two fingers cut off at the first joint and at the grimed coaldust round the nails. 'Stomach not so good now I'm old ... It's too hard work,' he said. Then he stuck his chin out. 'I'm glad I'm old. Soon don't work no more.'

A Reformer's Life

My friend was through his meeting, and stood with a cashbox under his arm beckoning to me from the door of the bar. As we walked slowly down the narrow winding road from the Social Hall towards the town he talked in a low even voice. He was sixty years old, he said. That was why he was glad my coming had given him an excuse to get away without taking any drinks. Drinks made him sick next day.

He'd been in this country thirtyfive years. He'd been a miner in his own country, and a miner in Germany, and a miner in this country. From a young man he'd been a Social Democrat. He believed in a slow reform of the social system by democratic means. Now one thing a little better, now another thing a little better. You couldn't go farther than the people were ready to go. If you did, you would get a reaction like the last twenty years in Europe.

He was a peaceful sort of fellow, he said, but he'd been in trouble all his life. He settled down in this town years ago, and married and bought him a house. Then he had to do with organizing a strike, and way back before the last war he'd been blacklisted. He'd tried to sell his house and move out but nobody would buy it; everybody had been afraid to buy off a blacklisted man.

'It's funny the companies ruled us with such an iron hand in those days, and now they've all moved out, let the county have the mines for the taxes.' Sure, there was a little coal left but methods had been so wasteful he doubted if anybody ever would be able to get it out.

Well, when he found he couldn't work in a mine any more, he'd bought a team and done trucking. Made pretty good money. One stormy day the team had run away and when he'd tried to stop them they'd run over him, and he'd been months in hospital and come out with a bad hip. Well, he was pretty wellknown to the miners, so when he got out of hospital he took a job soliciting for a beer concern. But then he made a speech at a political meeting about Karl Liebknecht and the brewery told him they liked him fine as a solicitor, but that unless he promised to keep off politics he couldn't work for them any more. Then some friends who were miners had put up some money to get him started keeping store, and he'd kept store seventeen years until when the crash came in thirtytwo they managed to break him. The company had been after him because he gave credit to miners during strikes and competed with the company store. Well, the wholesaler he dealt with went into the hands of a receiver and the receiver came down on him for his back bill and he couldn't pay suddenly like that, not at that time, nobody could, so they put him into bankruptcy and sold him out. Since then he lived by being secretary of fraternal orders. He was agent for liberal and foreign language papers. He'd raised a family and his children had all had good technical educations.

'At least, you are glad you didn't stay in the old country?' I asked.

'Sure,' he said with a dry laugh. 'Hitler, he'd have killed me ... In fact he nearly got me over here. They threw me out of all my foreign language societies four years ago. You wouldn't think it now, but they all thought he was coming over here and get 'em. Me, I've been all the time Social Democrat. Two or three years ago they thought I was crazy. Now, they think different. You'd have thought they'd had better sense, American citizens and all. You'd be surprised how many of 'em thought democracy was all over.'

We had reached his house and were going through a little picket gate that opened into a grape arbor with big bunches of green grapes hanging down into the rosy slanting sunlight of late afternoon. The house was very clean and polished. His wife was a friendly broadfaced woman with straight dark eyebrows. She had supper ready for us in the spotless kitchen, a Viennese sort of supper of breaded cutlets and tomatoes and salad and coffee and cake. She'd just gotten back from her work in time to cook it, she said smiling. She worked at the junction, handling freight.

'Handling freight?'

Sure, she said, with a broad smile. It was her war work. At first it had seemed awfully hard, but now she liked it. She knew how to handle packages up to seven hundred pounds. 'We transfer them from one freight car to another,' she said. I asked her if she wasn't worn out. 'Oh, no,' she said cheerfully. She didn't think she was any more tired than she had been when she just did the housework. She made six dollars a day with overtime.

'Pretty good for a woman of fifty who has three grown children,' said my friend smiling.

'At first I lost weight, but I'm gaining now. It must be muscle,' she said.

'It don't bother me having the wife make more money than me,' my friend said, 'because I got liberal ideas. But it makes the miners sore. Their kids, boys and girls, go to town and make two or three times what the old man makes a week . . . and he asks himself: Here I've worked in a mine all my life and my kids make better money than I do. What good am I?'

The Big Wind

The streaming rain shimmered on the windows of the bus whenever a car passed on the highway. Then I could see the square outlines of the face of the man beside me. His eyes were set deep and there were deep hollows in his cheeks. As he talked he looked straight before him at the raindrops flashing in the light of the headlights. I had asked him what the men in the mines who had struck were saying about the things the newspapers were printing that the boys in the theatres of war thought they ought to be taken out and shot.

'The newspapers in this country have always been against the working people. We all know that,' he said. 'We miners have got as many boys in this war as anybody else, and we're more patriotic than most.'

Well, hadn't his union's leader, the man with the eyebrows, broken his pledge not to strike in wartime?

'The President of the United States has broken every pledge he ever made ... Thank God we've got a leader who can talk as fast as any of 'em.'

I suggested that he'd pretty near talked a lot of the boys into jail.

'They didn't go, did they? That's what counts ... In this country there's one law for business and another law for the working man. Don't forget that while you people work in the sunlight, we work underground like a goddam woodchuck, and every time we go down that mine who can say we won't come out feet first? Ten years ago you could kick a miner around like a dog. Now we got a big wind to talk for us with the other big winds in Washington. We got one of the smartest looking out for our interests. Newspaper talk don't bother us.' He lifted a big hand off his knee and made a gesture across his face as if batting at a fly. 'When he says strike we got to strike. If we didn't have a big man to look out for our interests that War Labor Board would have us down on our knees begging the operators for a glass of water. It's the tough guys make themselves respected in this man's country, the tough guys an' the big winds. Mister, you know that just as well as I do.'

Pittsburgh, Pennsylvania, September, 1943

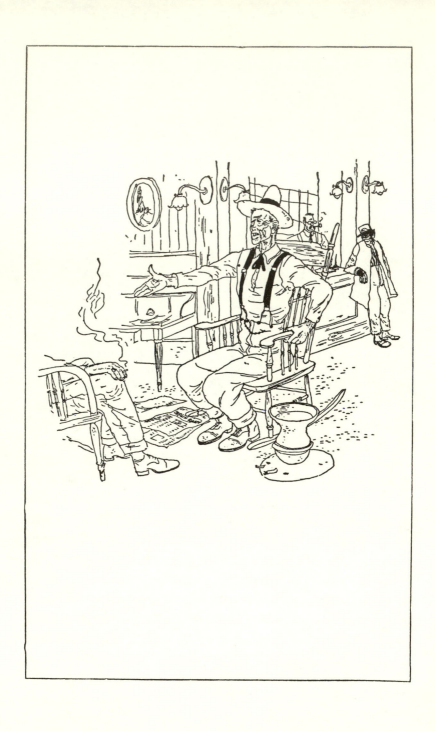

AT THE FRESHPAINTED WHITE HOUSE set behind the rosy dry blossom heads of hydrangeas among trees and broad lawns, they told us he was out in the field picking corn. We followed the ruts along the edge of the thicket that marked a winding silty brown brook until we came to the first tall rows of corn. The big ears hung so heavy they seemed about to break out of their dry gaping shucks. We walked along the edge of the cornfield towards the roar of the tractor's exhaust and the whir of metal, until we came out on an open space of wrecked and trampled stalks where the picker had been through. He was coming towards us down the rows sitting up high on the seat of the tractor while the cornstalks bowed trembling and crumpled and vanished between the shining steady shears and were spewed out in a dusty cloud in back, while the ears tumbled in a glow of gold and deep yellow into the towed wagon. Right at our feet he stopped the tractor and jumped down from the seat. The roar of the motor and the clatter of the picker stopped. The cornfield was all at once immensely quiet. We could hear the cawing of crows along the hedgerow. Without looking at us he knelt in front of the picker's shining perpendicular jaw and began yanking pieces of tough stalk from between the snappers. When he got to his feet again, he turned and walked

[251]

towards us pulling off one heavy work glove as he came. He greeted my companion and we shook hands.

He was a tall grave man with clear gray eyes. The stubble on his cheeks and chin was gray. When he pushed back his sweaty denim cap to look at us better, he exposed a tall white forehead much paler than his windburned nose and cheeks.

My companion, possibly to bring him out, asked him how he was stepping up production for war. Standing very still and straight, he looked at us steadily and unsmilingly for a moment. Then he said quietly and without warmth, as if he were answering the silly questions of a couple of children, 'We know that this thing is not of God, but it does not go against our conscience to get production out of the land.' A smile almost flickered round the corner of his thin wide obstinate mouth. 'You can't make a farmer happier than by offering him a good price and telling him to produce. Now can you?'

My companion stammered a little when he explained that I was trying to find out how all this effort for production was going to affect the growth of the county cooperative.

The farmer stood there straight and tall, with his feet a little apart and his arms hanging easily at his sides, for a full minute before he answered. 'You know very well that it is my opinion that we farmers should do for ourselves what the government is doing for us and doing very badly with a political purpose,' he said. 'This is a time of organizations. We farmers must develop organizations to protect our families and the things we hold dear.'

'Do you think we are succeeding?'

'You have the figures in the office. Why do you ask me?' He pointed with a long blackened forefinger at a cloud that was spreading over the dappled sky above the bare trees at the end of the cornfield. 'That's rain,' he said. 'A little rain will help us . . . the corn is too brittle now . . . but a long spell of rain would

spoil the crop. I'm too busy today to talk of politics.' He fixed his
level gaze on my face. 'You must excuse me. We speak plain
here,' he said. 'If you could come back when the crop is in, we
should have time to talk.' He lifted one arm in a gesture of dis-
missal as he turned and strode back to the tractor. The whirring
roar of machinery drowned our voices out. We turned and walked
back along the ruts towards the house. 'He's the best farmer in
the county,' said my companion, in an apologetic tone, when we
were enough cut of earshot to hear our voices. 'I can see why,' I
said.

CHAPTER 12

Three Hundred Acres and a Tractor

Driving west, across Southern Ohio, cornfields spread out over the flat land on either side of the straight concrete road. The white farmhouses with green roofs had a wellkept look. They were very small beside the immense barns and cowstables and the tall silos that towered above the tattered russet of the trees round the houselots. It was prosperous looking country. The high wire fences were neat. The gates hung straight. A high tension power line went looping along on tall steel towers to the right of the road. At regular intervals olivecolored four-motor bombers roared overhead on their way out from the airplane reconditioning plant in the industrial town we had just left. In some fields the corn had been cut by hand and stacked in rows of wigwamshaped shooks; in others the mechanical picker had gone through, leaving a confusion of mangled stalks where tall black hogs rooted and munched; in others the corn still stood in twelvefoot ranks of pale silvery yellow that rustled drily in the fading breeze of the late fall afternoon. There were occasional patches of pumpkins or warty nilegreen Hubbard squashes humped among their wilted vines, or strips of green alfalfa, or stubble where beans had been cut off, but mostly it was corn, corn, corn, and tall black hogs that looked bigger and taller and blacker as the evening mist closed in.

It was dusk when the highway swerved south and plunged down through a wooded rolling country that smelt of dead leaves towards the river. In the driedout weeds along the roadside a rabbit now and then sat up looking at us with twitching nose for a second, before he turned and showed us a white blob of cottontail as he made off into the darkness of the underbrush. By the time we reached the redbrick rivertown where the meeting was being held, it was night and the streetlights swam ruddy in the streaky mist off the river.

Farm Bureau Supper

It was the yearly gettogether and business meeting of the local county Farm Bureau organization. The meeting was being held in the basement of a rambling old Methodist church off the main street. Smells of frying steak and baked biscuits met us as we hurried past a few lanky sunburned men in store clothes standing silent round the entrance treating themselves to a last chew of tobacco or a last puff on a cigarette before going in. The ladies of the organization had prepared the supper. The tables were set in the long basement room under the steampipes. We were greeted at the door by the minister, a redfaced young man who had the healthy cornfed look of a prize carthorse. While we were being shown our places at the crowded narrow boards, everybody was singing to the tune of 'O Mother dear, Jerusalem':

> Oh, beautiful for spacious skies,
> For amber waves of grain . . .

At first the women carried it, but gradually the men and little piping children's voices joined in:

> For purple mountain majesties,
> Above the fruited plain . . .

The minister stood on a piano stool and led with as much energy as if he were leading the cheering at a football game:

America, America,
God shed his grace on thee;
God crown thy good with brotherhood
From sea to shining sea.

They sang well. The song roared among the low rafters. The glasses along the tables rang on the high notes. On 'sea' they ended up with a bang that left the hall so silent you could hear the puffing of the ladies with frilled aprons over their party dresses as they hurried in with the last trays of dinner plates.

The minister boomed out a short grace. With the amen chairs scraped, throats were cleared, crockery clattered as we all sat down simultaneously to the steaming meal of fried steak, stewed corn, string beans, fruit salad in pink jelly, and biscuits and hot bakers' rolls and butter. Opposite me sat a longfaced man in a black suit with black hair and a leathery skin, who looked like a member of Lincoln's cabinet. Farther along, several old ladies in their best frocks, with dimpled marshmallow faces chirped and squeaked among themselves. On my left was a freshfaced white-haired man in light gray tweeds. I asked him what folks round here thought about the presidential election.

'We are mostly Republicans bred and born,' he said. 'If a man votes the Democratic ticket it's a pretty sure sign he comes from across the river. We pretty near fell for the Administration once. I came near voting for the man in the White House myself. I'd just about made up my mind to vote for him, when I went out to talk to some old tenants on part of our farm. The old man's father had been a tenant of my grandfather's. I asked him how he'd take it if I voted the Democratic ticket. His face got so long you would have thought I'd told him about a death in the family. "How do you think your father and grandfather would have taken it?" he asked me. That saved me from doing what I see now would have been a foolish thing.'

I asked him what kind of a Republican nominee they'd vote for down here. They'd vote for any Republican, naturally, he said, but they'd prefer a candidate as different as possible from the present incumbent. They would go all out for a general.

They were singing again, this time men's and women's voices carrying alternate verses of 'When you and I were young, Maggie.' With the dessert of icecream and cake, child entertainers were herded by their mamas into the open corner of the room where the piano was. Two little girls in pigtails sang 'Oh, lay that pistol down.' A glassyeyed toddler in a white rayon naval uniform with a great deal of gold braid on the shoulders was stood up on the piano stool and howled out mournfully 'If I could call you sweetheart.'

Then the meeting was called to order. We pushed back our chairs and listened to a series of seriousfaced men giving an account of the year's proceedings. Most of them dealt with their efforts to start a cooperative to sell gas, tires, feed, and fertilizer. Though the cooperatives had been a great success in the rest of the state, this county organization had had poor luck. Two fires had set them back. In this coming year they were determined to get her over the hump. A young man with blond hair cut in a brush gave a talk on the food needs of the nation for next year. Prices would be good, he said. It was up to the farmer to produce as he had never produced before. A sharp volley of handclapping accented the word 'produce.' There were reports from committees. There was an election of officers. Then the man who had brought me over, who was making the trip to organize a membership drive, gave a talk on what the Farm Bureau could do for the farmer and urged everybody to go out and get new members, and we all sang *America* and filed out.

The Cooperative Idea

As we drove out of town under a last quarter of moon that shone wanly on cobwebby tangles of mist among the trees in the hollows, the Farm Bureau organizer said apologetically that this county we had just been in was one of the worst in the state from the point of view of farm organizations. In this state, he went on to explain, the Farm Bureau wasn't so political as it was in the South. They were building the most progressive set of consumers' cooperatives in the county. Already their gasstations sold enough gasoline to set the price for the whole state. They were on the point of buying a factory to build farm machinery. When they got that going it would help keep prices down for the nation. I mustn't think this county was typical. I assured him that nobody could go through the big office building of the Farm Bureau cooperatives as I had that morning without getting the impression of an immense going concern.

This blueeyed young man who had invited me to come along on part of his organizing trip, was a Virginian. After working his way through college he had gotten a scholarship to go abroad to study the cooperative movement. He'd been in England, France, and Sweden just before war broke out. He'd stayed on in Sweden for a while after the shooting started. Everywhere he'd seen self-government and individual liberty, everything we had been brought up to prize in this country as making life worth living, going down the drain. How could we keep that from happening here, was what he'd been asking himself ever since. Of one thing he was sure. No human institution ever stood still. It either grew and progressed or else it decayed. That was why the conservatives were always wrong because what they were trying to conserve was always spoiling on their hands. When he came home he had gone into cooperative work because he thought that if anybody could bring selfgovernment back to life in this country the farmers could. In this state they had really inspired leadership, he thought. The plan was to build up consumers' cooperatives for economic selfhelp at the same time they built up a political lobby to influence legislation. He didn't think one could go ahead very far without the other.

There was one interesting development I ought to know about ... Now, in his opinion one of the great mistakes of Farm Bureau leadership was opposition to labor. There was just no doubt that farmers were naturally prejudiced against labor organizations. Nobody had ever convinced the farmer that he had anything to gain from high industrial wages. But in this new development he saw a chance of bridging the gap between them

There was springing up in this state a chain of cooperative stores operated by labor unions in the cities which bought their products directly from the farmer. It had begun with poultry. These stores cut out the middleman's expenses and assured the farmer a good profit for his product, and the union man the lowest possible price. Outside of the expense of hauling, they shared between them the entire markup of the commission merchant, the retail storekeeper, the jobber, the wholesaler. More important than the economics of it was the fact that it constituted a bridge between farmers and workers in the industrial cities. 'That's the sort of thing I call practical politics,' he said.

The Nature of Argument

One reason why liberals and progressives in this country have had so little success in convincing anybody, he went on to say, was that they had never tried to puzzle out for practical purposes how the human mind worked. You can talk yourself blue in the face, using the closest reasoning in the world, and all your audience will get out of it is the part that jibes with what they were thinking before they walked into the hall. People will accept a strange fact more readily than they will a strange idea. Often it's years after they've cheerfully accepted the facts of a situation before they'll be able to call it by its right name. That was why if you get a bunch of farmers looking at a labor union as a customer, you had done more than all the political orators in the country could do, laying it on the line night and day, to convince these people their interests ought to coincide. 'At least,' he said modestly, 'that's how I look at it.'

Where General Grant Went to School

The town where we'd planned to spend the night was nothing but a square of old storefronts around a redbrick courthouse at a crossroads and a scattering of old peakedroofed brick dwelling-houses under broadly branching trees along the roads. A little way beyond the square, my friend drew up at a small hotel, also of neat red brick. At the desk in the lobby we found, sitting hunched in his shirtsleeves over an oldfashioned black ledger with a red binding, the lone man who served as nightclerk, bellboy, manager and landlord. Above the desk hung a portrait of a desperate looking man with a creased up face, in a darkblue uniform. It was an odd work, obviously by a local amateur, daubed with love and conviction. We asked who it was. Of course it was General Grant. This wasn't his birthplace? No, this was the town where he went to public school.

'Doesn't seem to have changed much since,' I said.

The hotelkeeper wore a pained look as he led us upstairs to our rooms.

After I'd put out the light in the clean square room I lay in bed looking out beyond black barns and houses at misty cornfields of ripe standing corn stretching off into a blur of distance under the frail moonlight. It was hard to go to sleep. To the tune of 'O Mother dear, Jerusalem,' the talk I'd heard during the day came trailing back through my ears. I kept thinking that here we were again a nation in arms. Again, for the first time since the Civil War, military brains were coming to the top. Sure, the farmers would go for a general at the polls. But what would the generals do with us now that they were back at the top? Would the brass hats of today show the restraint and civic decency of the brass hats of eighty years ago? Here in this little crossroads town was where Grant had learned to behave as he behaved. How had the new generals learned to behave where they went to school? Argument wouldn't change them now. The thoughts and fears went round and round. How many men, I kept thinking, in the last few years had felt the cold sweat of fear when they woke up at night and thought of their country's future?

The place was absolutely quiet. I lay on my back in bed smelling the rich fermented autumnal smell of crops and stock and rotting leaves that came in through the window, feeling the soothing security of the immense breadth of the plains between the rivers, where you feel so far from the quandaries and complications of the seacoast, and went to sleep hearing again the voices of the farm people in the basement of the Methodist church singing:

> And crown thy good with brotherhood
> From sea to shining sea.

A Program for Nineteen-Fifty

After breakfast the next morning we drove on westward across the state to another small town that consisted only of two rows of redbrick houses of the mansard period with creamcolored woodwork and solid carefully tooled doors. The widening of the highway had cut off porches and front stoops and gave the place a sunken and dejected appearance. At the end of the street near the railroad station we drove up beside a long corrugated iron building that housed the feedmill and the cooperative store.

The manager was a plump rosyfaced young man. He came out and sat in the car and told us his story. This was a dairy and poultry raising county. As the soil was poor, the grain crops were mostly for home consumption. Ninety percent of the feed had to be brought in. There was some tobacco and fruit raised. Mostly the county served as a bedroom to the nearby city. You wouldn't think it was the perfect setup for a cooperative, would you? Well, the cooperative was started in 1934, on a small scale, to distribute gasoline to Farm Bureau members. No, you didn't have to be a member to trade with them. They had bought a milling company so that they could grind their own feed and mix their own mashes, then another mill, then a feed and supply concern. Now they were ready to supply the farmer with almost everything he needed for his farm. In the last two years just about all the agricultural business of the county had come into cooperative hands. There were four small private feed dealers they kept going by furnishing them supplies because they were needed. Without the statewide organization of cooperatives, this county wouldn't have produced anything for the war effort because the private dealers weren't operating on a big enough scale to get the supplies. Private business hardly existed there any more. Oh, yes, marketing cooperatives were growing up too. They had one dairy, two poultry and egg, and three fruit, concerns. Without any increase in the plant, business had doubled in four years. Sure, that was good, but it was going to be better.

The manager rummaged among the papers in his inside pocket and brought out a mimeographed map of the district. 'Now, this isn't for publication yet,' he said, 'but it gives you an idea of what a complete cooperative servicing of the county will call for.'

On the map were marked the suitable locations for branch offices, grain elevators, coal depots, freezing lockers, dehydrating stations, a cannery, and a bakery. At the bottom were listed the main facilities to be offered. They included sheep dipping, grinding and spreading of lime, shelling of corn, spray painting, a training program for employees and directors and managers, a hundred cooperative councils of farm families and a weekly newspaper. A pink dimpled smile spread over the young man's broad face. 'Big, isn't it?' he sighed. 'But if we could do what we've done in the last five years, there's no reason on earth why we can't do that in the next seven.'

The Farmer Loves to Produce

'I'm seventyfour,' said the hawkfaced whitehaired man, as he let himself down from the wagon piled high with corn, where he'd been fixing a sideboard. He grunted as he straightened up in his neatly patched blue overalls and put his hand to his back above his lean hip. 'Ouch ... I'm beginning to find the work heavy.' He pointed to the new mechanical loader that was hitched behind the wagon. 'Boys bought me that. They think I'm too old to lift the corn up into the wagon. Never could have gotten this crop in without it.'

He took his hand away from his back, wiped it on his overalls and walked slowly towards us with the hand outstretched. We were standing beside the highway on a semicircle of grass heaped with redbrown leaves from the horse chestnut trees in front of the big mansarded house with broad porches. Whenever any one of us moved, the leaves crunched crisply underfoot. He was a tall slender man, remarkably straight for his age. After shaking hands, the old man stood quietly looking us over for a moment out of sharp blue eyes between narrowed red lids. 'Well, the government said they wanted production, and, by gum, we'll give it to 'em if it kills us,' he said. 'By the way, how's Pete Hawkins?' he added, looking towards the Dane. 'Those cornpickers are nasty things. Never put your hand near 'em without stopping the motor. That's the rule here.'

'He's gone to the hospital,' said the Dane. 'His hand's pretty badly mangled.'

'Picking some stalks out of the snappers that looked like they'd stick, I suppose. The hired man over at the Children's Home got a piece taken out of his finger that way only yesterday. Lucky he didn't lose it. We're so shorthanded around here we can't afford to have accidents. Well, we've planted eighty acres of wheat and we've picked six thousand bushels of corn, just me and the two boys. All this machinery costs a heap of money, but it surely does the work. If we can't get labor we've got to buy machinery. If we buy machinery we've got to get prices to pay for it.'

'Well, before long we'll have cooperative machinery,' said the Dane.

'They won't be able to cut prices much.'

'If it's a cooperative the price won't matter. The profits will go back to the membership.'

'They will if it's run right.'

'It's up to us to see it's run right,' said the Dane, warming up. 'The farmers around here do a pretty good job running their farms. There's no reason on earth why they can't run a few enterprises,' he went on, his voice rising as he spoke. 'Look at me. I've done both. I've kept a store and I've worked for cooperatives and I tell you storekeeping's a whole lot easier and a whole lot less satisfactory to the spirit of man.'

'I'd surely like to see the whole agricultural program taken away from the government,' said the old man, with a blue flash in his eye.

'You wouldn't want to see it fall into the hands of the Wall Street bankers, would you? Then we'd get our hides taken off for fair.'

'I've been through periods when the bankers ruled. I've had 'em skin me alive like the rest of the folks . . . I'd trust 'em before I would the politicians at that.'

'But suppose the farmers ran their entire business for themselves? Finance, furnishing of supplies, marketing right through to the consumer . . .'

'I'd like to see it properly managed. I certainly would like to be shown.'

A shining black Buick towncar drove up and parked in the shallow ditch beside us. A young man in a dark business suit stepped out. 'Folks,' he said, 'I just stopped to hear if you knew about Pete's hand. Down the road they are saying he may lose the whole hand. I hope it isn't as bad as that.'

'I don't think so,' said the Dane, furrowing his brow. 'I'm very much afraid he'll lose some fingers, though.'

The man in the business suit, it came out, ran a chicken hatchery and sold incubators and brooders. He was in the business in a big way. He'd even been as far as Soviet Russia before the war, installing his incubators. When we asked him how he liked it, he said he'd come back believing in private enterprise more firmly than ever. Of course, he admitted smiling, all he'd seen had been chicken farms and chicken officials, and he didn't know any Russian.

But what about cooperatives? we asked him. What about democratically run business? His face darkened. Hadn't we had enough bureaucracy by this time? he asked with impatience. We were up to our necks in it. You would think people would be sick of it. 'Frankly, I think businessmen contribute more to the community. That is, if you give them a chance to make a profit. We pay better wages. I don't mind a few cooperatives for the little fellows, but I'd hate to have them get their hands on everything. That'd be as bad as the federal government. It's the businessmen who contribute to community projects.'

The Dane had a thoughtful look as we drove off. 'Now, the curious thing is,' he said, 'that that man is a leader in our town in every committee for the public good. He's one of the most publicspirited men we've got. How can he be so shortsighted?'

As we drove farther along the highway we could see the flashing perpendicular jaws of the cornpickers mounted on tractors moving down the rows. The tall ragged cornstalks fell trembling and were swallowed up. Yellow corncobs glowed in the sun as they plopped in a stream into the towed wagons. 'One man can do in a day with one of those what five men did with a combine and what twenty men could do by hand . . . The weather looks almost too good,' said the Dane. 'But the farmers are breaking their necks to get the corn in. Can't trust the weather this late in the year.'

He had turned into a driveway that went to a neat narrow white house that sat up like a jackrabbit among smoothboled walnut trees. Their last yellow leaves spun as they fell to the grass of the dooryard. 'You were asking about stretching manpower,' the Dane said. 'This lady runs a three hundred acre farm all by herself. Let's ask her how she does it.' As we climbed out of the car a redfaced buxom woman in a Mother Hubbard and a blue poke bonnet came hurrying towards us from the barnyard, pulling off her workgloves as she came. 'I knew you were coming, Mr. Hansen,' she screeched, 'but I just had to do some work in the garden. There's so little time left . . . Do come right in and sit down.' Panting, she fussed around us as she ushered us into her clean kitchen that smelt of apples and milkpans and coal oil. 'This friend of mine wants to know how you do it,' said the Dane, with his broad disarming smile.

She sat down in a rocker facing us. As she talked she rocked fast. Well, she'd been a widow for sixteen years, so she'd had to manage her own affairs. No, she'd never had any inclination to marry again. What she did was get a young boy as hired man and bring him up right. Of course, people would talk if she got a man her own age living right here in the house with her, but, shucks, this way she was like a mother to the boys. She'd been very careful who she picked, of course. She picked clean steady youngsters who didn't use tobacco or anything like that, and they certainly had been marvels. This boy she had now was the third she'd had. The other two had grown up and married and she'd lost them. This boy she had now was going steady with a girl, but she hoped she could hold on to him until the war was over, anyway. He was a worker, all right. The last two weeks he had been picking corn by day and plowing at night. He'd rigged headlights on the tractor. But had we heard about Mr. Hawkins? Ground his hand off in the cornpicker. Might lose his arm. Dear land sakes, she hoped he wouldn't. He was such a civil man and a good neighbor. She had heard he was careless with machinery. So many things like that were happening round the country. People were in such a hurry. Most of 'em trying to get more work done than they could manage. Of course, we had to do it when the country needed the production. No, she didn't sell any corn. The cows took it all. She sold her milk. The cows took a lot of feeding, and what was left she fed to the hogs and the fowls. More profit that way. She had to buy feed as it was, and, my, it was scarce. She'd done right well with her hogs. Shipped them at the end of six months. The last lot the boy had shipped into Kansas City had been so fine the dealer had given her a premium on them. She heard it over the telephone . . . 'I slid down like I was about to faint. The boy said, "Let's shake. I fed 'em" . . . That boy sure can feed hogs.'

A tall young man with dark eyes and brows in a face crimson from the outdoors stood pulling off his gloves in the back doorway. When he noticed it was him we were talking about, his red face went even redder.

'I bet your ears are burning,' the Dane said pleasantly, as we got up to shake hands with him. 'Maybe you can tell us how one man and a tractor can take care of three hundred acres.'

'Well,' the young man said after a long pause, 'I let the tractor do the work.'

'How about next year?'

'Don't hurt to hope. We can't feed no more stock. We got

no more stable room. We're aimin' to shift to beefcattle a little It's gettin' so hard to get mash, but we're aimin' to produce a little more feed ourselves. We grind our own corn.' He showed a set of broad white teeth in a grin. 'The tractor does the grindin' ... Well, I'm glad to met you folks,' he said, coming forward gravely to shake hands again. 'I better be goin' about my business.'

Peace on Earth

Driving back into town, the Dane told me about his own life. He was an American citizen, he'd served in the army in the last war. He'd been brought up on a dairy farm in the old country and had come over because he thought he had better chances for schooling in America. He'd worked his way through college managing a dairy. Then he'd married and the itch to make money had gotten hold of him and he'd gone into the grocery business. He'd run a retail store in Pennsylvania, but he and his wife had gotten tired of just buying cheap and selling dear and he'd sold his grocery and come out here to take a position with the county cooperative. It was harder work and less pay, but he loved it. This was a Quaker community. His wife came from here and was kin to most of the old established Quaker farmers. They were the kind of people he liked. This town he lived in was the kind of town he liked, with its treeshaded streets kept so clean and its little college, a Quaker institution, and the sense of dignified community life these folks had. They were all working farmers. Most of them had been to college. The farms were large and took a lot of work, but the land was rich. They were awful tight with their money and set in their ways, but he liked them. The war was hard on them on account of their religion. Many of the boys were in C.O. camps, when they'd be more useful at home on the farm where hands were so scarce. The cooperative ideas fitted in with Quaker notions of how to do things. He felt that in this trying time when they were cut off from other folks by the war, the cooperative offered them a rea' constructive community enterprise to rally around. He believed himself that there was no other way to fight fascism than with arms — look what had happened to his own Denmark — but while we did that, he believed we had to build democracy at home. Otherwise, we would win the war abroad and lose it at home. That was why he was so happy in his work. He felt he was building practical democracy.

'As a merchant I was a very unhappy man, and now I'm a very happy man,' he said.

It was dusk when we drove up in front of his house. On the broad lawns of the treeshaded street, piles of leaves were burning, adding a deeper blue to the blue mist of the October evening. He sat at the wheel for a moment, staring ahead of him. 'How well we work together to produce for war that is all destruction,' he said. I didn't answer. Then he went on, 'It is my profound conviction that the cooperative movement is the only answer. We have reached a point where business economics can only survive through war and government subsidies. If we can get the farmers who grow the food, and the town people who produce the machinery, to gear their economy together through co-operatives we can eliminate the dangerous group conflicts within the state. It'll be only when these are eliminated that we'll be able to go ahead and try to eliminate wars between nations.'

His wife had come out on the stoop to see why we didn't come in the house. As we walked up the steps, crunching through the leaves that had fallen that day, she called out to him, 'Darling, I just called my sister on the phone. She says Pete Hawkins is doing very nicely at the hospital, but,' her voice choked, 'he had to lose three fingers of his right hand.'

When I left them to catch the bus I said to the Dane who was a very busy man that I hoped I hadn't taken up too much of his time. 'It's been a vacation for me,' he answered, smiling. 'Why, I'd rather ride around the country and talk to farmers than do anything else in the world.'

Wilmington, Ohio, October, 1943

2

Westward the Course

The train crossed the Mississippi in a flurry of snow. The line curved onto a levee along the edges of a great still backwater here and there blurred with snow, here and there streaked with blue from reflected patches of clear sky; then it crossed a bridge above a swirl of muddy water; then ran through a little wood. Beyond the smooth boles of the trees you could see the river and against the pale bluff opposite a little town that seemed to be on an island of green grass. There was a row of tall vaseshaped elms in front of some stately old white houses and a church with a slender pointed steeple. It was like one of the old untouched towns left over from the good times of New England. As the train lurched round another curve the little town vanished like something seen in a dream.

Meanwhile, the heavyset man with sunken eyes beside me was talking and talking in a deep husky voice in my ear. 'The man in the White House was all right,' he was saying, 'to tide us over the depression. What we needed in those days was compromise, temporizing, finagling. He gave the country time to get its breath and to find its way around in the modern age that came on too soon for us. Now what we need is conviction, a plain man of conviction. Such a man will rise up suddenly when the people need him, the way Lincoln rose up out of the people, the way Bryan rose up out of the people . . . The man this country needs is living today, doing his workaday work somewhere among the people of the United States. When the need comes for such a man he will rise up from among the people. I believe he's got to come from the west.'

The Wisconsin Drift

'What do folks around here think about? Why, they think about corn, corn and hogs, but corn mostly,' drawled my friend,

in his ingratiating singsong. He was a large sandyhaired man
with a large frame loosely put together and a large belly and
large powerful arms and large irregular features linked together
by thoughtful lines in a triangular ruddy face. Sprawling at the
table in the lunchroom over his second cup of coffee, he had the
look he often had of being just about to wriggle out of the workclothes that hung loosely about him. He had a slow persuasive
expository way of talking. His manner was between that of a
lecturer explaining the solution of a problem at a blackboard,
and a lawyer pleading with a jury. There was a disarming
friendliness in his voice that had a way of dissolving objections
before you brought them up. 'Around here they are the durnest
folks for growing corn,' he said. 'They don't know about much
else. They get out of growing corn what other folks in the East
get out of country clubs and the stockmarket and the international situation.'

We were sitting in a small plain lunchroom on the short main
street of a small plain town on a creek in a region of broad slow
lazy hills. The carefully scrubbed tables and counter and the
chairs were plain and old. The fittings were seedy. The middleaged waitress had a brisk homely healthy look. The men
hunched over coffeecups at the counter, or meditatively dawdling round the tables, were all in workclothes. Most of them
wore high boots. The highpriced cars parked in the centre of the
street outside were splattered with brown mud. Everything
was built for use in this town.

'You are sitting right now' — my friend went on with his
lecture — 'plumb in the middle of one of the richest agricultural
regions on the face of the earth, the Wisconsin drift of black dirt.
Since our grandfathers moved out here we've been taking crop
after crop off it without the slightest diminution in fertility.
Instead of getting poorer, the land is getting richer. I'll tell you
why it's getting richer. We are just starting to learn to use
fertilizer on this land. Hybrid seed corn has added about twenty
bushels to the yield per acre. A number of years ago we used to
hear a good deal about the hundred bushel club made up of fellers

who had managed to grow a hundred bushels of corn to the acre.
Now nobody talks about it any more . . . too many members . . .
A hundred bushels isn't the average yet, not by a long shot, but
it might be. Then new machinery, better tractors, better plows,
the mechanical cornpicker, have increased the yield per man . . .
Boys,' he addressed the men at the next table, 'how long is it
since an oldfashioned twenty mule combine was seen operating
in this county?'

'The last one was laid away two years ago,' piped up a short
blackeyed man, with a chin full of black stubble, who wore a
turtleneck sweater and overalls.

'Even then it was an antique. Now one good man on a picker
can bring in more corn in a day than ten men and twentysix
mules could.' He drank the last of his coffee. 'Now, suppose
we go and take a look around.' He gathered himself slowly together and rose to his feet. 'No,' he said gently, as I tried to pull
out a dollar bill, 'your Eastern money isn't any good here, is it,
Ellen?' The waitress, who was standing beside the table with
her hands in the pockets of her apron, smiled brightly and shook
her head.

I followed him out to his car and we drove slowly out Main
Street and past the sparse bare trees of the little park at the end
and across the bridge over the muddy creek already rimmed with
ice. 'You came just at the right time,' he was saying. 'I got
the last of my corn in yesterday. We've got plenty of time today
to loaf around a bit . . . First, we'll swing around past the plant.'

Hybrid Seed Corn

He drove down a side road past a row of small new white houses
that had the constricted look of the houses on the cover of a
builders' supply catalogue and crossed the railroad tracks and
stopped in front of a long gray galvanized-iron building. Behind
it, next to an elevator tower, rose a volcanoshaped mountain of
reddish yellow cobs. He leaned back in his seat and stared at
the pile with some satisfaction. 'What do you think of that foɪ

a pile of cobs? . . . And they've been carting 'em away every day
We burn 'em in the stoves here . . . When I first went into the
hybrid seed corn business eleven years ago folks thought I was
crazy. I had the hardest time persuading the fellers around here
to take a couple bushels for a trial. Now we can't begin to fill
the orders . . . Folks make me tired when they talk about the
frontier being gone. We are on a frontier all over this country.
Even back East there'd be frontiers if folks had the sense to look
for 'em . . . damn wonderful frontiers . . . You see the corn goes
in at the end over there, and then it's dried by hot air from mechanical blowers. Then it runs through troughs where they sort
out the grades, then it's shucked by machinery and shot up into
bins. Then we draw it off in bags and store it in that last building. That building at the end is jampacked full of the finest kind
of hybrid seed corn right now . . . If we could fill a couple more
warehouses like that we could fill all the orders we get . . . I tell
you, we have ourselves a time out here with our seed corn business.' He had started the car and was circling back onto the
main highroad out of town again.

Farm Management

'Politics,' he was saying. 'The only time folks worry about
politics around here is when times are bad and they can't get a
price for their corn. Other times they just naturally vote Republican. The way they're messing up the corn hog ratio in
Washington is what is worrying me. They are going to bring
about an acute shortage of feed in this country . . . Now and
then I get on the train and go to Washington and go around and
try to lay down the law to the boys, try to tell 'em how things
really are out where we produce the stuff. I'm working against
my own interests at that, arguing for a low price on feed, because
it's to my interest to have a high price for corn . . . but I get
something out of it just the same. I get kind of an idea of what
they are up to around there. That helps me in my business.'
He brought the car suddenly to a halt at the corner of a dirt

road that cut across the highway. His voice had a streak of impatience in it, unusual for him. 'Now look at this feller. See what he's done,' he said as he pointed to a farm that rolled in dun patches of pasture and bluegreen strips of winter oats and great squares of wrecked stubble of harvested cornfields up over the gradual hills. 'See, he's got a little pasture in the corner near the house no bigger than a nickel . . . Now, his houselot's all right, I don't mind that, but, you see, he's got some very good land there and he's ruined it with nasty little crisscross fences. How can he plow those fields? No place to turn the tractor around . . . I aim for milelong rows.'

He turned and drove up the sludgy dirt road to the top of a hill and then he swung out into a field through a gap in the fence and drove uphill over the bumpy grass that had spread over the old furrows where corn had been planted. At the very summit he slowed down to a stop. 'Let's get out and stretch our legs a little.'

We climbed out of the car beside a great stack of oatstraw. We were on the top of the highest hill around. In front of us a small unpainted farmhouse sagged black and vacant with gaping windows. Behind the house the great stretch of country rolled pale ochre towards blue hills along the horizon moving in slow undulations like an ocean groundswell in a calm. Here and there in a deeper hollow was a scrap of a bright blue pond or the green smudge of a swamp.

My friend pointed vindictively at the house. 'I'll have that out of here before long. You see the feller who lived up here was starving to death . . . I hate to see that . . . No decent well. No barn. It's quite easy for folks to starve to death on the richest land in the world if they don't manage it right. Now, the first thing I do when I get hold of a piece of land is pull out the fences and knock the houses down and cart 'em away. We got to have space to operate our machinery. Do you notice the roads? When this country was laid out years ago they laid out roads a mile apart each way. A square mile ought to be the unit for growing corn in this country. Then you can cultivate sixtyfive acres a day along milelong rows.'

He turned and pointed in the other direction.

'You see over there there's a gully beginning to wash. That's
a bad business. What we do is to put in an earth dam and fix it
so that the water comes up out of a standing pipe and flows over
the top. You'd be surprised how soon the space behind the dam
will fill up with mud. When it has filled up to the top you raise
the dam and set your pipe higher up, and in three or four years
your gully is filled up flat as your hand, and you've got a field you
can operate with. Well, I know what you're going to say, what
about the tenants? All you bighearted folks back East are
worked up about the tenants . . . Let's move on. It's getting
chilly. I'm going to show you a tenant.'

We drove down the hill to the main road again. 'Now, I'm
going to take you to see a tenant who has put twentyfive thousand
dollars in the bank in two years. I know because he is under my
management. Of course, I admit he's got one of the best farms
in the country. He's somewhat exceptional, but out here folks
don't have to starve to death. Mind you, twentyfive thousand
dollars was his share after the landlord was paid off and all expenses paid. Of course, he's a lively young feller who works
from before dawn till after dark, and who'll do what you tell him.
We used plenty of fertilizer. Some folks would rather lose money
than invest a couple of thousand dollars in chemical fertilizer.
One way I keep the boys interested is to lay bets with 'em. I
bet 'em such and such a piece of land won't bring thirty bushels
or fortyfive or eighty, say, according to what kind of land it is,
and they'll work their heads off to make a monkey out of me. I
lose quite a little money that way.' He looked at me and grinned.
'But it sure is worth it in bushels to the acre.'

He turned off on another rightangle crossroad and drove up to
a small plain white house. The barn in back was modest and the
cowshed and outbuildings were in poor repair.

A mildfaced lighthaired young man in blue overalls came out
of the house, stretching. After we'd asked about his wife who
had been feeling poorly, my friend started off:

'Joe. that feeding floor's in the wrong place. It's unsightly

We don't want your wife looking down into a hogtrough every time she comes out the kitchen door, now, do we? Specially when she's got one of the most beautiful views over the finest cornland on God's green earth stretching out as far as she can see. I'm goin' to tear that cowbarn down and cart it away this winter and build you a decent one and a concrete feeding floor . . . One thing about farming,' he added in an aside to me, 'that folks often forget is that you can't take out unless you put in . . . Say, Joe, we were talking about how much land one man could handle if he was the right kind of a man with the right kind of equipment. Exactly how many acres did you handle yourself this year?'

The man pushed his denim cap back thoughtfully on his head for a moment.

'Let's see,' he answered quietly. 'I had two hundred and eighty acres in corn and sixty acres in oats, and then there was sixtyfive acres in flax and sixtyfive acres in soybeans the government asked for, and the hay . . .' He paused and stood looking out over the rolling land pallid with winter. We looked the way he was looking. A big red squirrel had come out of the tangled cornstubble and was venturing in a series of little quick runs along the fence. Three belated bluebirds fluttered up and darted away into the sky. 'Well, say fifteen acres in hay . . . The wife takes care of the garden . . . Of course,' he added in a sober voice, 'I did have a hired man some, but the custom work I did for the neighbors with the tractor plowing and with the cornpicker picking corn, just about balanced that up.'

'And you're not worn out yet, Joe?' My friend burst out laughing.

'I'm in pretty fair shape, to tell the truth.'

As we drove back toward town, my friend was saying, 'And we haven't begun to produce in this country yet. Well, suppose we go and have us a cup of coffee and see what the boys have to say, and then I'll take you to see some really poor land, a farm I'm taking over nobody ever could make a living on. I have a hunch that with proper cultivation and plenty of fertilizer I can

make that grow corn just about as well as this good land ... I'll
have me a whale of a time trying anyway ... I know you folks
in the East are always saying the country's going to the dogs.
Maybe it is. But I tell you it's hard to convince us farmers it is,
when a man like that can bank twentyfive thousand dollars in
two years.'

Coon Rapids, Iowa, November, 1943

3

Cooperative Commonwealth

Every seat was taken in the coaches on the transcontinental train west. The breathed-out air was heavy and stale. People had the wilted look of having slept night after night in their clothes. Most of them had come clear from Chicago. There were sailors and soldiers and a great many young women out of textile mills and department stores and negro families all dressed up in new duds and middleaged mechanics and old daylaborers and cocky young kids out of highschool in leather jackets. They were all going through to the Coast. The civilians were headed for war industries. The soldiers and sailors were headed for the Pacific. Through all the travelweariness there was an air of adventure about the closepacked travelsodden crowd. People spelled out for each other the unfamiliar names of stations. They told each other about the jobs they were going to and showed each other their slips from the hiring services. At the rare curves in the straight track their necks craned towards the murky windows to get the first glimpse of the Rocky Mountains that were still hundreds of miles to the west.

The train had left the lake country tufted with birch and larch and spruce and scrubby pine and was jogging steadily across a wan wintry plain of endless wheatfields powdered with the first snow. I was standing in the vestibule breathing the cold air that came up through the floor when I noticed that a longlegged lighthaired dourlooking man beside me wore a Farmers' Union button. We got to talking and it came out that he was headed for the same convention I was headed for. A glaze of suspicion came over his gray eyes when I began to ask him questions. I was asking him about farmers' cooperatives. Reluctantly he admitted he knew something about them. 'Where I live,' he said soberly, 'in the extreme northwest corner of the state, we can still remember the drouth years when eighty farmers out of every hundred were on relief. We've taken a beating out there

and we know that if we don't help ourselves nobody's going to
help us.'

We managed to find ourselves two seats among a stack of
drowsy young gobs in a smoking compartment. I mentioned a
name he knew. I suggested that at the office they'd know I was
coming. At that, it was some time before he would open up.
'The newspapers don't like us,' he grumbled. 'Well, we don't
like them. Take this business about boxcars. We have the
hardest time getting boxcars for our cooperative elevators. The
wartime allocation authorities are rigging the regulations in
favor of the big milling interests and against us . . . Well, we're
getting pretty big ourselves.'

In the county he lived in, the cooperatives had just about had
to take over everything. Once he started to talk he couldn't
help warming up to the subject. Private business in the tank
towns was folding up. The cooperatives were able to handle the
situation fine. Business doubling, going up by leaps and bounds
. . . New services all the time. 'We can put together the chunks
of the business system as fast as they fall off,' was how he put it.

They would make a beginning of a cooperative commonwealth
if legislation didn't cripple them. There was a move in Washington to tax cooperatives like other corporations. That would
mean double taxation because the members paid taxes on their
profits. In his opinion, the business interests were out to nip the
cooperatives in the bud before they became too strong. Well,
they had a fight ahead of them. To tell the truth, they weren't
so badly off for a fight — they had a strong national organization
and strong consumer and marketing organizations. In the county
he lived in private business was just about gone. He used to work
in a chainstore himself, had worked his way up to manager —
what a gyp! Well, now he managed a cooperative grocery. They
were giving better service at lower prices with more profit than
the chainstore ever did. But they never would get away with it
without a political organization to keep hammering on the
legislatures. Out here the Farmers' Union and the cooperatives
worked together like your two hands; you know, when you wash
your hands, one hand washes the other.

The young sailors were sleeping all in a heap on their seabags. The man pointed at them with his thumb. Their pink faces with closed lids swollen with sleep looked almost babyish, they were so young. 'Let's get out of here,' he said, 'and give these kids a chance to sleep.'

While we were lurching our way down the aisle of the car again, he suddenly put his hand on my arm. 'Isn't it too bad,' he whispered, 'when you think of these kids, where they are going, what they'll have to go through . . . that the people of this country have to be tearing each other to pieces instead of working together to back these boys up? The kind of folks we are . . . we'd like to let down our guard. If we could put the energy into just producing we have to put into fighting the interests in this country, we'd finish this war up in jigtime. But we can't do that. We know through long experience that the minute us little fellers quit fightin' the big boys'll eat us up . . . And we don't want to forget, friend,' his voice grew loud and gruff above the racket of the train, 'that these kids are our kids and this country is our country. That's why we have to fight the enemy at home while they fight the enemy abroad.'

Resolutions Committee

The resolutions committee sat at a long table in the brick basement. They were big plainly dressed men with heavy hands thickened by farm work, and weathered faces engraved with fine wrinkles by the glare and the savage climate of the plains. They were men you would look at twice wherever you saw them. The chairman had dark curly hair and a decisive profile and a long thoughtful nose. He had a bad cold and kept blowing his nose into a big white handkerchief. Beside him sat the secretary, a little quickwitted brighteyed cripple who moved jerkily among his papers with the motions of a marionette when the wires are tangled.

From upstairs through the floor came the creaking shuffle of the crowd in the hall and the sound of men's and women's voices singing:

> We're in the Farmers' Union;
> We shall not be moved,
> We shall not be moved,
> Just like a tree
> Standing by the water,
> We shall not be moved.

The tiny secretary was reading in a taut voice:

> We are fully aware, however, that this worldshaking crisis, the mean-
> ing of which we cannot yet fully grasp, will not be over with the con-
> clusion of the military phase of the conflict. In the new age, struggling
> to be born, two powerful forces are at work. On the one side, the few,
> lusting for profit, would snatch the fruits of victory to further entrench
> their power at home and fasten a new imperialism, with the help of
> similar vested interests in other nations, on the whole world.

He paused. The men along the table had sat listening with
furrowed brows. There was a silence. 'Nobody will sacrifice
anything but their sons in this war . . . That's what that means
. . . Sure.' There was another silence. Their faces were grave.
In his head each man was struggling to bridge the distance between the notion and the phrase.

'Couldn't we say it plainer?' asked a handsome lighthaired
man who was leaning back in his chair blowing smoke up at the
ceiling.

'What we need is a Wagner Act for agriculture,' muttered a
broadfaced man at the end of the table.

'We ought to bring out clear and straight who our enemies
are,' came a bitter voice. 'Some of the newspapers, some politicians, the bankers, the big grain operators,' the sharpfaced man
went on slowly as if counting them off on his fingers.

'Sure,' said somebody else. 'How about more fight in it?'
The thought seemed to cheer them up. Smiles went from face
to face. 'Brass tacks, plenty brass tacks,' a man shouted cheerfully.

'And what about the family-sized farm? That's our platform, ain't it?'

'Most of that's in . . . After all, this is just the preamble. The
details follow in the body of the resolutions,' interrupted the

chairman, in his bland tones. 'It's tied up pretty tight.' He smiled a subtle smile. 'Suppose I read it again from the beginning,' he said insinuatingly. 'It reads to me like it was pretty well boiled down to the essence.' With a fatherly kind of smile he took the typewritten sheets from the secretary, who grinned and wiped the sweat off his forehead. He started again at the beginning. He read the words precisely and well. Hearing it a second time heads began to nod approval.

> ... millions of common people are striving to make the century theirs through developing economic freedom by acquiring democratic ownership ...

'That's the cooperative idea,' a man interrupted sharply. 'That's all right.'

> ... producing abundantly, trading without restraint, and by acquiring political freedom through the extension of education, civil liberties and participation in governments of their own choosing ...

'Good.' Somebody let out a genial growl.

'We've lost every legislative battle in Washington this year,' interrupted the sharpfaced man again. 'What are we going to do when the drouth comes back with no Youth Administration, and Farm Security just about gone?'

'... And when the banks have put the Indian sign on government credit,' echoed a voice from the end of the table.

The chairman paused and looked up attentively from the typewritten sheets. Again there was the silence of knitted brows round the table. From upstairs came the bass viol sound of slow voices singing:

> From the hills I gather courage,
> Visions of the day to be;
> Strength to lead and faith to follow —
> All are given unto me ...

The men were listening to the words of the song. By their slow breathing you could see they were stirred by its slow organ-like solemnity. 'That's *Peace by the River*, that's the one we sing

best,' one man turned to another and whispered with a smile
They waited till the voices in the hall above had finished:

Peace I ask of thee, O River,
Peace . . .

'We better get along. We can't stay all day on one sentence,
said a crisp voice. Throats were cleared. Chairs were drawn
closer to the table   The chairman blew his nose loud into his big
handkerchief and began to read again.

Jamestown, North Dakota, November, 1943

SERVICE MEN waiting in line to get into the diner are passing the word along that there's a carload of Russians in the back of the train. There's a carload of them all right, but they aren't Russians. They come from every state in the Union. Old men. Young men. Drunk men. Sober men. Only yesterday they got off the boat from Alaska. They've been up north in the northwest drizzle building a base on the coast. Yarning, smoking, spitting, laughing, shouting, kidding, cussing, they loll back in the soft seats of the overheated daycoach. They've had baths since they landed, haircuts, the best meals money could buy, they've been out on the town. All the clothes they are wearing are new, shoes, high boots, new corduroy pants, new leather jackets, new lumberjacks. Their wallets are stuffed with new bills; they have nuggets of Alaska gold in their vest pockets. Some of them still wear their beards, broad beards and chin beards, goatees, imperials, muttonchops, drooping walrus mustaches they are wearing home to astonish the folks.

The car's a bunkhouse on wheels. Shouting. Hooting. A continual hail of fourletter language . . . 'Sweet Jesus, that's the sun. Ain't seen the sun in three hundred and seventyfive aays.' . . . 'Is it good to see houses again?' . . . 'Boys, that's a woman.' . . . 'Is that a woman?' 'Ain't seen a woman since Christ was a

[283]

corporal.' 'You buckheaded son of a seabee, what was that wearin' skirts I seen you with in Seattle?' 'He was too drunk to see in Seattle.' ... 'We started afoot from the liquor store.' ... 'She took us right home in a cab.' ... 'We picked this gal up near the liquor store.' ... 'She kept feeding me drinks; nothing doing, I kept her at arms' length. If you once get the syph you're a goner.' ...'We met this jane in a restaurant.' ... 'We were looking for a steak, but chicken was all we could get ... Sure I slep' wid her. What do you tink I was doin', readin' the Gideon Bible?' ... 'We had three quarts in a paper bag.' ... 'Last place I saw those guys was the liquor store.' ... 'I lost my ticket on the way to the station ...'

Four older men are reverently nursing a quart of rye, talking over the finished job in drowsy philosophic style. 'Wasn't that a bastard? ... You'd go down a foot and hit mud and another foot and hit rock again and then a splash of water ... That bullhead didn't know nothin' about construction ... That Indian Joe, he wasn't a bad Indian, a good worker, a real hard worker.' 'Chief, he had a good deal of Russian blood ... Quicktempered though, got beat up about every time he went to town.' 'They were two very steady workers .. Our Indians back home, they wouldn't pitch in an' work like that' ... 'Remember that big Norwegian? He was as good as he was big. He'd pick up a hammer and he never did turn it off. When he'd drilled one hole he'd just lift it over an' drill another. He never did put his foot on it. He was a powerful bastard.'

The train was jogging slowly round the curves of a deep blue glacial river up a snowy canyon full of young spruces. A small buck that stood drinking on the ice rim of the opposite bank raised his head and looked at us. He sniffed for a moment with his head high and turned and leapt gently out of sight among the young spruces. 'Boy, if I only had my gun!' ... 'I left my gun and seventeen shells in British Columbia.' . . . 'Jeez, let's go huntin'.' . . . 'Knocked one off up the valley at a thousand yards.' . . . 'This was kind of a reservation, see? All you had to do was know where the warden was . . . We went up there an' shot us the fattest doe you ever saw.'

A tall man with a thin broken nose and weatherbleached yellow hair combed back on his head, lets himself down on the arm of the seat beside the four whiskey philosophers. He wants to know if they signed up with any of those hiring agents in Seattle. Headshaking. Downward gestures with the flat of the hand. Talk of jobs in India, China, Brazil, bonuses, vacations. He says thoughtfully he's heard of something that interests him in South Africa. 'In the vicinity of Cape Town . . . nice climate . . . After a year in Alaska you need to thaw out . . . I looked it up in the National Geographic. I'd like to see Africa.'

A redfaced sailor, somewhat breezed up, comes down the aisle singing 'I want to go back to West Virginia' in hillbilly falsetto. He hovers unsteadily over the broadest of the beards. 'Who do you think you are brother, Paul Revere?' The whiskey philosophers hold their bottle up to him as they roar in unison, 'You mean Paul Bunyan.'

CHAPTER 13

North and West of the Great Divide

I<small>T WAS A RAW NIGHT</small> of freezing fog. We were sitting in front of the fire in the ornate pink lobby of a big mineowners' hotel. This tall lawyer had been telling me he'd come out here as a boy, from the Middle West, had sold papers, gone to public school, studied law here, grown up with the country; the typical white collar man's career, he said. Yes, he thought it had been easier for him in a new country than if he'd stayed East. He didn't feel at home any more the other side of the Continental Divide. I asked something about the Columbia River and his face caught fire. 'Let's go over to my office and look at a map,' he said.

We walked with long strides through empty slippery streets that had a gaunt look in the freezing fog. Upstairs in a tall square dark building he let me into his office and switched on the light. There were maps on three walls. 'You probably find it surprising to see so many maps on the walls of a lawoffice,' he said with a shy smile, 'but the Columbia River's been my hobby for years . . . My wife and I go to look at it every time we get a chance. I think I've seen every speck of it you can reach with a car.'

He twisted the greenshaded lamp on his desk around so that the light fell on a map on the opposite wall that showed the region between the Rocky Mountains and the Pacific Coast from

Alaska and the Canadian North to the California line. 'Here's the Columbia River.' He followed the jiggly black line of the river down the map with a long knotted forefinger. 'It's the greatest glacial river in the world. It's got a course like a Chinese dragon, always clear green or blue. It starts out flowing northwest up here in Canada. Then it doubles back and pours out of a region of long lakes into the desert country of Washington and describes a gigantic S through the state. At Grand Coulee it breaks into the Cascade Mountains but is thrown back east again; then after the Snake River comes in out of Idaho, it breaks through for fair a hundred and fifty miles to the south at the Dalles and goes out through the gorges and into the Pacific beyond Portland . . . These are the dams already built. These are the dams we hope they'll build. Columbia River waterpower is the basis for the future wealth of this whole great inland empire. Then there is salmon . . . and wheat . . .' He brushed his fingers back and forth across the map. 'This is the dryfarming wheat country . . .' He placed his full flat hand against the middle of the map. 'This is the region that's going to be reclaimed when Congress appropriates the money for the storage reservoir in Grand Coulee.' He was pointing with his finger again. 'The fruit begins out here, apples, apricots, berries, everything you can imagine. The Cascades are the richest undeveloped source of rare minerals in the United States. Here's a great deposit of zinc . . . and all the rest is timber, the past wealth of the country, now headed straight for destruction. We can save it by sustained yield operations if we have the sense.'

He turned sharply away and sat down at his desk again. 'We are in a curious state of mind out here. We feel that with the opening up of airplane trade with the Soviet Union and the Far East we ought to be one of the most important corners of the nation, but that we are still dominated by Eastern financial interests who think of us as just another colony to exploit . . . We'd welcome them if they came out here to grow up with the country. The people in British Columbia feel the same, only worse, because the railroad monopolies and the like have a much tighter control in Canada than they have in the United States. The feeling's growing that the Pacific Northwest is one separate unit and that we ought to work together on both sides of the line to keep Ottawa and Wall Street from reducing us to the level of poor whites . . . Well . . .' He picked up a pencil and twirled it thoughtfully between his fingers for a while. Then he said sharply: 'Men can't expect to survive without a struggle.'

Where the Volcanoes and the Glaciers Worked

The next morning a man from the power administration drove me out of town before day through a gray land of hoarfrost and fog. We headed westward out past the glare of floodlights over army airfields, through a region of scattered pines. 'This piney stretch is all scabrock from an old lava flow. The volcanoes and the glaciers both worked on this country.' Intent on the road he spoke without turning his head. With full daylight through the mist we came out on immense flat lands, white with frost. 'The wheat country begins here,' he said. 'In summer the wheat's shoulder high . . . we have hot days and cool nights. That's what wheat likes.' I asked him how many acres the average farm had through here. He didn't move his head because the road was a glaze of ice, but the corner of his mouth stretched towards me in a grin. 'A quarter section, a half section . . . we don't talk about acres much.'

We were passing a long farmhouse with wide porches and big barns and outbuildings and a small grain elevator in back. He pointed out an oblong bin built of freshsawed boards. 'See, he had to build himself an extra bin. Everything's still chockablock full of wheat around here. Every farm has one of these, or two, maybe . . . This land was homesteaded about fifty years ago. They've never had a real bad crop yet . . . Down further south where the reclamation project's going to be they tried wheat and had to give it up. Too many dry years . . . These houses are like townhouses for conveniences. They have just about everything there is and they still want more . . . What we are looking fo:

after the war is an electric furnace that will store heat in some way at nights, during the period of least load, and distribute it during the day. There's one that heats up granite blocks that's pretty feasible but it's not quite right yet. There'll be a demand for electric appliances around the barn. This region has the highest per capita consumption of electric power in the nation. There was a good deal of tenant farming, but the owners are taking the farms back into their own hands. With modern machinery it's too darn profitable to farm them themselves ... I wish the sun would come out and thaw the road out a little ... I lose just about one car a year this way, running off the road from ice ... I don't want to lose this one just yet.' We sat silent, looking ahead, as he drove down the smooth straight slippery road. It was hard not to clench your teeth.

After another couple of hours the road forked and the country began to break into great duncolored folds. The mist had lifted a little and the frosting was gone off the road. Some blurry dots far in the distance turned out to be a flock of sheep. Ten miles farther a little truck with a house on it stood alone on the spot where wheeltracks turned off to wander out of sight into the sagebrush. 'Chuck wagon,' he said. 'Somebody herding those sheep.' The road began to wind by slow curves down into a depression. As we swung towards the north, the country began to heave and roll. Overhead the mist bunched up into clouds. Ahead of us an immense flock of birds spread upwards in a dark streak like a snapping whip.

'Those ducks?'

'Geese. They'll form up in a V in a minute.'

As the road wound down, the hills grew steeper and through curtains of mist we began to see dark slopes rising again miles away across the valley. Far below in the shadow a patch of silver showed up for a second with a light streak cutting it off. 'That's the dam,' the power man said, without changing the tone of his voice. 'That's the largest edifice man has yet constructed.'

Waterpower

The dam in the immense misted fold of the buffcolored mountains
looks neat and exact as an architect's elevation. The whole
Columbia River pours roaring over the spillway as smoothly as in
a draftsman's wash sketch. The buildings and offices look like
the prizewinning effort of a class in mechanical drawing. The
engineer in charge is large and quiet and blueeyed, with a memory
of the State of Maine in his voice to give a twang to his ruminative
way of understating his story. Only in the eyes of the gnomelike
elderly man with a white beard on his chin, who shows us around,
is there an occasional sparkle of excitement. The hall in the pow-
erstation, ten stories high, where the generators whir like big tops
in a row, is full of quiet business. An extra generator is being installed. The war has increased the demand for power beyond anybody's imagining. The overhead crane is lowering vast concave
sections of burnished steel gently into place at the end of the line
of generators. Stairway after stairway down underneath, we
crawl through the snailshaped scrollcase lined with bituminous
paint. Soon another spout of the river will churn through there
into the turbines. The control room with its charts and dials is as
quiet as a physics laboratory in summer. A skinny man in a
green eyeshade sits at a plain little desk the size of a kitchen table
with boards full of dials set round him on the floor like mansized
dominoes. 'Every four hours we get Naval Observatory time,' he
says. 'We regulate our time by that or else all the electric clocks
would go screwy on account of slight variations of current. The
whole Northwest is hooked up in a grid. That means power can
be equalized anywhere the load gets heavy. Without the grid our
war industries would be up against it.'

'By the way,' I ask the gnome, as we are walking back towards
the car, 'how do the people who fought public power say we could
have fought this war without it?'

'They've been very quiet on the subject,' he said, his eyes snapping. 'The truth is we would have been out of luck . . . I mean
. . . out . . . of . . . luck.'

At the thought we shivered as we stood there in our overcoats in the warm sun of the valley.

'The Northwest has been pretty well sold on public power,' my friend said, once we were out of earshot of the roar of the great spillway. Our road had started to climb up out of the valley again. 'Tacoma has had municipal power since 1893. Seattle's had it since 1902 and its development has been an outstanding success ... We can't imagine the Northwest without it. We'd be just like the Okies, without public power, a lot of miserable poor whites starving in the midst of plenty.'

We had driven up into the altitude of mist and frost again Nothing moved in the great billowing landscape of dry grass and sagebrush, here and there powdered white, except miles away a single tractor drawing two disk plows that left a dark scrape of turned dirt behind it as it moved slowly across the hillside. Three miles farther on we saw a house. We turned down into a wide canyon with precipitous walls and a great rock mesa in the middle of it. 'That's Steamboat Rock,' my friend said. 'That will be an island. This is Grand Coulee proper. This is where the river flowed during the last glacial period. You see it's left lakes ... good duckshooting there ... Where we are now will be a hundred feet under water. They'll build an earth dam at both ends and make this a storage reservoir for the reclamation project. Two extra generators will pump the water up from the present dam during the period of least load. Then it will flow down into the irrigation canals by gravity.'

We drove for miles down a wide valley mottled with sagebrush between sullen cliffs hung with mist. The north wall was patched yellow green with lichen. Over the rolling hills at the end we caught sight of a grain elevator and a few iron roofs. 'That's Coulee City. That'll be below the dam. Now I'm going to take you a couple miles off our direct road to show you something else the Columbia River did.'

'Dry Falls,' said a sign on a turnout on the road along the steep flank of the mountain. Two young men in khaki had gotten out of their car. One of them was looking out through a fieldglass and pointing. 'Isn't that the damnedest?' they kept saying. 'In some period of melting glaciers,' said my friend, in his even voice, as we got stiffly out of his car, 'the river flowed in a fall over those ledges . . . as much water as half a dozen Niagaras. Those green lakes where the ducks are were the plungepools.'

Across an immense canyon behind a dapple of patches of tattered mist we could see the darkstreaked alcoves pouring water had left in the high brown cliff. At that distance the smooth grooving the water had left had such a look of motion that you could fancy you still saw the churning glacial river plunging over in a cataract that stretched as far as you could see across the valley.

'It was at that time,' my friend was saying, 'that the geologists say the river deposited those beds of silt, hundreds of square miles smooth as your hand, and without a stone on it, that we want to reclaim with the irrigation project. The river gave us the silty land, but the Cascades rose up and took away our rain.' He laughed softly. 'Now it's up to public power to give us back our water.'

Booster

When again we drove down into the valley of the Columbia River, it was at a much lower altitude. The river was dark green. The trees still had their leaves that glowed with every warm dry color of sunset in the rosy afternoon light. On the hillsides apple orchards were yellow and russet. Chrysanthemums were still blooming in the farmhouse dooryards. Where there was grass it was bright green. The air had a moist rainy feeling of early autumn. We drove across the bridge into the little rivertown just as the lights were coming on along the broad main street.

When we called at the onestory newspaper office we were greeted by a tall blond man in his shirtsleeves. 'He'll be in in a minute,' he said. 'Sit around.' We sat in the corner of the press room while he leaned back from his typewriter and talked about his boss:

'Next to Grand Coulee Dam, he's the most important monument we've got. I suppose you know his story. He was born in
Nebraska and went up to the Klondike when he was still a kid,
and finally settled down in this country and he and his newspaper
grew up with it. He's one of those people who always goes to see
for himself. If something's going on he's interested in, anywhere
in the world, off he goes. He went to Soviet Russia and to Germany, and I don't know where else besides, and of course he goes
all over the United States and Canada and Alaska, but he always
comes back to the Columbia River and to fight for the development of this country. For years now that's meant his fight for the
dam. Maybe he wasn't just the first man to get the idea . . . when
you get a good idea a lot of people usually think of it at once . . .
but he was the first man to put up a day to day fight for it. He
had this paper and the means to do it and the tact and the gump-
tion and the drive . . . you wait till you see him . . . He had some
tussle with the Chambers of Commerce of our two biggest cities.
They're all filled up with stooges of Eastern interests, or managers
of branches of Eastern concerns. What do they care about what
happens to us out here? . . . Now a lot of them are trying to
make out they thought it was a good idea all along.' A car drove
up outside. 'Here he is.'

He was a big grayheaded man in a light gray suit with a gray
felt hat on the back of his head. He had a wide decisive mouth
and explosive opinionated eyebrows. As he strode in, he swept us
all into his office with him. 'You've come by just in time to see
our glucose plant . . . down by the river there . . . it's just started
operating. It's the kind of local enterprise we mean when we say
we want to develop this country . . . makes glucose out of wheat.
Here's some. Taste it.' He had a bowl of clear white glucose on
his desk. He snatched up a little wooden paddle, whirled it
around, and poked it in my mouth. 'Isn't it delicious? That's
the first glucose we produced. That means the farmers of this
section will have something to do with their grain when the price
drops . . . always a market for glucose. Let's go take a look at it.'

He swept us out of his office again and into his car and drove

across town a couple of blocks to a group of new wooden buildings
beyond the railroad tracks. We poked around in the semidarkness
while he pointed out the copper stills and the vats and the elaborate network of pipes. Here and there he switched on a light.
Meanwhile he went on talking: 'You can't start anything in this
world without bucking some kind of interests. You'd think a
bunch of farmers could get together and decide to distil a little
glucose without stirring up all the great corporations in the country, but they fought us tooth and nail like they fought the dam
. . . Of course on a smaller scale, because this is a small operation
. . . ' He laughed. 'Fortunately, we're a tough bunch around
here. Farmers remember when they had to grind their own wheat
in a coffee grinder to get something to eat. We got hold of a little
Polish Jew chemist who had a process. He'd built a lot of
plants in Poland and Germany. They say he'd made himself quite
a fortune. The Nazis chased him out of there with a bayonet for
his pains. Well, around here everybody yelled that the process
was no good. But it works. We've proved that. Then we
couldn't get the equipment: priorities. Well, he collected it piece
by piece, some piping here, a vat there, a kettle here . . . through
refugees in the junk business. Those boys stick together . . . and
now she's a rollin' . . . ' As we were about to step out the door
into the night again, he put his arm across it to get our attention,
and said in a breathless voice: 'Now, the next thing is alcohol . . .
alcohol to make synthetic rubber, plastics, and all the rest . . .
then we'll be really bucking the big boys . . . but when we've got
that we'll have the basis for a wellrounded industrial and farming
setup . . . Of course, without cheap and abundant power we
couldn't have done a thing . . . public power plus private initiative, that's our story.'

Peddler of Power

Here the Columbia River burst through tall cocoacolored portals
of cliff into a green raindrenched country of ferns and tall shaggy
spruce and fir and waterfalls lacing the green shadow of the south-

ern wall of the great gorge with flashes of white. We had gotten out of the car where the road curved round a high head of rock to look back at the low dam and the locks and the fishladders. The man who had driven me up from the seaport looked at the dam a long time with burning eyes, as if he had never seen it before. 'We're carrying an overload now,' he said. 'In another year we'll barely be able to produce the power that's needed for the war industries.' As we stood at the edge of the road looking down, to keep our footing we had to lean into the furious cold wind that poured through the mountain gap. When we got back into the car our eyes were streaming. 'I don't want ever to come back here after the war and see three or four of the lights out on those generators,' he said passionately. 'If I ever do, it will mean we are licked.'

I had known him as a youngster years ago in New York in a world that was made of books and concerthalls and theatres and little parties in walkup flats in the evening, when people sat on the floor and got drunk with phrases about politics and art and letters. We had talked about that world a little, driving out, as you would talk about some buried city out of some long extinct past. He could hardly imagine any more what it had been like. He had to go to Washington now and then in the course of his job. That was far enough East for him, he said. Out here in this raw coun try he could see a corner of the nation building itself a destiny It was real life instead of story books. 'I was born in Switzerland. It's the kind of landscape I like, anyway.'

Driving back to town through the shaggy ruin of mighty forests, we talked about the possibilities for the future there were in this foggy Northwest. If everybody didn't get to work and plan something, the possibilities were pretty damn grim, he said through clenched teeth; hundreds of thousands of people who had come West for the war industries out on the streets when they shut down. And out here people couldn't be trusted to starve quietly and like it. Cheap power was the answer. This was the only region in the nation where already power was cheap enough to compete with petroleum fuels. A rationalized lumber industry

could produce wood alcohol, high protein yeasts, plastics, char-
coal, lignin, if the lumber companies would only see it. There were
abundant clays for aluminum production if the stranglehold of
monopoly could be shaken loose from light metals. There were
the as yet unexplored possibilities of magnesium and all the alloys,
even steel, if the big boys back East would loosen up a bit. No
reason in the world why there shouldn't be a Northwestern steel
industry. There was the mining of zinc, copper, mercury, tung-
sten, chrome, antimony, phosphates.

He suddenly turned to me and laughed. 'I get that Klondike
feeling,' he said. 'I can't help it . . . We're on the great-circle
route to China and the Orient. There's no reason why there
shouldn't be an immense demand for our manufactured products
if ever some kind of a satisfactory peace is worked out after we've
smashed Japan and Germany . . . We have to go forward to keep
from going back.'

'That's what people have been telling me all through this section,' I said. 'They don't want to be Okies.'

'That's just what they are going to be, if we don't get together
and take advantage of electric power. A lot of the oldtimers have
just gone down in the cellar and thrown a blanket over their
heads . . . None of these things are going to happen just by
themselves, unless energetic people get together and make them
happen.' He stopped the car in front of the government garage
on the outskirts of town. 'I'd like to be one of the people who
makes things happen.'

In the Language of One Born and Raised Here

The streetlights are drowned to a ruddy glimmer in the soppy wet
fog off the river. The beer and wine bars along the downtown
street are crowded. At the corner of the vegetable market, a
middleaged woman with black hair and eyes stands all alone
preaching to the people walking along the sidewalk. A beaten
looking old man stands beside her with his cap in his hand. He's
the only one who's listening. As we pass we catch the words *sin,*

abomination, iniquity, shot out in a brisk brassy voice. 'In my
language,' the man beside me drawls as we walk along. 'In the
language of one born and raised here . . . Now, just look at that.'
He catches my arm. Two young boys in black leather jackets,
who look about fifteen and are obviously so drunk they can hardly
stand, brush clumsily past us as they reel by. They are poking
and gibbering at the women as they go. My friend catches his
breath. 'What I was going to say is, this used to be a nice town, a
homefolks town . . . See those two bareheaded men? They are
Russians. They never look to the right or the left. They go
through the streets like they were scared of something . . .' We
are overtaking a tall leathercheeked man with tight black pants
and a broadbrimmed black hat, who looks like a cowpuncher.
Beyond him are three sawedoff little men talking Yiddish. At the
next corner we have trouble getting through a bunch of highschool girls who are just in the act of picking up some sailors.

My friend is talking again. 'We never locked our doors. It was
the most natural thing in the world for a girl to go home by herself
at night, but now since all these Middlewesterners have come to
the shipyards a woman dasent drive out in a car alone. There's
murder. They snatch purses. There have even been rapes by
sixteenyearold boys . . . And we've got a negro problem on top
of everything else . . . Do you know you can't even go down to
the bank and rent yourself a safe deposit box? There are waiting
lists eight or ten names long for every one. Damned if these
Middlewesterners don't keep their money in safe deposit boxes
in rolls of bills. Some of 'em buy diamonds and get soundly
rooked, I can tell you. Either they don't trust the banks or they
don't know what a bank account's for . . . They talk about
housing. My God! We've got people housed in every barn, in
every rattrap, in every cellar . . . What kind of a country is this
we live in? That's what the people who were born and raised here
are asking themselves . . . And all these boosters tell us we've got
a great future in trade with Alaska, Russia, China, the Orient.
Now, mister, you just tell me what those folks are going to use
for money. Clamshells? I know a lot of things they've got we

don't want. Communism, fascism, dictatorship, bubonic plague, Asiatic cholera, and beriberi, but I'll be damned if anybody's been able to point out yet one single thing they've got that we do want.' We had broken out of the crowd and turned up a square full of trees still dense with brown foliage that dripped on us as we passed. 'I swear I wish you'd seen this place before all this mess began,' he was saying. 'It was a real nice little city before all these Middlewesterners ruined it for us. Folks like me who were born and raised here, we liked it the way it was.'

Blastfurnace Man

'So that Barnum's big boosters have you in tow, have they? Well, they sure do put on a show.' . . . We were sitting after supper over two glasses of scotch in two deep chintz chairs in front of the fire in an empty room in the silent lowceilinged clubhouse. 'I helped blow in his first blast furnace.' He was a thin-faced lowvoiced man with a quiet manner. He stirred his ice thoughtfully with the little glass stick. 'Now, I don't mean to say that they haven't produced results . . . showmanship's a great thing in building ships or winning a war or anything else, I guess. But I'm a blastfurnace man,' he repeated, looking down into his glass as he talked.

'Well, I'd been with an old concern for some time, pretty contented there except my salary was frozen, and I kept thinking I wasn't making enough money. This Barnum outfit had been after me for months, so finally I fell. Twice the salary, every conceivable inducement . . . So I went on down to the plant where he was building his blast furnace. The place is beautifully landscaped . . . Orange groves . . . They grow quite a crop of walnuts there. The units were put in without disturbing the groves . . . This was quite a ways back. Barnum had sworn they'd blow in his blast furnace by the first of the year. They had grandstands set up and flowers ordered and engraved invitations sent out and a banquet laid out and music and the governor of the state and senators and movie stars and all the publicity agents and public relations men in the world. Everything was ready except the blast furnace. Now, you can't hustle a blast furnace. So they decided they'd have the grand opening anyway. I was working down in the laboratory. They sent down to ask us if we could mix up some magnesium so that it would burn in different fancy colors. Sure, we mixed it up so that it would burn blue and violet and green and left some plain so that it would burn white, and they fixed the blast valves so that they'd make a hell of a roar — only they were blowing the wrong way — and when they threw the switch that was supposed to blow in the blast furnace, we had an electrician hidden away who set off the magnesium, and it made some very pretty fireworks, and all the senators and the publicity men and the movie stars thought sure enough they saw a blast furnace blown in . . . About that time I called up my old employer long distance and asked him if he wanted to take back a rather bedraggled blastfurnace man and here I am back at my old salary . . . I guess what I'd like to do is teach school, anyway . . . I'd like to go up to the University of Alaska and teach.'

The Big Tent

When we drove out of the seaport town the morning of the launching, white fog blanketed everything. All we could see was the white fourlane highway straight ahead of the car, that rose occasionally to cross railroad tracks. Now and then we passed a car or a brightpainted oil truck or a load of machinery under tarpaulins. Gradually the fog lifted so that we could make out the cranes of the shipyards along the river standing in rows of longlegged 4's above the long horizontals of the roofs of shops and the tangle of stumpy masts and girderwork.

'No.' The shiningfaced young man in a doublebreasted suit, who was showing us the sights, twisted himself around in the front seat so that he could beam into our faces. 'That's just another of our yards. We're going across the river.'

As the fog thinned over the mustardcolored flats between the yards and the highway, the outlines appeared of a checkerboard of small new white houses with green roofs, slatecolored roofs, ochre roofs, a tiny dollhouse pattern of three windows and a door and a garage endlessly repeated. Inland of the highway were other checkerboard settlements of similar houses between roads of rutted mud, reduplicated again and again as in a series of mirrors, as far as you could see into the fog. 'This isn't our housing project,' the young man intoned in his radio announcer's voice. 'These homes are the result of private initiative.'

At the crossroads we caught up with a long string of peasoup-colored busses moving slowly across country. As we passed them on the inside lane we saw that they were jampacked with men and women in workclothes, with grimestreaked faces under their yellow glazed helmets. Their clothes were all alike. Their helmets were all alike. Their lunchboxes were all alike. We were going too fast to make out their faces.

The first busses were already unloading in a square of prefabricated peasoupcolored buildings. 'Our outfit has built, according to government specifications, a town of thirtyfive thousand people,' intoned the shiningfaced young man. 'Eighteen months ago it was mudflats.' 'Looks kinda muddy now,' muttered a woman in the back seat, but he didn't answer. We drove round curving drives through ranks of peasoupcolored barrack buildings past schools, stores, recreation centers, postoffices, libraries, gymnasiums. Only the prettily contrived white kindergartens, that looked fresh as the coverdesigns for an architectural magazine, stood out. Shambling along hardsurfaced roads, picking their way through mudpuddles where the hard surface hadn't reached yet, the men and women of the returning shift moved wearily along, picking out their homes by the numbers on the doors.

As we crossed a green canal with yellow Lombardy poplars along it and turned back into the broad highway towards the Columbia River, the fog settled down about us again. Crossing the long bridge, we could see that here the water of the great river was a dense murky olive color. We could hear the hooting of tug boats. On the other side more stretches of new identical small houses, other reduplications of peasoupcolored barracks, stretching mile after mile in every direction into a vague blur of low roofs and windows.

When we finally reached the yard where today's launching was going to take place, the administration building loomed up suddenly in front of us in oblongs of mat white with broad low shining windows. The gates where the people who worked there got their cards punched were a series of jaunty little wickets with green peaked roofs over them like the entrances to a race course.

Inside the administration building the new pine floors shone with varnish. Everywhere shine and glitter, neat secretaries in high heels, with elaborate hairdos, young men in perfectly pressed doublebreasted suits as spick and span as if they had been cut out of fashion catalogues and pasted on cardboard. The bare desks were brilliant. The ashtrays were immaculate. Upstairs, in a diningroom flooded with light, the lady employees who had been invited to the launching were all in a bustle in their best clothes, arranging the flowers on the tables where lunch was to be served to the guests after the ceremony.

We were furnished with badges and went through the gate into an immense steel shed. Yellowhaired girls and young boys were welding steel plates. While the welders watched them through their goggled masks, the arcs like needles of vast sewing machines travelled by themselves across the clean blue steel. In the open yard beyond the shed, as in some giant's toyshop, parts of ships — smokestacks, ventilators, deckhouses, bows, quarterdecks, lifeboats — stood ranked in groups waiting to be lifted into place. Above them, through the girderwork of their cradles, loomed tall the rows of hulls under construction. As we stepped out into the open, a breeze sprang up and tore away the fog enough for us to see the manycolored pennants fluttering and the shine of new gray paint on the freighter that was ready to be launched.

The twelve o'clock whistle blew. Immediately the roar and the hammering and the screaming of cut metal stopped, and for a second the place was so quiet you could hear the complaints of the gulls as they circled overhead. 'They always come in at noon,' said the shiningfaced young man. 'People feed them sandwiches

while they are eating their lunch.' The loudspeaker started rattling off the noonday news. The yard had become a picnic ground.
On platforms and flatcars and piles of equipment, men and women
and boys and girls, with their helmets tipped back on their heads,
sat eating their lunches out of their tin boxes.

Under the bow of the boat to be launched a little staging had
been built. A bashful young woman in a fresh frilled blouse, surrounded by a group of young men and women in store clothes,
stood up there making trial passes toward the bow with a dolledup
champagne bottle tied to a string. There was a minister. There
were naval officers. Hats came off as, instruments shining in the
sun that had finally burned through the fog, a small band played
'The Star Spangled Banner.' A foreman made a speech. The
people on the staging were introduced in turn by a master of ceremonies. They were the sponsors and their invited guests, all
workers in the yard. The minister intoned a prayer. Down below
two young men in masks were burning with violetflashing arcs
through the steel plates that held the boat on the ways. The last
plate snapped with a sharp crack. At the minister's loud 'God
bless this ship,' the young woman smashed the bottle with a will
and, whistles blowing, the shining gray freighter began to slide.
She gathered speed. Pushing out a white surging wave behind
her dipping stern, she slid into the river. The cable from the bow
tightened; she lost momentum and sheered gently off into the fog.
At the moment that the cable snapped, two small chugging tugs
with yellow stacks were already nosing her around.

Before we had time to turn away, a crew of men were out on the
ways scooping up the grease, and over their heads the first section
of the keel for the next ship dangled from a crane ready to be laid.

In our group eyes were damp. Throats were being cleared.

'And they said private initiative was through,' said the shiningfaced young man, as he began to herd us back towards the administration building. 'Every day in some yard a ship is being
launched. As many as I've seen go down, it always gives me a
thrill. This ought to prove that private initiative can do anything.'

'Using unlimited public money and public power. Why not?' the woman who had sat in the back seat muttered into her muffler.

'How long will it be before she goes to sea?' somebody asked.

'Four or five days, maybe,' chanted the shiningfaced young man, 'for the final fitting up alongside the dock and to put the stores aboard. Then the crew'll come down and she'll be ready to sail down the Columbia River and out into the ocean to try her luck in the theatres of war.'

Portland, Oregon, November, 1943

A DRIZZLY DAY is ending up in fog. Along the lunchcounter grayhaired men in overalls and leather jackets are eating oyster stew. A set of hamburgers sizzling on the electric plate sends little wisps of scorching beef smell up through the cigarette smoke. From outside through the loosely slapped together boards of the frame building come the hoots and howls of steamboat whistles. Through every crevice the fog seeps into the tavern, bringing with it a tang of rotting evergreens and giving faint ruddy haloes to the unshaded lights. Against the windowpanes and the glass of the door the white fog presses snugly as flannel. Across from the lunchcounter, every stool along the bar is taken. Behind the seated drinkers stands a row of men waiting for places. A skinny yellowhaired waitress with buck teeth moves back and forth with trays of beer between the end of the bar and the booths of yellow varnished fir in the back of the room. Now and then the barkeep, a weazened grizzled man with a slabsided look as if at some time in his life he had been passed through a rolling mill, gives a hoarse exasperated bark like a seal's bark at the thronging customers waiting to quench their thirst at the bar, to get them to make way for the girl and her tray of empties.

In front of me a stocky blackjowled man in a tightly buttoned peajacket is addressing a very young blankfaced sailor who sits on the next stool with his blue pancake cap pushed far down on his head.

'You are the most hated nation on the face of the earth,' he is shouting in the sailor's ear. The sailor gives a gulp and looks down glumly into his glass. The blackjowled man raises his beer thoughtfully against the light and drinks it down and wipes his mouth with the hairy back of a hand that has the points of the compass tattooed on it in red green and blue. He makes the assertion again, louder: 'You are the most hated nation on the face of the earth and don't you forget it.'

'I only said mebbe it 'ud be a short war,' mumbles the very young sailor.

'Short war, hell!' shouts the blackjowled man, scowling under the visor of his seagoing cap that has weathered a streaky green. 'It's goin' to be all war from now on. You got to fight your way to the top yet ... Another beer, Joe,' he adds in a pleading aside in the direction of the barkeep who is staring at him with a sour look on his flattened countenance. The barkeep answers with one of his barking yawps and starts to draw the beer. 'And you're asking me,' the blackjowled man goes on, looking up and down the row of more or less weatherworn faces, turned blankly, most of them, towards the dusty cockpheasant standing guard over the winebottles above the barkeep's head. 'You are asking me why you are the most hated nation. I'll tell you; it's because you got the most to eat, and the most to drink, and the most to wear. You can sit down with the war on and eat a turkey dinner if you want one. You can sit down and drink a glass of beer.'

'Like hell I can,' mutters one of the men waiting for a seat at the bar.

'You can make yourself sick on wine or get yourself a snootful of whiskey. Maybe you can't get a steak whenever you want it, but you can fill yourself right up to the neck with good hot beef stew. And all those colored people all over the mighty oceans, they ain't got a goddam thing. The little yellow Japs, they fight on a handful of rice. In India they are fallin' down dead in the streets from hunger. The Russians live on a potato a week. The Limeys ain't none too fat. Every port you make across the mighty oceans, they are hungry and wretched and they see your cooks throwin' porkchops over the side . . . That's why you are the most hated nation . . . You got to fight your way to the top, boy.'

The old rednosed wino in a checked suit, slumped over a glass of port with a beer chaser at the next stool, raises his smeary eyes and stares thoughtfully at the blackjowled man and gives a long shuddering belch that makes all the flabby creases on his neck quiver. 'This beer,' he whispers peevishly, 'makes a man sick.'

The very young sailor's face is queasy pale. With a shaky hand he presses his cap down hard on his forehead so that the band presses the damp hair down in yellow spikes over his eye-brows. He straightens himself up and drinks his beer down at a gulp. His mouth puckers as if it were castor oil he's been drink-ing. 'That's all right, pardner,' he says briskly. 'We'll take 'em island by island.'

'Sure you will,' says the blackjowled man. 'And you and me'll be crows' meat before it's over. We gotta cross the mighty oceans and hit 'em in the solar plexus . . . but out there in the fog across the mighty oceans, they are waitin' to get you . . . Joe, another beer . . .'

For the first time the barkeep shows his yellow teeth in a smile. He is pulling a cardboard sign out from under the bar. Holding it in both hands he reaches his skinny arms up to place it on the shelf in front of the pheasant. He stands looking up at it ap-provingly as if he just finished lettering it himself. The sign reads, NO BEER.'

Already the men without seats are filing out of the door. Talk at the tables and along the bar quiets down. The tavern is all at once as quiet as a cage of birds that's had a cloth thrown over it.

CHAPTER 14

Pacific Waterfront

THE FERRY pushed off from the slip into mist as full of colors as an abalone shell. Walking forward into the bow, the breeze pressed mist into my face drenched with a dank smell of docks and lumberyards and steamengines and with the immense quiet chill of the ocean. Overhead was the crying of gulls. As the ferry sludged on out into the bay the mist thinned so that we could see the gulls circling and swooping above the deck. Standing in the driving mist in the bow, the crowd was made up of service men mostly, sailors, soldiers, girls in uniform. A sailor with a halfeaten ham sandwich was feeding scraps of it to the gulls. He would throw a scrap of bread as far as he could out into the wind and as it swirled down toward the crisp scalloped waves, a gull would follow it and swoop and hover a moment above it, braking himself with a backward flap of his wings, and stretch out his neck and catch it. They hardly ever missed. The sailor used up his ham sandwich and went inside for another. Pressed against the rail a tall private in a neatly pressed uniform stood beside a rosyfaced girl whose hair was blowing. They were eating popcorn out of a box held between them. They started flipping pieces of popcorn to the gulls. 'Imagine gulls eating pop-

corn,' they said. They couldn't get over it. There was a small
gull with only one leg that was their favorite. He came around
again and again.

When the ferry had passed the island the mist began to frazzle
out until we could see the humming bridge and gray freighters
at anchor and patrol boats and the cranes along the wharves
and above them the city steaming up white off its hills against
the rosy afternoon. The soldier grabbed the girl by the arm and
twisted her round till she was looking the way he was looking.
'Fortyeight hours left in the world,' he said.

She was looking down into the empty popcorn box. She was
blushing. 'Let's just stay on the ferry and feed the gulls,' she
said.

The Spout that Feeds the Pacific

'Come out here before it's too dark to see the military secrets,'
said the man I had come to see, ushering me right through to
the back of his apartment after he had opened his front door
for me. We looked down at the darkblue harbor sheened with
lights and the grim shape of Alcatraz and the gossamer elegance
of the bridge and at the high hills beyond, a smouldering burnt
ochre in the last flare of the afterglow. 'Gosh,' I said.

'Well,' he went on, 'that's the Golden Gate. That's the spout
our supplies are pumped through into the Pacific. Even if we
wanted to keep it secret we couldn't. This town is built to give
everybody a grandstand view of everything that goes on ...
That's why the little Japs had to be moved out ... The troop-
ships, the transports, the strings of freighters we've seen go
steaming out through that narrow tongue of water ... so narrow
Drake missed it and sailed clear past ...'

'We used to think of it as the back door of the continent.'

'Maybe it'll turn out to be the front door ... the military
phase has hardly begun yet ...'

The light had faded out of the sky. Everything was drowned
in transparent indigo. Pinpricks of light throbbed yellow in the

moist air. Right under our feet at the wharves where freighters
were being loaded and unloaded clear round the clock shapes of
smokestacks, hoists and cranes stood out inky against the white
glare of floodlights. Across the bay a shipyard glowed like a
forest fire.

Waterfront Politics

We turned away from the window and sat down in the warm
orange light of the room. His wife, who had been bundling two
small squirming sharpeyed children off to their suppers, came
back bringing in some drinks.

'The army and navy have done an immense job in the whole
bay region. The war's been the salvation of this city. That's
the truth. A few years ago we were dragging along the bottom.
Nobody could talk about anything but class war . . . now we are
a pretty darned effective machine for repairing ships and spout-
ing supplies out to the Antipodes. The state of mind around here
has changed so much we hardly know ourselves. I suppose if
I'd been away I'd feel more of a change than I do now . . . Five
years ago the San Francisco waterfront was a strictly capital
versus labor proposition. Of course, it's always been a labor
town. Black was black and white was white. The workingclass
leaders told their boys the businessmen were trying to introduce
fascism. The Chamber of Commerce boys thought Harry
Bridges was hellbent for communism. And in a way they were
both right.'

'What changed things? Hitler's jumping Stalin?'

'That wasn't the whole story . . . Of course, that changed the
line of talk of the comrades . . . The best example of the change
is in the election for mayor we had last week. Well, everybody
had come to feel that the present incumbent, an elderly florist
who can hardly write his own name, was hopeless. I don't suppose he's any worse now than he has been right along. But
everybody suddenly woke up to the fact that he was abject, so
we had three other candidates. One was an oldtime barroom

politician, who represented quite simply liquor, prostitution and gambling, strictly gravy train. The other was a young progressive with what they call a good labor record. He was endorsed by labor. The third was the man who had been president of the American Hawaiian Steamship Company, who was way out front in the employers' groups and bought tear gas and brought in scabs to fight the longshoreman's strike ... Halfway through the campaign the C.I.O. people decided their man, the young Galahad with a good labor record, was running behind. They promptly knifed him and switched to the old wardheeler with the gravy train to try to beat the steamship king. The result was that everybody got sore and confused, and the steamship magnate got elected though he spent less money than the other candidates ... What I'm trying to bring out is that he couldn't have been elected without getting a good slice of the labor vote ... Of course, he's changed too. He's been to Washington on one of the labor boards and he's probably learned a good deal. He's a man of ability. I think he's going to make a very excellent mayor.'

'And the ships are getting loaded.'

'We're not loading as fast as the East Coast, but efficiency is improving all the time. The railroads have simplified the handling of freight trains so that the terminal yards now run clear across into the mountain states. The central control boards take a lot of the load off the dispatchers. Trains aren't run out to the wharves until the boats are ready for them. At the central control the position of every train is marked with lights on the board. Switching is done automatically just like toy trains.'

'Doesn't that mean that the men of the rank and file are pretty keen for the war effort?'

'You better go ask 'em.'

His wife came in to tell us that dinner was ready. Before going to the table, we looked down again into the inky gulf of the bay as full of busy twinkling lights as the sky overhead.

The Guy Who Knows How

Outside it was raining. We were sitting in my small hotel room. There was something oldfashioned about the lamp and the armchairs and the window curtains, something about the scrubbed white paint on the often repainted woodwork that made me think of a room I'd had years ago overlooking the old port in Marseilles. The young man had walked in bareheaded with a longlegged stride, shaking the rain out of his hair and sliding out of his wet raincoat as he came. He didn't smoke. No, thanks, he wouldn't take a drink. Just getting over a stomach ulcer. Working too hard? Maybe. After we had talked of one thing and another, I asked him if getting the waterfront straightened out was such a tough job as all that. Plenty tough, he said.

Then after a pause he leaned forward in his chair and burst out, 'Goddam it, people in this country are wonderful, they are so wonderful it makes me feel like crying when I think of it.' He paused again and then started talking eagerly. 'You have to get around out in the Pacific a little to see how much some guys are doing with how little. I was out there four months. I work with the army, though I'm not in the army. That gives me a better chance. I don't get tied up with the ritual. They even had me talk to one of the grand moguls in Washington over the phone. He'd sent orders a certain boat had to be turned around within twentyfour hours and somebody had to tell him why it was impossible. Loading ships is a business full of definite limitations. It's like packing a trunk. There's a limit to the number of men you can put to work in the space . . . My, he was mad when I explained the setup to him. He asked me who the hell I was. I was just a mere civilian so there wasn't anything he could do. It just was not possible . . .'

He leaned back in his chair and moistened his lips with his tongue. Then he brought the fingers of one hand across his forehead with a gesture of brushing away fatigue, and straightened up. 'Now, at least, all the stuff that comes into this town gets loaded and pushed out into the Pacific as fast as they can handle it on the receiving end . . . Well, those guys on some of those islands out there, they just about do the impossible. Honestly they do. Unloading alongside a dock with wharfing facilities, and unloading heavy equipment on a coral reef or with lighters on a beach full of mangroves, with nothing to work with but a few hoists and the principle of the lever, is something else again. Enemy action is the least of your troubles. Usually there's one guy, a corporal or a sergeant or at most a second loot, who's had longshore experience and he's expected to unload the stuff and carry it up to the depots in the jungle. And that's that. He has to imagine up the tools and the men to do it with. What each one tells you is for God's sake send me a couple guys who know how . . . Only a couple guys.'

He paused again. 'I hope this is the sort of thing you want to hear. I'm so full of it I can't talk about anything else. Alongshore here we're not doing so badly now. The main trouble is trying to get the boys to put in the kind of work they used to put in in the old days before the strikes. The old speedup system was slavery and it was stopped and it ought to have been stopped . . . The longshoremen were down then and now they are up. Harry Bridges did a wonderful job as an organizer . . . my people weren't exactly on his side of the fence in that little argument, so we ought to know . . . He got the longshoremen their porkchops. He did it for sincere and idealistic reasons . . . But at running the union once it's set up he's no good at all. He can't carry his people with him. I don't know whether he's a member of the Communist Party or not and I don't care, but he certainly believes in their philosophy and he put up a wonderful fight for it. He convinced a lot of people around this town, but he didn't convince the longshoremen. They are no more communists than rabbits. The longshoreman around here is a special kind of critter. He's a Scandinavian, mostly. He's independent as hell. He tends to be a middleaged man with not too much brains or ambition, or he wouldn't have stayed a longshoreman. Or else he's just too ornery to do other kinds of work. He'd been getting a raw deal all around the lot and he was sore and Bridges came along and showed him how to get his porkchops. Now he's got a pretty good system worked out to spread the work, he's got all the work he wants to do, he's getting good pay and you can talk to him from hell to Christmas about the Second Front and how this is a people's war and all that, and he won't bat an eyelash. He's sitting pretty. He's got plenty to eat and plenty to spend for whiskey and plenty of work to do tomorrow and he's sitting pretty. Hell, I can't exactly blame him. I can understand that point of view . . . But it breaks your heart to see one of these same kind of guys — he gets something in him that's more than porkchops — literally splitting himself in two to do a job unloading material on some godforsaken atoll . . .'

He got to his feet. 'Well, I've got to run along. Did you ever notice,' he added grinning, 'that it's a hell of a lot easier to talk about things than to get them done? Don't get the idea that we aren't going to speed up the loading of ships around here. It can be done and it's going to be done.'

Uncle Sam in the Hiring Halls

The next morning I was in the office of the committee the government put in to get the various elements along the waterfront working together. A seriousfaced grizzled man was drawing a curve for me on the back of an envelope. 'It's been a long pull,' he said, 'but in the last few months there's been a steady improvement in efficiency.' He tapped the place with his pencil where the ascending curve left the paper. 'As far as the longshoremen are concerned, our business has been to get the idea of the slowdown out of their heads . . . It took the union a long time to drive it in . . . You remember "the Yanks aren't coming" and all that talk . . . When it came to driving it out again the comrades were helpless. It was at their request we took over supervision of the hiring halls.'

He introduced me to a stocky Irishman with crisp dark hair and darkblue eyes, who was acting as troubleshooter for the government along the waterfront. His broad shoulders and big thickfingered hands gave him the look of having done some mighty heavy work in his day. His hands were white and smooth now. He'd been an organizer in the union in the knock- down and dragout days of the fight for organization. Now he was organizing for Washington. He was headed down to the wharves. I asked if I could go with him.

We walked down Market Street together. 'One thing,' he was saying, 'is it's hard to get the boys to believe the work's goin' to last. They been on the bricks so much in the old days they can't help tryin' to spread the work out so it'll last; they can't get it into their heads that now there's plenty work for years to come.'

'Do you think there is?'

'Sure. This Pacific business ain't begun yet.'

The hiring hall was a little like a smalltown railroad station. It was noon and most of the gangs were out. Only a few big shaggy men in workclothes belted tight at the waist were looking up at the bulletinboard where jobs were announced. Beside it there was the ticketwindow where they handed out the work- slips. On the other side was a larger board full of numbered holes with small plugs in them. Every man had a number, and by the position of his plug the men in charge of the hiring hall could tell where he was working and what gang he was on. 'If a man don't turn up we ring him on the phone to see what's the matter. If we can't get him that way we send somebody after him to see what's what. If he's off fishin' or on a drunk or somepen' we want to know the reason why.'

'It looks simple enough.'

'Wasn't so simple till we got it worked out.'

He led me up a stairway in back. 'I'll show you where they make out the pay checks.' At the door at the head of the stairs a sharpfaced man with his big workgloves tucked in the back pocket of his overalls was knocking and knocking.

'What's the trouble?' my guide asked him.

'Been off sick. I want to know about my compensation.'

'This ain't the place. That's way across town.' He told him

an address. He waited until the man had shambled off down the stairs and then gave the door a couple of sharp rattatats with his knuckles. When the door opened he showed his big white teeth in a grin. 'You have to know the combination to git in here,' he whispered to me. 'Or else the boys would have them driven crazy . . . I thought I'd spare yez the trouble. I sent him off to chase hisself,' he announced in a loud roar as we stepped into the room. I was introduced to several elderly men who sat stooped over ledgers in the gray light that came in through tall old-fashioned windows. My guide explained: 'The men are paid through the union. If there's any dispute about time or over-time, we have the figures right here. Since we had this system goin' we've had very little trouble. I think everybody's pretty well satisfied all around. Well,' he said, as he ushered me out again. 'You wanted to see some longshoremen. Suppose we step around to a couple bars. Some of 'em'll be trickling in for a bit of a drink. This is the hour they knock off for dinner.'

A Spot of Irish on the House

As we walked around the corner to the broad waterfront street full of the racket of trucks and streetcars he explained a little sheepishly, 'I don't go around to the bars much any more. Everybody wants you to hear his mournful tale and then he treats you to a drink and you have to treat him back and first thing you know you're full up to the ears.'

There was an air of wellbeing at the long bar that stretched from the window full of war posters into the dim interior of the building. Along it stood a row of big men bulging out of their workclothes. Big profiles stood out in the slanting light, chins thrust out, Adam's apples, hooked noses, jutting cheekbones, brawling mouths, snaggleteeth under mustaches tobaccostained to the color of shredded wheat. Along the line tiny whiskey glasses winked and bobbed, lightly held between the grimy thumb and forefinger, or rose to puckered mouths hidden in big encircling mitts. Beer chasers were tipped into gullets. Lips smacked over the spirit of the grain or the prickly cool draught of the brew. Cusswords shot out of the corners of mouths, filthy phrases were wiped off casually on knotted backs of hands.

Among the faces along the bar there were some with bleared eyes and boozy mouths, heavy and battered as the packingcases they handled all day, but here and there a countenance stood out: a ruddy fisherman's face full of fine creases radiating from the mouth and eyes, or the leaneyed leanlipped face of a hunter, or a canny hired farmhand's face, or one of those faces, clearcut in repose, that stamp on your mind the damned human majesty of a man at ease in strength of body and the certainty that what he knows how to do he knows how to do well.

The proprietor kept his own bar, a bit of the green isle of saints if I ever saw one, laying about him at his customers in a brogue so rich you could grow shamrocks on it, storming up and down back of the bar on his toes like a boxer at work with a punching bag, drawing the beer and pouring the whiskey and wiping the timedarkened mahogany off with a rag and bringing a big white paleknuckled hand down fast on a stack of coins, and all the while ducking mock reproaches and slinging a stinging wad of abuse out of his big mouth. He had a pair of rotten eggs ready for every custard pie they threw.

'He's a terrible moneylender,' my guide whispered in my ear. 'He gives the boys advances against payday.' We were standing at the bar in an eddy of the torrent, drinking a pair of modest beers. When the barkeep laid eyes on my guide he leaned over towards him. 'It's a cold day, Freddy,' he said in a throaty fatherly whisper. 'You'll have a spot of firstrate Irish on the house, you and your friend, won't you now?'

We couldn't very well refuse, so we put it down with some pleasure. We ordered up a couple more. 'Pat, my friend here's askin' me what you think of the New Deal?' my guide asked with a twinkle in his eye.

'Washed up,' said the barkeep, cutting the suds off three glasses of beer. 'Goin' from bad to worse,' his voice rose. 'The dirty deal I call it. And the worst is these subsidies. Of all the dirty deceitful measures for tying the farmer and the producer and the consumer up in another net of government red tape regulations. We're regulated off the earth already. And it's liberty they say we're fightin' for.'

'You talk like a Republican. Aren't your customers mostly Democrats?' I asked.

'The boys was Dimocrats sure when they was hungry and sore, but they are sittin' pretty now and the way things are goin' in Washington with the waste and the chicanery and the taxation and the bungled up rationin' it wouldn't surprise me if every man jack of 'em voted the Republican ticket.' He stood with his shoulders spread looking up and down the bar. My guide blinked and made a face. Men stood listening with their glasses poised. Nobody answered back one way or another. Then the horsing and the kidding started in again. Time for one more drink before going back to work.

2

The Hills of San Francisco

The hills fill me with an irresistible desire to walk to the top of each one of them. Whoever laid this town out took the conventional checkerboard pattern of streets and, without regard for the laws of gravity, planked it down blind on a peninsula heaped with steep slopes and sandhills. Wherever you step out on the street there's a hilltop in one direction or the other. From the top of each hill you get a view and the sight of more hills to the right and left and ahead that offer the prospect of still broader views.

This one is Nob Hill, I know that. I remember it years ago when there were still gardens on it and big brokenpaned mansions of brownstone and even, if I remember right, a few windbleached framehouses with turrets and scalelike shingles imitating stone and scrollsaw woodwork round the porches. Now it's all hotels and apartmenthouses, but their massive banality is made up for by the freakishness of the terrain. At the top in front of the last of the old General Grant style houses, I stop a second to get my breath and to mop the sweat off my eyebrows.

Ahead of me the hill rises higher and breaks into a bit of blue sky. Sun shines on a block of white houses at the top. Shiny as a toy fresh from a Christmas tree a little cablecar is crawling up it. Back of me under an indigo blur of mist are shadowed roofs and streets and tall buildings with wisps of fog about them, and beyond, fading off into the foggy sky, stretches the long horizontal of the Bay Bridge.

Down the hill to the right I've caught sight of accented green roofs and horned gables painted jadegreen and vermilion, that must be Chinatown. I find myself walking along a narrow street in a jungle of Chinese lettering, interpreted here and there by signs in our alphabet announcing Chop Suey, Noodles, Genuine Chinese Store. There are ranks of curiostores with their windows filled with knickknacks. Soldiers and sailors on leave brood over the showcases. The street tempts you along. Beyond the curioshops there are drugstores, groceries giving out an old drenched smell like tea and camphor and litchi nuts, vegetable stores, shops of herb merchants stocked with the same goods Marco Polo saw with wonder on his travels. In another window there are modern posters, plumcheeked pinup girls and stern lithographs of the Generalissimo, a few yellowing enlargements of photographs of eagerlooking young broadfaced men in cadet's uniforms. Next, there's a live-chicken dealer's crowded with customers. Then a little store that sells you don't know what. The gilt lettering amuses the eye. The decorative scrollwork of dragons and lotus flowers leads you along.

Coming out into a broad oblique avenue full of streetcars and traffic the Chop Suey signs are suddenly gone and now everything is Spaghetti, Pizze, Ravioli, Bella Napoli, Grotta Azzura, blooming in painted signs along the housefronts. There are Italian bakeries and pastryshops breathing out almondpaste and anise. In small bars men sit talking noisily as they drink black coffee out of glasses. Restaurants smell of olive oil and spilled

wine. I cross the street and at the top of another hill catch a
glimpse of a white tower shaped like a lighthouse. That must
be Telegraph Hill.

Walking up through a shabby lightgray cheerful quarter where
the doorbells have Spanish names and where the air out of door-
ways smells of garlic and floorpolish, and there begin to be pots
of geraniums on the tops of scaly walls that conceal small
gardens, or carnations now and then on a windowsill, it suddenly
feels like the quiet streets back of Montmartre or, so many years
ago, Marseilles. I reach the top of Telegraph Hill just in time
to take refuge in the tower from a spat of driving rain.

The tower is a memorial to somebody. Inside the walls are
all painted over with frescoes in the style of Diego Rivera. The
elevator is running. For a quarter it takes you smoothly to the
top. You look down into a swirl of mist, shot with lights and
shadows like the inside of a shell, that pours in from the ocean.
Now and then the hurrying mist tears apart long enough to let
you see wharves crowded with masts and derricks, or an expanse
of bright ruffled water and once a row of sullenlooking gray
freighters at anchor. Two young men in khaki are standing beside me squinting to see through the rainspattered glass.

'Boy, it won't be long now,' said one.

'Before we are stuck down in the hold of one of those things?'

'You said it.' They notice that I am listening. They exchange
reproachful looks and their mouths shut up tight and they move
away.

Seafood Carnival

When I leave the tower the sun is beginning to burn through
the white dazzle. There is blue in the puddles on the paved
parking place on top of the hill. I plunge down the hill in
the direction of the harbor, lose my bearings in a warehouse
section and after a good deal of walking find myself following
a set of signs lettered, 'Fisherman's Wharf: Pedestrians.' They
lead me along lines of railroad track immensely crowded with

freightcars bearing the names of every railroad in the country, patrolled by army sentries in tin hats, past streets cut off by wire fences and down alleys between corrugated iron sheds down to a stagnant inner harbor packed with small motor fishing boats painted up Italian style like the Guinea Fleet in Boston. The place, hemmed in on every side by military barriers, still has a holiday air, a reminiscence of the cheerful charlatanry of oldtime international travel. Along the wharf are brightly daubedup fish restaurants ornamented by paintings of the Bay of Naples and luncheonstands with outside racks stacked with great rockcrabs crimson from cooking and kettles where Pacific clams are steaming. On one of the glass fronts is the familiar name of Joe Di Maggio. Beyond are more restaurants and curiostands with the same beachresort look of weekend whoopee about them. They face what had been a wide space that stretched for blocks in front of the covered wharves of the Pacific steamship lines. Wire fences have been built right across the face of the seafood carnivals and against them, blocking the view as far as you could see, are piled packingcases of military stores. In canyons through the packingcases move strings of trucks and freight engines slowly shoving long strings of boxcars.

I turned back and paused a moment to lean over the rail above the fishing boats. Overhead the sky had cleared a robin'segg blue and the mist had drawn itself up into cottony white clouds. On the hills behind me the umbrella pines spread out a violent bluegreen above their wet red trunks. The buildings on the hills shone curdwhite and crumbly buff and yellow as if drawn in with chalk. Beside me two elderly and redfaced Italians with a good deal of wine under their belts were arguing as to who should take home a small gray shark with brown tortoiseshell markings one of them had just brought in. 'No feesh today,' said the drunker of the two. 'You take it, cap.' They made a lunge with the shark in my direction. I dodged and started to move along. 'Heem Okie, heem scared of feesh,' croaked the drunker of the two. The shark slid out of their hands onto the pavement and they stood there shaking with silent laughter.

Chinatown

We were sitting around a table in a Chinese restaurant heaped
with white rice and a multiplicity of shredded dishes and hashed
dishes and dishes floating in thin amber gravies. There was a
philosophic professor of law with historical perspective, there was
a smart young lawyer who had his fingers on the wires of progressive politics, there was a liberal newscaster with a warm heart
for the underdog. As we crunched the noodles and the crisp
peapods in the sweetsour gullion, the young lawyer told us
about the local Chinese. He had been busy with China Relief and
the entertainment of the Generalissimo's lady when she came
through, and was looking forward with some interest to the
Chinese vote in the coming election. Since he'd known them,
he said, there had been a great change in the attitude of the Chinese towards us, towards white Americans. People used to talk
about our prejudice against the Chinese. But when it came to
prejudice we were pikers compared to those boys. Now, even
among the older people, it was beginning to break down. They
were inviting us into their homes. They weren't nearly so ex-
clusive any more. After supper he'd take us around to meet a
really modern Chinese, the young fellow who ran the Chinese
radio station. 'The old Chinese used to think we smelt and that
we were disgustingly hairy.'

Somebody told a story about a friend of his who had taught
for several years out in the Orient and who had gotten to feel,
among all those hairless people, that there was something really
immodest about his legs and armpits when he went out to play
tennis. He got so he would never show any piece of his skin in
public. When somebody suggested that our real allies in the
Far East would turn out to be the Hairy Ainu, the young lawyer
frowned. No, the Chinese were our allies, probably in all the
world the steadiest allies we had; but we had to play straight
with them. He'd had dealings with the leaders of the Seven
Companies, the Chinese Merchants' Association, in getting up a
war-loan drive. Right at the beginning they'd said frankly,

'You better meet us fifty-fifty because if we begin to bargain we'll get the better of you . . . We've had more experience at that sort of thing than you have.' Everybody had put their cards on the table and things were working out fine.

When we got up to go, he introduced us to a Chinese lawyer with a smiling face as round and yellow and expressionless as the rising moon. Quick as a wink our check was paid. No way of getting it from the waiter who insisted that we were the Chinese lawyer's guests. As we went out the newscaster shook his head. 'Chinese hospitality,' he said, 'is something.'

Celestial Radio Station

We crossed the main stem of Chinatown with its floodlit gold lettering and its glimmer and glow of nightspot signs in neon light and walked up a steep dark narrow street. 'Now we are going to a basement. Everything in Chinatown's in basements and sub-basements. They are terribly congested here,' said the newscaster. At some steep stone steps leading down to a faintly lit glass door he stopped us. 'Let me go ahead,' he said, 'and get clearance . . . With the Chinese you always have to get clearance.'

In a moment a slender brighteyed Chinese, with entirely American manners and speech, ran up the steps and ushered us down through a hall past a tiny dim room where four old men were playing Mah Jong, and through another hall with a red carpet into a big brightly lit room stacked with Chinese musical instruments. At one end there was a glass partition with a desk behind it. This was the broadcasting studio.

As our host disappeared again, the newscaster told us his history in whispers. He'd been born of the poorest kind of Chinese parents, left an orphan, and had worked his way up from a little fellow, working in stores, going to trade school. He had managed to open a record shop on his own. The record shop had grown into a radio studio and now he probably was pretty well off and had as much influence over the younger progressive Chinese as any one in town.

Our host came hurrying back tearing the paper off a bottle of rye whiskey. He was evidently excited and pleased that we had come to call on him. He didn't drink himself, but he kept filling our glasses. Meanwhile, the members of a Chinese orchestra he had hurriedly gotten together came straggling in. In our honor, it was explained, he would have an orchestra on the air tonight instead of records. The mike was brought out and a slender little girl in black appeared and began reading the news in the resonant nasal tones of their language.

After listening for a while to the lilting music with its unfamiliar chords and dry clopping insectlike percussion we moved into the hall so that the young lawyer and our host could talk politics. Chinatown could muster about ten thousand votes. The Chinese had not forgotten the Chungking declaration of the voluble man who had been Republican candidate in 1940. They liked him all right. Our host began to talk very clearly and seriously. Something must be done to give the Chinese in this city more space. They were hemmed into an overcrowded ghetto. They had to have new housing, opportunity to come out in the light and air. Opportunity. Housing. Those were the two things they wanted. The young lawyer was very sympathetic. Sure, a progressive Republican administration could do a great deal for the Chinese. As we were getting our coats to leave our host turned to me. 'Our people,' he said severely, 'live in cellars. The tb. is terrible among our people. We must have light and air.'

As the broadcast was over he left with us. Outside his wife was waiting for him with their car. They were going out to his farm for the weekend. Eighteen hundred acres. A big potato crop. Hard work to do there. As they drove away we turned down the street towards the bright lights.

That Russian Winter

We ended up in a big paleblue amphitheatre of a night club in the Italian section of town. An old old variety actress out of the gaslit era was strutting her spangled bust back and forth in the powdery light of the spots, hoarsely reciting the song about 'That Russian Winter.' When the song was over, there was a certain amount of growling among service men at the tables round about us. 'Why don't she sing about Americans?'

At the next table there was a young officer and his pretty wife, who turned out to be friends of the newscaster. He leaned back in his chair and asked the officer through the hum of voices and jingle of glasses: 'Well, what about the Soviet Russians? You see them all the time?'

The young couple moved their chairs around and we all leaned towards him to hear what he had to say.

'Well, what do you want to know about them? They aren't so different from other people.'

'What I'd like to know,' I said, 'is how the Soviet citizens react to American life when they really live in the middle of it.'

'Well,' he said, 'I've seen a good many in the course of some special work I've had to do . . . It takes them a long time to thaw out . . . There are a good many in towns up and down the coast in connection with Lend Lease . . . The crew particularly seem scared to death when they first come. You see them walking up the street with blank faces not looking to the right or the left. People offer them lifts in their cars coming up from the wharves, but they always refuse. They won't even answer when they are spoken to.'

'Scared they'll be corrupted with capitalism?'

'I reckon they are scared the N.K.V.D.'ll take away that one potato a week their old mother's living on or something like that . . . After four or five trips the officers tend to thaw out a little, at least with their opposite numbers here. They love music. My, they sing well! After a good dinner and some accordion playing and a suitable ration of grog they'll finally loosen up and talk about themselves . . . It's always the same thing . . . They wish to God they could pull themselves out of the whole bloody mess and get themselves a little farm up in Alaska or out in the woods somewhere, any place where no damn government

can bother them . . . most of them want to raise chickens . . .
and to hell with the brotherhood of man.'

The place was closing up. People were streaming towards the
cloakrooms. On the way out our friend the lawyer wanted to
introduce us to the old variety actress. She was sitting at a
large round table all freshly set for supper in the midst of the
desolation of cigarette butts and spilled glasses of the emptying
nightclub, and the racket of waiters in a hurry to upend the
chairs on the tables and go home. Beside her, a little back from
the table, sat a stately old racetrack character with cottonwhite
hair over a red barroom face. His pale gray fedora hung on the
end of his cane gripped between his crossed knees. His folded
yellow kid gloves were tucked in the brim. The rest of us hovered
round the table while our friend tried to catch her eye. He'd
just managed to get her attention when a waiter set down a big
bowl in front of her and whisked off the silver lid. Steaming
inside was what looked like Irish stew. She pounced on it with a
spoon that she held ready poised in her fat beringed old hand and
started ladling it into her plate. She broke a roll in half and set
to work with a will. No way to attract her attention now. The
powder scaled off her sagging cheeks and the aigrette in her hair
went slightly askew as her stout jaws began to chew. We were
all sleepy and yawning and thinking of how we were going to
make morning appointments. We called out goodnight in her
direction and sidled away. She didn't look up from her plate.

Taste of the Pacific

Eventually, I had to ask my way to the ocean. Somebody said
I ought to take a car to the Cliff House. Connected with that
name, somewhere in the back of my memory, there was a park
on a cliff full of funny beergarden statuary under pines, and dis-
appointment as a child at not being able to spot a sealion among
the spuming rocks of the headland. The streetcar rattled along
through a suburban section of low stucco houses, across wide
boulevards planted with palms, described a reversed curve through

pines down a steep slope, and finally came to rest in a decrepit barn beside a lunchcounter. I stepped out on a road lined with souvenir stores on one side that swung down the steep slope to the old square white restaurant and farther round the headland to the broad gray beach fading into mist in the distance where slow rollers very far apart broke and growled and slithered inland in a swirl of white water, and were sucked back in spume.

I went out and leaned over the parapet of the observation platform. The bluegray Pacific was clear far out to where a fogbank smudged the horizon. Coming around from the Golden Gate, that was hidden behind a fold of the coast, a gray patrol boat showed white teeth as it chewed its way seaward into the long swells. Still no sealions on Seal Rocks. A few gulls circled screaming over the platform.

Beside me three very black G.I.'s stood in a huddle staring out at the ocean. Farther along two sailors had their backs turned to the view and were watching with envious looks a boy and girl who looked like highschool kids, both in sweaters and slacks, who were pushing each other around, giggling. A sergeant of marines, very snappy in his greens, came out of the building that houses the slotmachines with a girl with a blue handkerchief tied around her yellow head holding onto his arm with both hands. For a couple of minutes the two of them stared hard out to sea as if their eyes could pierce the fogbank. Then they hurried back to the slotmachines.

Family Parties

In the restaurant on the level above, the tables are all full, but the eaters are very quiet. There are many family parties. Old people and middleaged people, and a young man or woman in uniform. At the table next to mine there's a whitehaired man and woman and a stoutish lady with pixie frames on her glasses who's evidently a doting female relative and seems to be somewhat in the way. None of them take their eyes off a first lieutenant in khaki with a closecropped black bullet head and ruddy cheeks, who looks barely old enough to be in highschool. The minute you see them you know that the old people have come to say goodbye. Maybe it's their last meal together. They are all trying to be very selfpossessed. The father is always starting to tell little jokes and neglecting to finish them. They keep forgetting where the saltcellar is on the table. The mother handles the plate of rolls when she passes it around as if it were immensely breakable. They fork the food slowly into their mouths. None of them knows what he's eating. All their motions are very careful and precise, as if they feared the slightest false move would break the fragile bonds that are holding the day together for them. The slightest fumble and these last few hours will be spilt and lost.

It's very different at the table next the window. A slender young air force major with dark curly hair already thinning on either side of a high forehead is taking out a strikingly pretty darkhaired girl. She might be his sister. There's something slightly similar about the build, about the way the nostrils are set in their noses. Or she might be his girl, or just the right chance acquaintance. They have had cocktails and oysters. The waiter is bringing them a bottle in a bucket of ice. They've ordered abalone steaks. They aren't saying much, but their eyes are shining and they keep looking at each other and at the wineglasses and at the food on their plates and at the fogbank creeping towards them across the black ocean, as if they'd never seen anything the least like these things before. They think they are alone in the restaurant. It's not so much that they are smiling at each other as that smiles are bubbling up all around them. Time, you can see, stands still for them.

Lunch alone doesn't have much flavor to it. Better get going. Coming out of the restaurant the fog pressed clammy against my face. I turned up my coat collar and went shuffling up towards the streetcar line. My coat felt suddenly out at the elbows. Everything about me felt shabby and frayed. There are things a civilian in wartime feels out of.

3

Elysian Fields

At a corner where a hilly street ended in a blank wall above the wharves, a cablecar was just ready to go. In short order it rattled me up to the top. I got off and set out along a street of framehouses. The houses were all alike, painted cream color with jutting bay windows and odd little columns that might have belonged to the architecture of a calliope, on each side of the front door. Occasionally there was a plot of grass or a bit of garden full of featheryfoliaged flowering plants held up against the hill by brick buttresses up which fuchsias grew into great vines large as rose vines. I walked on and on through the pleasant mild sunlight expecting to see the ocean from the top of each hill. Eventually, the sight of a hill taller than the rest and topped with tall gray pillars of blooming eucalyptus trees made me change my course. I got up there puffing after a stiff climb. The hilltop was a park. All the city and the Bay clear to Oakland and the bridges and the hills opened out in every direction at my feet. But not the Golden Gate, though I could see the high dark hills beyond. Towards the ocean there was only a bright haze.

An old Mexican was raking fallen eucalyptus leaves and scaled bark into a bonfire that trailed stinging sharp tonic-flavored smoke across the path. At the very summit of the path, cut off from the wind by a hedge of shinyleaved privet, four whiskered old men were seated round a green board table playing cribbage. It was quiet and sunny up there. The billowing blue smoke cut them off from the city. There is something very special about the smell of burning eucalyptus leaves. In the light fragrant air of the late morning the old men sat in relaxed attitudes of passionless calm. They held their cards with the detachment of gods on Olympus. They weren't smoking. They weren't talking. No one seemed in any hurry to win the game. Their pleasure wasn't in the sun or the air or the immense view. It was just in the ambrosial coursing of the blood through their veins, in the gentle pumping of the heart. That was what the Greeks meant when they wrote about the shadowless painless pleasures of the dead.

I had stopped in my tracks to look at the four old men. I was squinting to see just what kind of a game they were playing with their cribbage boards. They all four turned their heads to look up at me, stiffly craning their necks at the same moment. Their eyes were beady with surprise at seeing me standing in the path beside their table. They stared at me as they might have stared at a spook from another world.

Town of Hello and Farewell

In the seat next me in the limousine going out to the airport was a little redheaded girl from Memphis. Her husband was a naval officer. He had just been ordered to Rochester, New York. She'd never been to Rochester, New York. What was it like in Rochester, New York? Did I know whether it was on the lake or not? Wouldn't it be nice to live on a lake? Golly, she hoped she'd get on the plane. Her seat was conditional. She sure had her fingers crossed. If she could get off on that plane she could make Rochester as soon as he did. Wouldn't that be fun?

In the front seat on one side was a quiet palefaced army captain and on the other the pretty little stewardess, neat as a mouse, who was going out on this flight. Between them sat a sailor, a redfaced browneyed bombardier off a navy plane.

The sailor was high. He'd gotten in that morning from the islands beyond the blue bulge of the Pacific. He had eighteen days' leave. He'd been out in the theatres for a year. He'd just gotten over malaria. He was going to get home that next morning before day. 'The wife's waiting for me and I never seen the baby . . . it's a little baby boy,' he kept saying. He was high. He had a pint of whiskey in his blouse that he kept hauling out and offering to all and sundry. The stewardess said if he drank too much of that she might not be able to let him on the plane. 'Sure you will, sister,' said the sailor. 'I only got eighteen days.'

The army captain, who seemed a stiff West Point sort of fellow, finally was prevailed upon to accept a drink. 'Where we was,' said the sailor, 'it was fifty dollars a quart . . . I only paid fifteen for this from the bellhop at the hotel.'

'You oughtn't to have done that,' said the stewardess. 'That's too high.'

'Better than fifty dollars a quart. It was after hours and besides there was more of it,' said the sailor. 'Considerable more . . . Where we was the Japs came down every evening to bomb right along the same grove between the hills like they'd built a railroad track up there. They sure gave us plenty hell. Brother,' he said to the army captain, 'those Japs are good.'

'Oh, we'll clean 'em up in short order,' said the army captain gruffly.

'I didn't say we wouldn't clean 'em up. I said those Japs are good.'

'Sailor,' said the stewardess, 'you'd better put that flask away before you get to the airport. I wouldn't like not to be able to let you get on the plane.'

'Sure, you'll let me get on the plane . . . I got eighteen days to see the wife and the little baby boy.'

When we reached the neatly starched building at the airport the young lady at the ticket counter was very sorry. No place for me or the little girl from Memphis. She had a long telephone conversation with somebody to check again, but after it she was still very sorry. No places on that flight. At least no place for us or for the man in the camel's hair coat. But none of us cared much when we saw the sailor, his bushy brows drawn together into an expression of portentous dignity, walking out through the gate towards the plane shoulder to shoulder with the pokerfaced army captain. He didn't drop the bottle. He didn't fall down. He made it.

The little redheaded girl from Memphis sat down on a bench in a corner and suddenly hunched over her suitcase and began to cry.

Meanwhile the incoming passengers were milling around

waiting for their baggage. There was a very young roundfaced fellow in an ensign's uniform, who came in with an army lieutenant. When they said goodbye they looked each other seriously in the face and said, 'So long, feller . . . Let's hope for a short war.' Immediately the ensign became the centre of a group of old people, young people, small children, and started hugging first one and then the other, and saying to each one, 'Well, that completes my first trip around the world . . . I started out towards the west and I'm coming back from the east That completes my first trip around the world.'

THE END